ANTARCTICA AND BACK
IN SIXTY DAYS

To the ~~Peter~~,

~~Christmas 1991~~,

with love from
Betty & Don.
(HOBART)

ANTARCTICA AND BACK
IN SIXTY DAYS

Tim Bowden

an
ABC
BOOK

Published by ABC Enterprises for the
AUSTRALIAN BROADCASTING CORPORATION
GPO Box 9994 Sydney 2001

First published 1991
Reprinted November 1991

National Library of Australia
Cataloguing-in-Publication entry
Bowden, Tim, 1937–
   Antarctica and back in sixty days.
   ISBN 0 73333 0113 4.
   1. Antarctic regions—Description and travel. I. Title.
919.8904

Designed by Helen Semmler
Set in 10½ pt Century Old Style by Midland Typesetters, Victoria
Printed and bound in Australia by Australian Print Group, Victoria
5-2-1995

For Ros

COMING HOME

Fat droplets of warm rain
Slither slowly down my porthole window
Where frozen fragments of ice
Whirled wildly past only days ago.
I am coming home.
To you.

Perhaps palm trees grew all the time
In Antarctica once.
Now patches of green algae stain
The underside of fragments of quartz rock.
A smear of lichen, patches of moss
Struggling for survival
Are an Antarctic forest.

I wondered if you would like it here,
But I could not think of you without pain—
Until the last iceberg ghosted past my porthole
And the first raindrops signalled I was coming home.
To you.

Icebird, Southern Ocean, 23 February 1989

FOREWORD

Publicity has always been important to polar endeavour. In 1915 Sir Douglas Mawson wrote the following in his Preface to *The Home of the Blizzard; being the Story of the Australasian Antarctic Expeditions, 1911-1914*:

I should specially mention the friendly help afforded by the Australasian Press, which has at all times given the Expedition favourable and lengthy notices, insisting on its national and scientific character.

The establishment of the Australian National Antarctic Research Expeditions (ANARE) in July 1947 under Group Captain Stuart Campbell saw a number of journalists, photographers and authors among both wintering and supernumerary staff. Dr Phillip Law, the first Director of the Antarctic Division, who took over from Campbell in January 1949, clearly saw the need for recognition of the wintering staff and the results of their exploration and scientific programs and made sure that there was adequate publicity for ANARE.

Such publicity continued into the early 1980s despite the lack of berths for journalists on the small ice-strengthened vessels used by Australia. The chartering of *Icebird* in 1984 doubled the berths available per voyage and an increased number of voyages allowed more film crews, authors, journalists, artists and photographers to travel south with ANARE.

Many produced creditable work, others nothing that can be remembered.

As Voyage Leader on *Icebird* to Mawson and Davis Stations in January 1989 I was most interested in the passenger list. This voyage was no exception to many of my previous ones and had an interesting array of people. One name, well known in ANARE circles but without previous Antarctic experience, was Tim Bowden of the ABC Social History Unit. He had specialised in radio documentaries based on oral history techniques, and had made a significant contribution to the history of ANARE by recording the recollections of expeditioners who had been in Antarctica in the period 1949 to 1970.

The staff of ANARE have traditionally been reticent to talk about themselves, their colleagues, their work and ANARE, but with skill and sensitivity Tim Bowden has brought the culture and human side of the early years of the expeditions to the public. One wondered as we departed Hobart if he would be as successful on a relief voyage as he had been with the veterans.

I can say with confidence that Tim Bowden with his tape recorder, years of experience in journalism and enthusiasm for Antarctica has succeeded again. The present volume, as well as being valuable as a record of such a voyage in the 1980s, will also make interesting reading for those who are not fortunate enough to travel on a voyage to Antarctica and observe the contributions in both science and exploration that Australia has made to the fascinating, and inhospitable, continent of Antarctica.

D J Lugg
Antarctic Division
Kingston, Tasmania
April 1991

CONTENTS

ACKNOWLEDGMENTS

I thank my shipmates of Voyage Six, 1989, for their company and their reminiscences, and beg their forbearance for how some have been portrayed in this extremely personal memoir of an Antarctic journey. I am grateful to those Antarctic expeditioners I met during Voyage Six and on Mawson and Davis Stations who not only spoke frankly about their experiences and memories of Antarctic life, but in some cases contributed photographs as well.

None of this could have taken place without the Antarctic Division according me a berth on *Icebird* for the 1988/89 summer season, and providing this journalistic Jafo with Antarctic clothing, transport, food and accommodation for two months. Voyage Leader Des Lugg, Deputy Voyage Leader Ian Hay and the Cargo Supervisor 'Pud' Taylor were ever helpful and courteous even at times of maximum stress and activity. Mawson Station Leader Diana Patterson facilitated two utterly memorable excursions, a husky dog-sled run on the sea ice, and the helicopter trip to rediscover the 'Lost Tractor Train of Frustration Dome'.

Captain Ewald Brune and his officers and crew on *Icebird* answered most of my new-chum questions with good humour and, Ewald, I'm sorry I whistled on your bridge.

The Army Larcies—yes, they *can* be trusted—were not only good companions but contributed substantially to this narrative.

I am grateful to fellow Voyage Sixers Chris Sattlberger, Keith

Scott, Clare Robertson and Barry Batts for permission to quote from their personal diaries. Graham Robertson was particularly helpful not only with his superb description of his experiences with Emperor penguins, but with photographs, and former Antarctic expeditioner Jonathan Kilpatrick contributed some of his remarkable wild life photographs.

Naming names almost inevitably leads to leaving out those whom you most want to mention, so, with some nervousness, I thank the following individuals who made valuable contributions to the narrative:

Icebirders: Third Officer Roger Rusling, Bosun Peter Hadamek, Radio officer Nils Grell and Geoff Taylor;

Pilots: Leigh Hornsby, Pip Turner, and Dave Pullinger;

Contemporary ANARE expeditioners: John Gill, Doug Thost, Adam Darrough, Greg Hodge, Ian Fitzsimons, Bob Orchard, Trevor Lloyd, Peter Newman, Allen Rooke, Rob Easther, Simon Young, Kevin Donovan, 'Wok' Bromham, Dave McCormack, Phil Barnaart, Peter Crosthwaite and Graeme Currie;

Voyage Sixers: Bryan Smith, Scotty Davis, Mal Ludgate, Tony Gill, Greville Turner, Konrad Muller, Dennis Quinn, Garth Varcoe, John Hackwell and Lawrence Johnson;

The Pollies: Peter Milton, Colin Hollis, Allan Morris, Bob Chynoweth and Ian Cameron;

Larcies: Phil Clark, Tony Hambledon, 'Dutchy' Holland, Steve Koutsouras, Kevin Maugher and Scott Dempster.

Earlier ANARE expeditioners: Phil Law, John Bechervaise, Doug Leckie, Tom Manefield and Nils Lied.

After enduring some of my verbal Voyage Six reminiscences, ABC Books Publisher Richard Smart suggested I write this book, Senior Editor Nina Riemer encouraged the process and steered me clear of gross excesses, and it only took one photograph of an Antarctic husky to yoke that most elegant of designers, Helen Semmler, to this particular project. My salutations also to Nora Bonney for her reading expertise

I thank you all for contributing to this book, as well as those who have been inadvertently and shamefully omitted.

AUTHOR'S PREFACE

My *Boys Own Annual* fascination with travel to exotic lands
was profoundly influenced by the adventure stories of R M
Ballantyne, found in Bowden family bookshelves. They were
the adventure stories of my father's generation but, as a small
boy, I read them avidly. Many of Ballantyne's books were based
in polar regions, like *The Young Fur Traders*, drawing on his
experiences with the Hudson Bay Company in northern Canada
in the mid 19th Century. *Coral Island* was his most popular,
where three teenage boys are marooned on a South Sea island
and have myriad adventures with creatures of the deep,
marauding savages and pirates.

Robert Michael Ballantyne, clearly an economical Scot, made
good use of the encyclopedia in his writings. If one of his
characters came across an unusual-looking tree in the jungle,
and ingenuously asked a companion what it was, the answer
was uncommonly well informed. You could almost hear the
pages being turned over.

'That is the pizzicato tree usually only found in the Amazonian jungles
of Brazil. You will notice its small green pointed leaves with a short
spike on each end which protects its brightly hued yellow fruit from
foraging birds. The fruit, about the size of a small apple, has a firm
aromatic flesh which can be eaten. The kernel of the pizzicato seed,
however, is deadly poisonous, and is crushed and smeared on the
tips of arrows used in the blow-pipes of head-hunting pygmies . . . '

His chapter headings were also extremely detailed and informative, for example—

We Examine our Personal Effects, and Make a Happy Discovery • A Description of our Immediate Location • We Experience a Dreadful Fright • The Mysteries of the Deep enlarged upon • And Our Leader Proves himself to be more Learned and Sagacious than his Companions.

I am indebted to R M Ballantyne for this approach.

T. B.
Sydney 1991

INTRODUCTION

Some Facts about Australia's Presence in Antarctica • We learn about Jafos and Jafas • Tenuous Bowden links with Polar Exploration • Uncharitable Reflections on the Character of a 'Gallant English Gentleman'

Going to Antarctica in modern times remains one of the last great journeys left on the face of the earth. Travel to Australia's Antarctic stations has to be by sea, and the transition through the storms and hurricanes of the Roaring Forties, the Furious Fifties and the Screaming Sixties to the tranquillity of the pack ice gives a sense of adventure, purpose and historical meaning to the journey that no plane trip could ever match— even if flights were an option. Australia has three main stations on the Antarctic mainland, Mawson, Casey and Davis. Mawson Station, Australia's westernmost Antarctic settlement, is geographically under the Persian Gulf. It is five hours behind Eastern Australian time and ten days steaming from Hobart. It is a long way from home.

I never, never thought I would journey to Antarctica. But in 1987 I began work on a series of radio documentaries based on oral history interviews with the Australian expeditioners who had pioneered Australia's post-war push south after World War Two. Australia claims nearly forty-two per cent of the Antarctic Continent, largely based on the pre-war voyages of the Australian explorer Sir Douglas Mawson in 1911 and his BANZARE (British and New Zealand Antarctic Research Expedition) voyages of 1929–31. But we had no permanent stations there until 1954. The sub-Antarctic islands of Heard and Macquarie were occupied by Australia in 1947 and 1948,

The Antarctic Field Manual must be carried at all times! Here intrepid Voyage Sixers display theirs on the icecap behind Mawson. From left: Allan Morris, Tim Bowden and Colin Hollis.

spurred by increased American, British and French interest in the area. A lack of funds and, most significantly, the lack of a suitable ship delayed access to the Antarctic continent until the mid 1950s. At that time, ANARE (Australian National Antarctic Research Expeditions), led by Dr Phillip Law, began a determined series of summer season voyages to explore and chart the coast and inland regions of Eastern Antarctica and, fortunately for Australia, secure the prime pieces of ice-free real estate for our stations.

Exposed rock makes up only two per cent of Antarctica, which can be described in metaphorical terms as like a huge dome of candied honey, with the honey (ice) continually on the move and slipping down to the edges to break off as icebergs. Some mountain peaks thrust up through the ice that is moving relentlessly past them and in certain coastal areas the ice cap has retreated, leaving small areas of exposed rock. Unless you build on rock in Antarctica, structures will eventually move off and fall into the sea.

The resupplying and remanning (and some rewomanning in recent times) of the three Australian mainland stations,

Mawson, Casey and Davis, can only take place during the summer 'window' in Antarctica, between December and March when the 'fast ice'—the unbroken sheet that extends out to sea—breaks up in the warmer conditions and drifts away before refreezing from late March. For many years the Danish Lauritzen Line provided a whole series of chartered *Dan* ships for this purpose. *Kista Dan* was the first, the *Magga Dan* and *Thala Dan* have voyaged south, and the last of the breed, the much loved *Nella Dan*, was wrecked on the rocks of Macquarie Island on December 1987. Since the summer of 1984–5, the main resupply of fuel, food and personnel to the Australian stations has been by the German ship *Icebird*, a 7000 tonne vessel with a specially strengthened ice-breaking bow. The Australian-built polar vessel *Aurora Australis* made its first trip to the Antarctic continent in October 1990.

Some of these resupply voyages also carry 'Jafos' and 'Jafas', individuals who have been judged by the Antarctic Division to have projects useful enough to justify being transported, fed and boarded for the six to eight weeks needed for the round trip south. (This is Antarctic slang for 'Just another effing observer' and 'Just another effing academic'.) Journalists can sometimes be Jafos, and on the strength of my ABC Radio Antarctic oral history project, and the promise of some more contemporary publicity, I applied for and was granted a passage south by the Antarctic Division on *Icebird* on Voyage Six. This was the main resupply voyage for Mawson and Davis Stations, to sail from Hobart on 3 January 1989.

This put me definitely on the lowest rung of the Antarctic totem pole as a round tripper—and only marginally below the next grade of Antarctic visitor, the Jafas, or visiting summer scientists. The elite, of course, are the hardy souls who occupy the bases for the whole year, experiencing the full polar winter.

I have a family-related 'brush with Antarctic fame'. On 11 March 1912 the Norwegian polar explorer Roald Amundsen sailed into Hobart in the doughty little wooden vessel the *Fram*. Amundsen had beaten Scott in the race to the South Pole, but nobody knew at that stage except the members of his expedition. My grandfather, Frank Bowden, then Director of Telegraphs in Hobart, met with Amundsen to send his telegram to the King of Norway announcing the success of the expedition. For some days, my grandfather was the only man outside the

Fram's company to share the knowledge that was about to excite the world.

My grandfather later said Amundsen was very stiff and formal over the telegram. He had reason to be cautious. Expeditions then, as now, were very dependent on sponsorship, and the news of his discovery of the North-West Passage in 1905 had been scooped when the Hearst news agency eavesdropped on the cable he had Morse-coded to his backers after skiing 500 miles down the Yukon to Eagle City in Alaska from his ice-bound ship. American newspapers pirated the story, and it was widely reprinted around the world. Legitimate recipients, like the London *Times* who had contracted for exclusive rights, refused to pay. Amundsen was intensely embarrassed, personally and financially, and after waiting in Eagle City some two months for a response to his cables, had to ski 500 miles back to his beset vessel in the knowledge that all his troubles would be waiting for him when he eventually got back to Norway in the summer of 1906. It was obvious he wished to avoid a rerun of that public relations disaster from Hobart.

I have a prized photograph of the *Fram* at anchor in the Derwent River in 1912. One day I hope to see her, where she lies in permanent dry dock in Oslo. As a young boy growing up in Hobart, I read and reread Nansen's *Farthest North* describing his ingenious attempt to reach the North Pole by freezing the specially constructed *Fram* into the moving polar ice, and drifting her there.

Nansen's expedition did not reach the Pole, but the *Fram* performed superbly, her stout timbers and specially designed bulbous hull lifting her above the fantastic pressures of the pack ice. She survived three winters, from 1893 to 1896, until she broke free.

By the spring of 1895 Nansen realised that his theories of polar drift would not take the *Fram* near enough to the North Pole, so he selected a companion, Hjalmar Johansen, from the other twelve men on the expedition, to try a dash to the North Pole with husky dogs, skis and a sledge—also carrying kayaks as the ice was expected to break up on their return journey to the nearest land. Long ridges of pressure ice frustrated their dash to the North Pole and they only just made the coast of Franz Josef Land as the sea ice broke up around them. It was

The Fram at anchor in Hobart in March 1912, following Amundsen's successful dash to the South Pole. Grandfather Bowden, then Director of Telegraphs, organised Amundsen's historic cable to the King of Norway.

then too late to travel any further and they were forced to spend a miserable winter in a stone and ice igloo, subsisting on seal meat and burning blubber to keep warm.

Incredibly, the *Fram* arrived back in Oslo under the command of her master Otto Sverdrup in June 1896 within a week of Nansen and his companion Johansen who had been away from the ship for fifteen months! *Farthest North* remains one of the great polar sagas, and kindled in me a life-long interest in polar literature.

Hjalmar Johansen was on the *Fram* when she came to Hobart in 1912, as a senior member of Amundsen's party. Poor Amundsen, he won the race and lost the contest. He was preparing to leave on a triumphant world lecture tour when the news of Scott's death eclipsed his triumph. The Norwegian explorer had done everything right. He had used dogs while Scott had put his faith partly in primitive petrol-engined tractors and the ludicrous decision to use ponies (reportedly because an Englishman could never eat a dog, even *in extremis*). Amundsen had not lost a man while Scott had led his polar party of five to their deaths.

Amundsen's biographer, Roland Huntford, says the Norwegian 'recoiled from the martyrdom of man-hauling, to which in a spirit of self-mortification, official British explorers had become addicted'. Amundsen won the race to the South Pole and back, but Scott struck out from the grave with his elegantly penned diary detailing heroic failure.

'A Gallant English Gentleman' was the title of one slim pamphlet in the Bowden post-war household, glorifying this useless sacrifice in the snow. It would have been more aptly titled 'A Bone-Headed Pommy Bungler'. As a schoolboy, I thought the 'Gallant English Gentleman' line was a load of cobblers forty years before the Scott 'legend' was debunked by writers like Roland Huntford. But no one wanted to hear anything from Amundsen. He was understandably miffed by Scott's posthumous literary revenge and never really recovered the historical initiative.

During my own voyage to Antarctica in the summer of 1989, a cheery glaciologist calculated that—based on the speed of the inexorable movement of polar ice towards the edges of the Antarctic continent—a perfectly preserved Scott, Wilson, Bowers, Oates and Evans were about due to break off and float out into the Southern Ocean on an iceberg!

I am leaping ahead. Back to 3 January 1989. It was time— as R M Ballantyne might have expressed it—to embark on the Great Adventure.

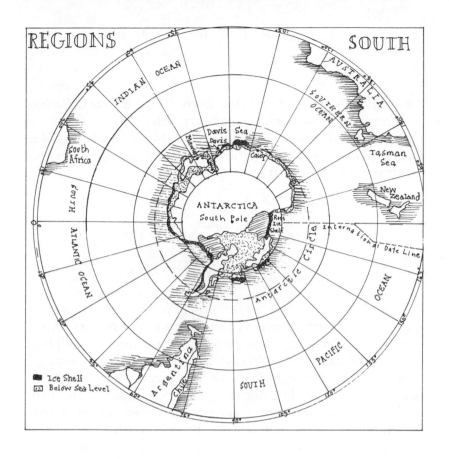

REGIONS

SOUTH

INDIAN OCEAN

AUSTRALIA

SOUTHERN OCEAN

South Africa

Tasman Sea

Davis Sea
Davis

Casey

New Zealand

Mawson

ANTARCTICA
South Pole

Ross Ice Shelf

HIGH

International Date Line

ATLANTIC OCEAN

Antarctic Circle

OCEAN

PACIFIC

Argentina

Chile

SOUTH

Ice Shelf
Below Sea Level

7

CHAPTER ONE

I am Equipped for the Great Adventure • My Curious Collection of Travelling Companions • Salutory Facts about Death in Antarctica and Frozen Eyeballs • An Introduction to the Ship and our Captain • The Departure • A Cautionary Tale about the Dangers of Double Dipping

All Antarctic journeys begin at the Store where you are issued with your polar apparel, beginning with a heavy windproof cotton jacket and trousers known as ventiles. Curiously enough these are not waterproof; there is no rain or moisture in Antarctica, the world's biggest and driest desert. (You can, however, be doused with freezing sea water, but that was something we found out later!) The end result is a bulging kit bag stuffed with gear including heavy woollen socks, felt liners for the clumsy rubberised boots, and assorted woollen garments including a grey balaclava of the style sported by Sir Douglas Mawson on the Australian $100 note. Mine had a rather quaint knitted eye-shade as a bonus.

I was reminded of stories I had taped about the Antarctic Division's first storeman, the redoubtable George Smith, who reigned over the Tottenham Store in Melbourne from 1947 to the late 1970s. George used his great height and matching bulk to loom over rookie expeditioners looking mournfully at their grossly ill-fitting issue of ex-World War Two left-overs. His stock response to any complaints about wrong sizes was to glower balefully at the complainant and say: 'There's nothing wrong with the *clothes* I've given you. The trouble with you is, you're *deformed*!' As a last resort he used to brandish a machete snatched from behind the counter and offer to trim off the trousers which were generally at least six inches too

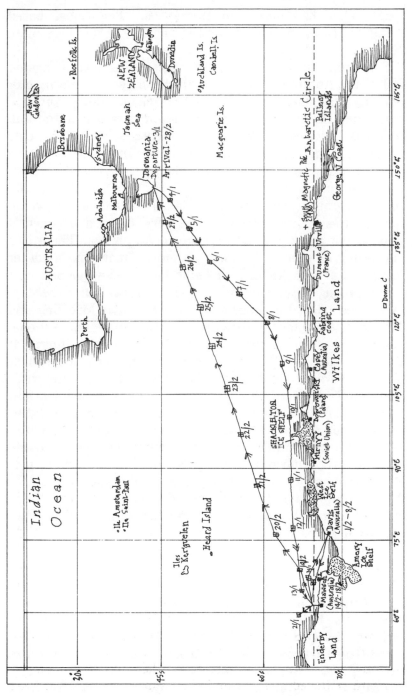

Voyage Six, 1989. Icebird's *route to Antarctica and back.*

9

long. (They had inches in the 1950s.) The Hobart-based Antarctic Division storepersons of the late 1980s were more polite, but the result was about the same.

Some sixty-six Voyage Six passengers gather at the Kingston HQ of the Antarctic Division near Hobart on the morning of our day of sailing for the final briefing, including Division personnel, Australian Army 'Larcies' (operators of the amphibious LARC vehicles), riggers, scientists, politicians, cine and still cameramen, journalists, and people with assorted occupations judged to have relevance by the Division. We are a diverse lot, including a writer of children's books, a wild life photographer, an artist from Darwin, a pathologist (would his services be needed?) and the very first environmental philosopher to be granted passage to Antarctica. There is a sprinkling of women, but we are mostly male and a rather WASP lot at that. No black or Asian faces on Voyage Six.

Our 'Voyage Leader' (as distinct from the captain of the ship) is Dr Des Lugg, the Division's Head of Polar Medicine and Research, who joined the original ANARE (Australian National Antarctic Research Expeditions) in 1962, and had wintered at Davis Station in 1963 and been south on many subsequent summer voyages. I had interviewed him during my Antarctic oral history project and knew him to be a man of forthright opinions, a critic of many aspects of current Antarctic policies, an ironic observer of the human condition and a most entertaining raconteur. Certainly a man with the experience and qualities to be lumbered with Voyage Six, the thorniest prospect of the summer season—not only the major resupply effort for Mawson and Davis Stations, but the most 'Jafo' and 'Jafa'-ridden, with a clutch of Federal politicians and media types thrown in for good measure.

DIARY

3 JANUARY, 1989

Des Lugg apologised for all the paper work, but said the days had gone when expeditioners had their briefing by going down to the pub for a beer with Phil Law (the Director of ANARE from 1949 to 1966) and colleagues. After our roll call (the National Party's Member for Maranoa, Ian Cameron stood up and solemnly intoned 'Queensland' when his name was

A bevy of Tasmanian Bowdens farewell the adventurer. Note the covered lifeboats on Icebird.

called) we were inducted into the very real dangers lurking for the unwary down south.

Apart from accidents like walking into helicopter tail rotors, hypothermia is a major hazard. The Division's Medical Director, Dr Peter Gormly, told us that the shock of falling into the super-chilled Antarctic sea water is such that it can stop your heart instantly. We heard the cheery news that the Scandinavians have redefined the description of death by freezing as: 'Failure to revive on rewarming'! Apparently you have to be warm *and* dead before they can be sure you have carked. If your eyeballs are frozen, though, they don't bother to rewarm you to confirm death. If there is no red light reflex from the back of the eye you are definitely brain dead.

We saw some amazing slides of what remained of three helicopters after they had broken loose in *Icebird*'s hold only a matter of hours after leaving Hobart in Storm Bay on the previous voyage; the most expensive collection of scrap metal you would ever hope to see. We were then issued with our sea-sickness pills and dismissed. The Antarctic Division's Acting Director Rex Moncur did not appear at our briefing to give us his blessing, but I heard later that he did invite our five Federal politicians to his office after the main mob departed clutching packets of sea-sick pills.

It was clear that political balance had not been achieved on Voyage Six. There were four Labor back-benchers, no Liberals, and one National Party representative.

We were to sail at 5 pm. Just time for a quick *sushi* lunch at Muires seafood restaurant at Constitution Dock with Keith Scott from the *Canberra Times* and it was up the gang plank of the bright red-hulled *Icebird*, the German-owned resupply vessel and our home for the next sixty days. The two big cranes on the port side of the ship were still loading the last of the cargo.

There is much talk of sea-sickness, and many Voyage Sixers were sporting their Scop patches behind their ears before we sailed. (This Scopolamine motion sickness remedy is in vogue on *Icebird* although the Division recommends a mix of Avomine and ephedrine tablets). I am sharing a cabin with a medical team conducting experiments into why Antarctic expeditioners suffer a drop in their immune systems while they are away. Konrad Muller is the Professor of Pathology at the University of Tasmania and his lab assistant is Dennis Quinn. They seem amiable souls, and I am sure we will know each other much better before the voyage is over! Our cabin is on the top deck of the accommodation module and is one of the smaller ones, into which they have crammed four bunks, nevertheless. Fortunately we are only three-up for the moment. At least it has an en suite bathroom. The lesser mortals on the level below have communal showers and toilets.

Apart from leaving and entering port, all passengers on the *Icebird* have access to the ship's bridge at all times; a very civilised and much appreciated gesture by the skipper

First lifeboat drill, while heading down the Derwent Estuary, under the stern Teutonic eye of First Officer Horst Wolmeyer.

Captain Ewald Brune and his German crew. I met the blond-bearded, surprisingly young-looking Master on the bridge while showing my father over the ship. 'Yes, I am the captain', he said cheerfully, acknowledging my unspoken doubt that he was old enough to be.

Paper streamers, tooting car horns and the *Icebird*'s siren, mingled with shouted goodbyes in the time-honoured tradition of leaving port, were carried out vigorously before we moved slowly down the Derwent Estuary. Our bows were already turned to the south as we glided past the Wrest Point Casino complex, on the foreshore of Hobart's exclusive waterfront suburb Sandy Bay, the brooding bulk of Mt Wellington dominating the western skyline. The weather was fine and the forecast for Storm Bay good. This was important. Apart from the all-pervading nervousness about sea-sickness, what Storm Bay gives is what you get. There is no way of using radar to slip in front or behind the low pressure systems that sweep eastward across the Southern Ocean until you have some sea miles behind you. That is what mashed up the helicopters on the previous voyage.

13

I decided to play it safe and affix my Scop anti-sea-sickness patches behind my ears, and felt better immediately.

Next day one dropped off and it was pointed out by a kindly soul that I had not removed the plastic coating from the adhesive—so they could have had absolutely no effect on me at all!

I stood on the flying bridge to farewell the last sight of land for quite some time. A superb sunset threw South East Cape into relief, and the ubiquitous and graceful shearwaters turned on a fine display as they swept along the troughs of the waves, not quite brushing the crests with their wings on their way to God knows where. There were countless thousands of them. Someone told me there are more shearwaters distributed over the oceans of the world than any other species of bird on the planet. It certainly seems possible on this random sampling. I found our Voyage Leader Des Lugg gazing moodily at the shearwaters from the corner of the flying bridge. I don't think this is going to be an easy assignment for him.

Decided to front up for dinner. Hospital hours! We dine at the uncivilised hour of 5.30 pm, army canteen style, and line up at a servery and battle for places at long tables in the rather cramped mess room. Stew and macaroni! I had hoped for German cuisine, but our French chef, Roger, is apparently under instructions to serve Australian tucker, which means basically boring food for the next two months, I suppose.

At dinner I heard a wonderful story. During the 'Australia Live' telecast at the beginning of Australia's Bicentennial in 1988, one of the most effective segments was beamed live from Antarctica, from Davis Station. The technology, involving satellite links, was awesome and there were some memorable scenes portrayed by the hand-held amateur video cameras. One involved expeditioners in bathers with beach towels supposedly heading down to the beach for a 'swim'. Later, in a two-way exchange, one of the expeditioners who had become a father during his time in the Antarctic, was shown live scenes of his new born babe in Australia. It was an emotional moment, and there was hardly a dry eye among the audience of millions in Australia and overseas.

14

Historic flashback: First landing, Oates Land, 1959. From left:
Dr Phillip Law (ANARE's founding Director), legendary storeman
George Smith, Bruce Coombes and Group Captain Robert Dalton.
Antarctic Division photograph.

There was a less happy follow-up. Apparently the Department of Social Security noted this emotional exchange with unfeeling bureaucratic efficiency. The mother of the child, allegedly, was claiming a deserted wife's pension while her partner was wintering down south. That is, until shortly after the telecast!

Visited the bridge before retiring. There should be no problem keeping fit on this voyage. To get from my cabin to the bridge, I walk down three sets of stairs in the accommodation module, along a companion way, and up four sets of stairs to the bridge. The weather is so good we are to take a more direct route south, and then head west closer to the Antarctic coastline, towards Mawson.

CHAPTER TWO

Nasty Happenings in the Night • Heaving on the High Seas • Alarming Toilet Explosions • Exploring the Ship • A 'Wives Lottery' • Frightening Experiences at Sea • I Grace the Captain's Table • We Hear of Broken Legs at Davis Station • Why do Penguins Like Cocoa? • Sad Story of the Death of a Polar Ship

JANUARY 4

Horrors! One of my cabin mates snores abominably! Great trumpeting bellows, snorts and grunts, little whines and the occasional monumental self-wakening explosive sort. It is the Professor. I asked the ship's doctor, Kevin Donovan, if he has any ear plugs, but he hasn't.

Dennis Quinn, who sleeps underneath the Professor's bunk, gave me a meaningful, mournful look as our eyes met first thing in the morning. As well as losing sleep with his boss's snoring, it was apparent Dennis was not a good sailor. His pallid face gave new dimensions to the metaphor of wet putty. So far he has put his faith in two elastic bands which press a metal button into a pressure point on the inside of each wrist. Losing faith, he disappeared into our little en suite shower and toilet cubicle to take a regulation issue sea-sickness pill. While he was inside, the cabin was shaken by a curiously explosive combined roaring and sucking sound. The *Icebird*'s toilet flushing system is a dramatic affair, involving compressed air as well as water.

Dennis is worried about being fit enough to carry out his medical experiments in the ship's surgery later in the day. I am worried about being part of them. There seems no way out as I am sharing a cabin with the practitioners, and am

17

The Professor in noisy slumber, Cabin C3.

assigned an appointment for blood letting and other personal indignities.

I decide to risk breakfast and, although Storm Bay is not living up to its name, the gentle movement of *Icebird*'s 7000 tonnes forging south at fourteen knots is more than enough to thin the queue for bacon and eggs. A crew from the television program *BEYOND 2000* is in the adjacent cabin. The reporter Bryan Smith is testing an anti-sea-sickness device that looks like a Walkman radio and constantly plays musical sounds of certain frequencies through headphones. He let me listen for a few moments. I think I'd rather be sea-sick! It didn't seem to be helping Bryan much, judging by his pale green complexion and wretched demeanour.

The first ship to take Australians south to the sub-Antarctic islands of Heard and Macquarie in 1948 was an ex-World War Two LST (Landing Ship Tanks). A big shallow draught landing craft designed to run up onto beaches and unload tanks and

18

troops, it had all the seaworthy qualities of a kerosene tin. In fact, it used to buckle and flex as it thrashed and bashed its blunt bows into the raging seas of the Southern Ocean. One Macquarie Island expeditioner was so chronically sea-sick on the voyage down that, a year later, he became nauseated while still on the island, simply watching the amphibious Army DUKWs ply back and forth to the LST that was to take him home!

At breakfast I met an Austrian photographer, Chris Sattlberger, who is to make a photographic record of the voyage for the *Icebird*'s owners. He is on the crew list, the only Austrian among the Germans—a bit like being the only New Zealander with the Australian passengers. There's a lone Kiwi too, Garth Varcoe, an observer from the New Zealand Antarctic Research Program. A chorus of sheep-like 'baa's' invariably greets him whenever he walks into the mess. He gives as good as he gets.

Chris Sattlberger is finding it a bit heavy going in the German officers' mess and has come to fraternise with the Australians. The Second Engineer, Manni, is in charge of the *Icebird*'s explosive toilet system and is obsessive about his filters. His sole topic of conversation at meal times, according to Chris, is a description of the amount of pubic hair and other un-mentionable substances recovered from these filters. A bout of sea-sickness on board is bad news for Manni's filters and equally unfortunate for his table companions.

Chris says the ship's officers refer to the passengers as the 'occupants', although he told me the German *okkupanten* has a lighter, friendlier connotation in translation. Most of the officers are amiable enough, but the Chief Officer Horst Wolmeyer seems surly. I went to the bridge to watch the *Icebird*'s high bows ploughing forward into an empty watery horizon. Horst was on watch, sitting in the elaborate 'conning' chair in front of a bank of radar screens and engine controls.

    TB: Good morning.
No reply. A few white caps seemed to indicate a freshening wind.
    TB (brightly): What weather are you promising us?
    HW (muttering): I don't promise any weather.
    TB (unwisely): What weather are you *suggesting* then?
    HW (peevishly): Nothing.

The barograph, however, was obviously heading down rather than up, and the satellite print-out of the weather seemed to feature a great cluster of lows ahead. It is intriguing to think of the empty ocean ahead of us. No icebergs—yet. Almost certainly no other vessels. Just a great expanse of nothingness. It hardly seems worthwhile having someone on watch at all. There is no wheel on a modern ship, just a toggle switch like something on your hi-fi set or PC, to operate the automatic pilot.

We have just under one hundred souls on board with a capacity for 120 or so. The numbers will ebb and flow as we pick up and drop expeditioners and summer scientists between Mawson and Davis Stations, and for the run home. The bridge is situated aft, on top of the superstructure housing the crew's quarters, captain's and voyage leader's cabins, crew mess and galley.

'The Module', with the passenger accommodation, mess, and a small cavern-like bar underneath, is plonked on the deck just in front of the bridge. I am fortunate to have a cabin on C Deck, the top level. There is a reading room on D Deck, but otherwise most group activities take place in the mess— a long narrow space divided off by a third for the smokers. It is not possible to feed everyone at once, so we have two sittings. Unfortunately there is no space big enough on board to have everyone attend a meeting so we have to cram in as best we can for important announcements. The long, bench-style tables are difficult to access carrying your meal. The technique is to hop up on the bench seat and walk behind the backsides of those already eating, trying not to slop gravy down their necks. In the evenings the mess is turned over to the video freaks.

Nicknames have started to appear. Lawrence Johnson, the environmental philosopher, is at first called 'The Philosopher'. He is a softly-spoken American with an unruly shock of grey wispy hair, a high forehead and wide-apart slightly staring eyes. His habit of dressing up in ventiles and Douglas Mawson-style balaclava and prowling round the decks of the ship braving wind and weather will later change his sobriquet to 'Lawrence of Antarctica'. Deputy Voyage Leader Ian Hay is quickly dubbed the 'Head Prefect'. He is a pleasant fellow in his early thirties with a King George V beard, but his manner can be a trifle officious at times. (I find out later he is the most formidable Scrabble player I have ever encountered.) The Cargo Supervisor and veteran of many Antarctic resupply voyages is the jovial 'Pud' Taylor. He has on board his wife Robin who also works for the Division. My world-champion snoring cabin companion, Konrad Muller, professor of pathology at the University of Tasmania, is simply known as 'The Professor'. The five Federal MPs are simply 'The Pollies'.

Women are much in the minority on Voyage 6—nine in all. One is Sandra Fahey who won the Antarctic Wives Association 'lottery', where a selected wife of an expeditioner is allowed a round trip to visit her husband on a particular base. Sandra's husband Brendan is an electrician at Mawson and she is highly excited about her first major journey anywhere. They have only been married for eighteen months. She has never even seen snow before: 'The only time I've seen ice is in a freezer'.

JANUARY 5

Boat rolling and pitching more. Clocks were put back an hour during the night, so arrived at breakfast an hour early. Ian Cameron, National Party Member for Maranoa, was in the mess holding court. He gave a detailed account of how sand moves along coastal beaches in southern Queensland and finished by saying how he ought to get a tax deduction for sending his kids to private schools!

Our Voyage Leader Des Lugg has appeared looking wan. He told me earlier that he is one of the worst sailors who ever embarked with ANARE. My Scop anti-sea-sickness patches behind the ears seem to be working. The side effects make you dry-mouthed and you can't focus your eyes to read. Some people find they can't pee, as well, according to Dr Peter Gormly during his pre-departure briefing. No trouble in that department yet. The Head Prefect said I am to grace the Captain's table this evening. Apparently there is a kind of roster organised by the Antarctic Division and the skipper has little say in the matter.

Enjoying a post-breakfast nap in my cabin (what a life!) I became aware that as the ship rolled, the whole accommodation module was shifting slightly against its chocks or whatever held it in place. I heard later it had shifted more dramatically in earlier voyages. The thought of accompanying this big steel box over the side is not attractive. Apparently a German expert was sent out to investigate, having pooh-poohed the concerns about its at-sea movement from afar. After the first blow, I heard, he was seen to be looking extremely thoughtful, and on return to Hobart some modifications were made to secure it more firmly to the ship.

In the late 1940s and early 1950s there was much more concern about the behaviour of the 'floating kerosene tin', the famous LST 3501 (later named HMAS *Labuan*), when it headed south to the sub-Antarctic islands of Heard and Macquarie as Phil Law told me on tape during an earlier interview:

PL: It was a unique vessel in a storm. An LST is a very long ship, about 300 feet long, I guess, and all the works are at the back. All the engine, all the accommodation, everything—the whole of this great long front part—is really a floating hull for carrying tanks. It doesn't have a pointy bow like an ordinary ship, it has a blunt bow, so it's like bashing into a wave with a brick wall. It's such a long ship that she'd climb up on one great wave in the Southern Ocean and then bash down and there'd be this tremendous crash like a thousand kerosene tins being bashed. Then the whole of this front part of the ship would act like a springboard and it would just vibrate up and down like a springboard. As it flapped, waves would come back through the steel decking! If you were standing on the deck you could see one of these waves coming, bending through the steel.

TB: Like a ripple in the steel?

PL: Exactly. And these were not small, they were four to six inches almost and they'd throw you off your feet as they came through. You'd be lying in your bunk at night and you'd hear this great crash of the bows hitting the oncoming wave. Then it'd go 'yoong . . . yoong . . . yoong . . . yoong' and the sides of the ship would go in and out, 'clonk clonk, clonk clonk', rather like bending a tobacco tin. So the whole ship was moving and flexing and bending. No wonder on the final trip, in 1951, I think it was, after weeks of storm it just literally shook to pieces.

HMAS Labuan *unloading cargo on a rocky beach at Heard Island during the establishment of the first Australian station there in 1948. Antarctic Division photograph.*

On one trip down we were heading into a violent storm—hurricane stuff up around 100 miles an hour—and it was a terrible night with all this movement and bashing and everything. Apparently the crew became very worried that the ship would break in half. I couldn't sleep either so I thought I'd better go down and see how the ANARE boys were getting on. I was berthed at the stern of the ship in the officer's quarters but our men were in the bunk rooms down the sides of this great flapping fore-deck. I found them all sitting up looking very worried and they said, 'Phil, the crew's all gone, there's no one next door'.

So I went to the crew's quarters and sure enough there was no crew there. I went back aft and all the crew were sitting with their knapsacks packed. I said, 'What goes on?' They said: 'Well, if this ship is going to break in half we're going to be in the half that's got the works in it'.

Icebird seems reassuringly high tech by comparison.

Dinner at the Captain's table was quite pleasant. Captain Ewald Brune seemed reserved, and not like the ebullient character described by Stephen Murray-Smith in his book on Voyage Six in 1985–86, *Sitting On Penguins*. He eats very sparingly, just a few pieces of bacon on a plate and some cheese. Chris Sattlberger told me later he rarely eats the food Roger the chef cooks for the passengers. I enjoyed a splendid thick German pea and ham soup. After dinner Ewald insisted I drink a liqueur he called 'Half & Half'—a great goblet of half cognac, half Benedictine. Three more were placed in front of me!

There is a God after all. Barbara Graham, a representative from DASETT (the Antarctic Division's parent department in Canberra) has some foam ear plugs. I swapped them for a music cassette. Now for some snore-free sleep.

JANUARY 6
Dennis has alleged I snore too—very hurtful. But I am not in the Professor's league. He has managed to get some foam ear plugs, too, from the ship's engineers. The quality of life has picked up in Cabin C3.

The *Beyond 2000* crew next door have labelled their cabin door 'Beyond Help'. I think Bryan Smith almost is. The synthesised anti-sea-sickness remedy has failed him utterly. His cameraman Mal Ludgate (an Antarctic veteran who has actually dived under the pack ice in a wet suit to film seals, penguins, and Antarctic fish) is goading him mercilessly around the ship to do stand-up pieces against the background of heaving sea. Heaving is the operative word. I don't think Mal has ever had a moment's sea-sickness in his life. He is the most dedicated cameraman I have ever encountered. If it moves, Mal is there shooting it. Scotty Davis the sound man is looking a bit wan around the gills also but is carrying on.

JANUARY 7
We were called to a meeting in the mess by the ship's PA system (known as the 'Bing Bong' because of its two-note attention-getting signal). Des Lugg said there

24

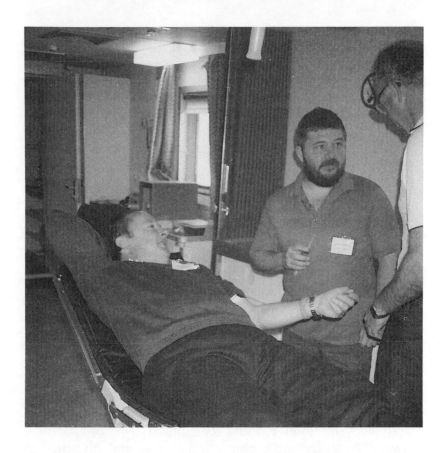

The author is subjected to bloodletting and other medical indignities in Icebird's *surgery in the interests of polar research. Dr Kevin Donovan prepares his attack, watched by Dennis Quinn (far right).*

had been an accident at Davis Station. There were two men with three smashed legs, caused by falling over an ice-cliff while travelling on motorised skidoos. The other supply ship in the region, *Lady Franklin,* is now several days' steaming from Davis, and is to turn back as they have a top orthopaedic surgeon on board.

Not long afterwards we were told that the *Lady Franklin* was back on course to Hobart and the injured men will be flown out by the Russians via South America. It is a first-rate example of the kind of international co-operation common in Antarctica.

The Russians (and now the Chinese) have stations at the Larsemann Hills, only an hour's helicopter ride west from Davis. They have an ice airstrip on the Antarctic plateau which can handle fixed wing aircraft. Had the accident happened in winter, it is unlikely the men could have been evacuated. It is a reminder that Antarctica is still the most isolated area in the world.

Des Lugg has instituted a program of after-lunch lectures every few days, where different experts can talk about what they are doing in Antarctica, using slides and diagrams where appropriate. It is a polar tradition dating back to the expeditions of Nansen, Shackleton, Scott and Mawson—and prolongs the life of the replay heads on the over-used video. The New Zealander Garth Varcoe, triumphing over a chorus of 'baas' and tasteless gumboot and sheep jokes, showed slides and talked about the Kiwi Antarctic base, near the Americans at McMurdo. It is a very modest operation in contrast to the great double-story steel structures indulged in by Australia in recent years, which have to be erected by skilled tradesmen. The New Zealanders have prefabricated single-story buildings of modern materials, linked by covered walkways, which can be put up by the expeditioners themselves—as were the huts that housed Australian Antarctic expeditions in the 1950s, 1960s and 1970s. Garth enjoyed himself making some unflattering comparisons between New Zealand's cost effectiveness and his view of Australia's Antarctic building extravagances of recent years.

The privilege of access to *Icebird*'s bridge at all times is deeply appreciated. The Third Officer is an Australian, Roger Rusling (later to take command of the Australian-built Antarctic supply and research vessel *Aurora Australis* which went into service in 1990). Unlike Horst, he was happy to chat about the Antarctic experience. On *Icebird*'s previous voyage, the Antarctic Division was helped by Australian adventurer Dick Smith who, with pilot Giles Kershaw, had flown a Twin Otter aircraft to the South Pole. (Sadly, Giles Kershaw was killed on 6 March 1990 in a gyrocopter crash on the Jones Ice Shelf, east of Adelaide Island off the west coast of the Antarctic Peninsula.)

Icebird carried helicopters on its previous voyage but needed to get within eighty nautical miles of the coast to be able to fly off cargo and personnel to Casey, Davis and Mawson Stations. Roger said they managed to chopper into Casey, but heavy pack ice kept them 135 miles from Davis. Dick Smith offered to land on a suitable ice floe—if one could be found—and take in cargo to Davis.

RR: We used our helicopters to find a suitably large ice floe about eight miles from the ship. The ice was marked with strips of black paint to indicate a runway. But the greenies on board the ship, the biologists and zoologists and all the other 'ologists, didn't like the idea of degrading the environment with paint. So, later on in the trip when we were off Mawson Station, Dick Smith offered to fly in and land on the ice again to take expeditioners and cargo in to the Prince Charles Mountains—some 400 kilometres inland —to begin their summer program because time was running short. The Twin Otter can actually carry two tonnes of cargo, where a helicopter can only carry 800 kilos.

We found out from the greenies that we weren't allowed to use paint on the ice again to mark out a runway, so we had a problem—what could we use? It had to be something dark which could easily be seen from the air, and bio-degradable. So they came up with the ship's cocoa! It was poured onto the ice in stripes to mark the runway. That was OK until the penguins became interested in all this activity and the cocoa, and waddled up to have a look. The guys who were out there doing the cargo transfer were trying to scare the penguins off the runway and were giving them a few kicks up the backside to get them away.

The greenies didn't like the idea of that happening at all, so they were chasing the cargo guys around trying to deter them from chasing the penguins. Anyone who has ever seen penguins knows how crazy and inquisitive they are. So of course more of them came across to see what all the kerfuffle was about, while others waddled up to the other end of the runway to inspect the cocoa up there. All in all it threatened to be a bit of a disaster. Finally we got enough people to stand in two rough lines, to indicate the runway, because the cocoa had run out at that stage.

The landing was fine—but we didn't have any cocoa for the rest of the voyage.

I found out that Roger had been involved with the final, sad story of the loss of the Danish charter ship *Nella Dan*. The

Nella was much beloved by those who had sailed on her over the previous twenty-seven years and was the last of the four Danish *Dan* ships that had explored, and transported Australian Antarcticans since Mawson Station was established in 1954. ('Lovely wooden and brass fittings, table service with damask napkins and superb Danish food', sighed one expeditioner. 'Not like the canteen chew-and-spew on *Icebird*. The *Nella* had real style.') She dragged her anchors and was blown ashore on the rocks at Buckles Bay at Macquarie Island in December 1987.

Roger Rusling was the skipper at the time of a Bass Strait oil rig tender the *Lady Lorraine* which had the advantage of being a shallow draft vessel which could get in close enough to the stricken ship to take on board the 600 tonnes of fuel and was powerful enough to tow her off the rocks if salvage was possible.

The first priorities were to stop the oil pollution, then inspect the damaged hull to see if the *Nella Dan* should be scuttled or towed back to Australia. On the third attempt, and the last highest tide of the month, the *Lady Lorraine* managed to pull her off the rocks. According to Roger, the pumps could not keep pace with the water coming in and the decision to scuttle the ship came from Denmark. Early efforts to salvage equipment had to be abandoned when the *Nella Dan* suddenly listed as though she was about to sink again, and the decision was made to take her out to deep water rather than have her wrecked permanently in Buckles Bay—the only anchorage and resupply point for Macquarie Island. But the *Nella Dan* had decided to die hard.

RR: We decided to slowly steam up and down in deep water overnight and see what would happen in the morning. If it did sink, well, it would have scuttled itself. If not, we'd make a further decision in the morning. But in the morning, there she was still behind us, so we decided we would steam back into shallow water and make some attempt to get off some of the more valuable cargo.

I turned and steamed back in, and called the amphibious LARCS out by radio from Macquarie Island to meet us. We were less than a mile off Macquarie Island when I saw this little puff of smoke come out of the aft end of the accommo-

28

dation. Within about ten minutes the whole accommodation block was a roaring inferno—so we turned and went back out to the deep water again to await developments.

TB: It has been suggested by those who thought the *Nella Dan* could and should have been salvaged that she was deliberately fired. What is your view on that?

RR: No, definitely not. When we left Buckles Bay in a hurry, everything was left running, the pumps, the compressors, because we literally thought it was going to sink there and then. It had been a dead ship for a fortnight in a very cold climate, so things like the toasters and the stove were left running twenty-four hours a day in the galley just so people could keep warm. Some 350 tonnes of oil had been discharged through the ship as best we could, and people had put newspapers down on the oily deck to clean their boots. The ship was really a bit of a fire trap. When we left Buckles Bay all this machinery had been left running unattended during the night, so it was surprising it didn't catch fire earlier, actually.

TB: Did things move dramatically after the first puff of smoke?

RR: The whole thing was a roaring inferno within minutes. We thought it would surely sink shortly. So we steamed up and down for another few hours with the *Nella Dan* behind us, and it settled a bit more. But it wouldn't sink. We couldn't put the salvage crew back on board because of the fire, and it didn't appear as if it was going to sink. So we used our water cannon on the *Lady Lorraine* to pump water into the ship, through doors and portholes, to make her sink more quickly. That was very hard to do because she was rolling in a seaway, and it was not very successful and went on for quite a few more hours.

After the fire had virtually burnt itself out we backed up very close to the *Nella Dan* and the salvage crew did go back on board. We rigged a hose between the two ships and used the ballast pumps on the *Lady Lorraine* to physically pump water directly into the *Nella Dan* and that is how she eventually sank.

TB: Last night I saw the video of the sinking taken by your cook, and there was absolute silence in the mess.

RR: It is a moving thing to watch any ship go down,

especially one with a career like the *Nella Dan*. I had Arne Sorensen, the skipper of the *Nella Dan*, standing at my shoulder when we were going through all these manoeuvres. What could I say to the man? He didn't say anything. He just stood there and watched. A bit of a Danish ice-man really. Anything I said would have been a platitude. We both stood there in silence and watched her go down.

CHAPTER THREE

Storms and Superstitions at Sea • The Morally Deep Aspirations of the Philosopher • The First Iceberg Triggers Major Koda-chrome Alert • Recollections of the Orange Bellied Parrot • Can Larcies Really Be Trusted? • Giant Bird Wrestling and Cardiac Massage for Elephant Seals

JANUARY 8

A wild and stormy sea. Went up to the bridge to record some wind and storm sounds. Noted that *Icebird* was rolling thirty degrees at times. A lone albatross was skimming over the breaking crests of the waves. The sun broke through low cloud in the afternoon revealing a brilliant stormy sea flecked with white crests and trailing streaks of foam.

Although the *Icebird*'s crew have been shaking their heads in disbelief at the smooth run south we have been having this voyage, the Southern Ocean is turning on some more charac-teristic behaviour. It was exhilarating to stand on the bridge (and occasionally out on the flying bridge) and watch *Icebird*'s bows rear up and crash down over the wind-whipped swells in a welter of broken seas and foam, drenching the amphibious LARCs lashed down on the foredeck. I looked up the Beaufort Scale chart and estimated we were in a Force 8, with winds from the south-west at around forty knots—technically a gale. 'Moderately high waves of great length: edges of crests begin to break into spindrift. The foam is blown in well-marked streaks along the direction of the wind,' was the official description. That looked pretty right to me.

It is bad sailor's luck and absolutely forbidden to whistle on the ship; to do so on the bridge is a

*An unusual cloud formation, photographed beside a rare clear view of
'Big Ben' in 1948.*
Antarctic Division photograph by Alan Campbell-Drury.

**particularly heinous crime. I was so carried away with
the excitement of watching *Icebird* punching through
the dirty weather that I began to whistle the first few
bars of Mendlessohn's Italian Symphony and was
pounced on by Captain Brune. Cut flowers are also a
no-no, and he performed to some order in Hobart,
apparently, when someone sent a bunch of flowers on
board for Ulli Feddern, the stewardess.**

Sea-sickness has cut a swathe through attendance at meal
times. No need for two sittings at the moment. Dr Barry Batts,
a Macquarie University geochemist in one of the cabins almost
opposite, tells me one of his cabin 'Okkupanten', meteorologist
David Turner, has been flat on his back since we sailed. There
are two kinds of sea-sickness pills, downers and uppers. The
uppers are supposed to get you up and about in the daytime,
but David, according to Barry, just takes the downers and
spends as much time as possible unconscious. Sea-sickness

is a terrible scourge. Mercifully I seem to be coping all right with the help of the Scop behind-the-ear patches. I'm told all the rolling stops when we get to the pack ice. The third man in cabin C9 is the environmental philosopher. I was intrigued to find out what he was planning to do down south, but after interviewing him on tape I am still not sure.

He says he will look at all living things in Antarctica including seals, penguins, birds and other wild life—even lichens and mosses—and how human beings interact with and affect those living things. 'I don't think the moral sphere stops with the human race. Plants, animals, ecosystems and species are included', he told me. 'We live in a world morally significant in a number of ways.'

Lawrence Johnson is also interested in the political situation, including the activities of the Russians, Chinese and French in the region because 'political decisions lead to moral decisions'.

Was he some kind of moral watchdog then?

'I am an investigator and a theoriser. I want to think about all these things and develop ideas. I don't want to pontificate. I'll familiarise myself with field work and ask ethical questions. At this stage I'm not going to try and supply any ethical answers, though.'

The Philosopher has lent me one of his research publications. It is titled *A Morally Deep World*. He has dedicated it to his children 'in the hope that they may live deeply valuable lives in a morally deep world'. I think he thinks something matters!

My theory, expounded in the bar last night, that the Indian Ocean-style weather we have been experiencing was clear evidence that we were not really going to the Antarctic at all— that Captain Brune was actually sailing towards South Africa where he was proposing to hold us hostage in Mozambique— has been exploded. The first iceberg has been sighted, so we are unquestionably getting closer to Antarctica. This is a moment of considerable significance on the voyage. There has been much conjecture about what day, what time of day, and on what quarter that first berg would be seen. For the record a smudge of white was seen on the starboard horizon at 4.10 pm on January 8.

Clare Robertson, an artist from Darwin, is particularly excited. Since 1983 she has been concentrating on a long-term art project in which she is contrasting a number of the most extreme and dramatic geographical locations. Two are equatorial, two are polar; two are being formed by volcanic activity, one is being ripped apart by it. They include Iceland and Greenland, Kilauea in the Hawaiian islands, the Kimberley/ Pilbara area, Antarctica, and she hopes to paint the African Rift Valley. Her first priority is to sketch the icebergs floating majestically in the Southern Ocean, each one an ice sculpture with its own intrinsic fascination.

No matter how many photographs you may have seen of icebergs, it is impossible to comprehend their reality until you have actually seen them in three dimensions: these enormous chunks of glacier ice floating grandly away from the Antarctic continent to their inevitable doom and destruction. Most begin as 'tabular' bergs with square tops—like a skyscraper floating along with only the top five stories showing above the water. Yet some tabular bergs can be several kilometres long, and almost as wide. Eventually the warmer sea water erodes them and they topple over, or half capsize, exposing elegant, water worn pinnacles, domes and spires. Ice caves of a deep cobalt blue form at their base. The colours in their fissures and jagged vents range from aquamarine to pure jade. Eventually the crystalline structure of these floating bergs decays to the point where they simply disintegrate.

Those who saw the *Four Corners* television program filmed in Antarctica in 1988 from a cruise ship sailing from South America will recall the once-in-a-lifetime chance to see—on film—the final collapse of a rare 'jade' berg. These particularly beautiful icebergs are most spectacular, formed of deep green and dark blue ice. As the ship carrying tourists and the *Four Corners* crew steamed past, this jade berg tilted, half rolled, lost its structural integrity, and self-destructed in a boiling maelstrom of green ice and thundering, falling ice cliffs. Surely the photo opportunity of a lifetime.

Perhaps the easiest way to comprehend how Antarctica constantly delivers these huge icebergs into its surrounding oceans is to return to the metaphor of the continent as a huge

A magic moment. The first iceberg!

dome of candied honey. All the 'honey' is on the move, slipping down to the edges and breaking off as icebergs. Some have been noted at more than fifty kilometres long and have been tracked by satellites for years. At least seventy per cent of the world's fresh water is locked up in Antarctica, and at the top of the 'dome' in the centre of the continent the ice is up to four and a half kilometres thick.

It is impossible to forget the impact of the sight of your first iceberg forging its lonely path through the Southern Ocean. Indeed, as we got closer, it was a wonder it did not dissolve through intensive bursts of Kodachrome radiation. Yet even after the constant parade of these stately ice forms had become more common, they remained an endless fascination and the regular cry of 'Kodachrome Alert' would ring out as *Icebird*'s course took us close to yet another berg, or cluster of bergs.

Fellow journalist Keith Scott wrote in his diary on January 9:

'**. . . They are rising out of the ocean around us like great islands or castles from some mystical fairy- land . . . they vary in colour depending on the light but even on overcast days can glow a sort of translucent aqua blue. One particularly spectacular berg passed us**

close on the starboard side this evening, catching the full reflection of the sun in brilliant orange–pink against an almost charcoal sea and sky.

'It is somehow humbling to think that such incredible beauty can exist so far from where we live and would exist whether or not we were here to see it.'

On her own admission, Clare Robertson has gone into 'iceberg overload', sketch pad in action, pen flying over art paper. Captain Brune is amused by her transports of delight, and offers to steer close to one particularly spectacular tabular berg ahead, with great ice cliffs and purple ice caves at its base into which the low swell is breaking with a distant boom and clouds of spray. He is as good as his word. I note that even the outwardly blase old Antarctic hands still sneak the occasional photo. It is simply the most stunning spectacle we Antarctic first-timers have ever seen.

JANUARY 9

There is talk in the mess about the psychological effects of Antarctica on human beings. We are simply not meant to be here, and we merely cling to the edges of Antarctica, bringing our own civilisation with us in capsules. Des Lugg said that people always slow up going to Antarctica. I am certainly sleeping much more—an afternoon nap as well as through the night.

The medical project for which I am one of many guinea pigs is trying to find out why those who go to the Antarctic—even only for six to eight weeks—suffer a measurable drop in their immune systems.

Richard Ferguson from the Mawson Institute in Adelaide is doing a photographic project associated with the work of the pioneer Antarctic photographer Frank Hurley, lent me a most interesting book by Stephen J Pyne called *The Ice—A Journey to Antarctica*. Pyne argues that no one has ever achieved a full adaptation to Antarctica. There is usually a period of initial disruption lasting from two to four weeks, after which a relative degree of adjustment is achieved; so summer transients like us never really have time to adjust.

Some of the effects on the winterers, according to Pyne, are disruption of diurnal sleep rhythms, deprivation of sensory stimuli, weight gain, dehydration, hypothermia, decreased blood circulation in the extremities, sleep arrhythmias, and minor frostbite. Sights, sounds, smells and feelings erode away, opines the rather gloomy Pyne. One year is about all an individual can stand at a time, and occasionally two! Yet I know some Australian expeditioners have, through necessity, wintered twice without complaint of apparent ill effects.

I am getting to know more of my shipmates. Dave Watts is a wild life photographer now living in Tasmania. He told me a remarkable story of how he managed to film the rare Orange Bellied Parrot in the South West Tasmanian wilderness. It is only the size of a budgerigar, and unfortunately there are only about 200 remaining. These tiny birds fly down to Tasmania from the South Australian and Victorian coasts, to nest.

Dave said that the parents return to the mainland before the chicks, but their offspring know through instinct to follow and fly over Bass Strait. No one had ever filmed them nesting. He was told by National Park rangers that a nest was ten feet up a tree, but it was actually twenty-eight feet. He had to build a substantial camouflaged tower of tea-tree poles as a hide. By a great stroke of luck, the afternoon sun actually shone through into the nest hole high in the tree so he did not have to use a flash. The site was a two-hour walk from his base camp!

He successfully photographed the parent birds and their chicks, and became so emotionally involved with them that he actually cried when the chicks finally flew away. He checked in later years, and the rare little Orange Bellied Parrots he had photographed were still returning to the same nest.

Both Dave and Keith Scott are spending a great deal of time aft of the bridge, photographing the albatrosses and petrels at the stern of the *Icebird*.

The Professor snored so loudly last night he crashed through my foam ear plug barrier. Dennis claimed to have had no sleep at all.

The water temperature is now below 2 degrees C, and we are making contact with the occasional

'growler': small bergs so called because of the grumbling noise they make as they slide along the side of the ship as we hit them.

After dinner there was quite a gathering up on the bridge. There was a clear sky to the horizon and the sun looked ready to set but it seemed strangely reluctant. We are already in the zone of permanent summer light. As the sun curved down towards the horizon it threw the most beautiful glow on the steep ice cliffs on the bergs off the starboard bow, initiating a frenzy of photography. I wish I'd bought shares in Kodak before I left.

I have made contact with the Larcies—an ebullient bunch of lads! There are Bargies and Larcies actually, a group from an ANARE Detachment from the 10th Terminal Regiment, who come down each year on the Antarctic resupply voyages to operate the amphibious LARCS (Lighter Amphibious Resupply Craft) and the powered barges that can ferry the huge containers of equipment and supplies to equip and maintain the stations for the coming year. LARCs are effectively a boat with four big wheels tacked on. They evolved from the World War Two Army DUKW which was essentially a truck with a hull built around it. Both DUKWs and LARCs can cope with quite large seas and surf and then drive straight up on to land with their cargo. They have been essential on the Antarctic run since they were first used at Macquarie Island in 1948, and later on Heard Island.

The Larcies train during the year, I was told, by loading boxes of rocks on and off their LARCs in Sydney's Middle Harbour, so the annual Antarctic expeditions are a welcome break. There are officers as well as other ranks, but their easy camaraderie and civilian dress seem to make these formal structures irrelevant.

Their unofficial motto is: 'Trust me—I'm a Larcie'. This is a necessity, apparently, when descending a rope ladder down the side of the ship to board a LARC which is heaving up and down on a swell. When the Larcie says jump—well, you jump! We have already been told to practise climbing on and off the LARCs lashed to the foredeck, by using the hub of their enormous wheels as a step. They are quite high off the ground.

Larcies don't normally spend a great deal of time in Antarctica, but several I met on *Icebird* had spent six months on Heard Island—a longer stay than planned because of the loss of the *Nella Dan* at Macquarie Island in late 1987. In effect they became expeditioners and helped the biologists and ornithologists—and all the other 'ologists they said—with their field work.

Heard Island is a most spectacular place, a 3000 metre volcano rising straight out of the sea. It has a particularly violent and tempestuous climate yet, being a sub-Antarctic island, is a haven for wild life. The Antarctic Division used to have a permanent station there from 1948 to 1954, but closed it down when the first Antarctic mainland station, Mawson, was established. Since then it has been occupied for short periods of time with summer science expeditions. Unlike Macquarie Island, which has introduced species such as rabbits and cats, Heard Island is pristine. I was interested to chat on tape to the three Larcies who had spent so long there, to see whether the experience had changed their way of thinking about Antarctica:

Dutchy: It did change my outlook. We had problems when we first got to Heard Island. I was a smoker at that stage. Through force of habit, I used to throw the butt off the end of my fingers when it was finished. Now don't get me wrong, I'm not a complete Greenpeace freak, I understand what they're trying for and that sort of thing—but I can't go the whole hog. I mean, I'm not going to lie down in front of a bulldozer. But after a couple of weeks experiencing Heard Island, even a cigarette butt sticks out like a Mini Minor in an empty car park. It's there and you notice it. It's introduced, and some animal might eat it and it's not going to do it any good. At Heard Island nothing has been introduced except Kerguelan cabbage. It's one of the few places in the world with no introduced species.

Tim: What stopped you flicking your cigarette butts about?

Dutchy: I did it myself. I walked around and I thought, 'There's nothing here'. I mean, sure, the huts at Atlas Cove have been there for many years and there's a lot of rubbish left over, but a lot of that has been cleared away now. It is actually historical rubbish for want of a better word. But a cigarette butt is obscene. And it is not only cigarette butts. We used to do a coastal walk around our end of the island and you would find fishing net buoys washed up on the beaches, plastic milk bottles, soft drink bottles, cartons, anything that isn't biodegradable.

Scott: We found three young fur seals that were about a year and a half old, and early in their lives they had swum into a fish net. These three guys were sitting on the beach about three feet apart with this eight foot trail of net behind them. We caught them so Peter our vet could free them, and he actually had to cut into their necks to get the square of mesh that they'd grown into. I'm very conscious now about rubbish. I don't throw bottles over the side or anything. I'll always remember those seals, those little fur seals with that bloody big green fishing net growing into their necks.

In the early evening, the scientists working on Heard Island and the Army Larcies used to meet in the mess hut for the evening meal. It was the only time of the day everyone was together.

Dutchy: We made the bread at night after the evening meal, which we'd take turns in cooking. There'd be chit-chat about what had happened that day or what people were going to do tomorrow. We'd have our radio sked with Davis Station. We'd talk to them—someone in the real world—and our people at Spit Bay on the other end of the island. Then some of the scientists would fix up their day's field notes and that sort of thing. It was like a family atmosphere, as though back in the old days when there was no TV and no radio. It was like family times, so I've heard, many many moons ago, pre-World War Two, when families used to just sit around the table and talk.

Tim: You're right, you know, not many of your generation have ever done that.

Scott: It was really good there, because some of the people were from absolutely different walks of life. We were Larcies, most of us had done a few years in the Services, done a bit of travel, moved around the country, and we were talking and working with people who lived for pool complexes—just a couple of puddles in the ground. That was their life, they just loved puddles. And birds—I've never seen anyone so infatuated with sea gulls. But it was quite interesting to find out that this particular guy knew every type of sea gull that there was.

Tim: Did you feel you learned something from the people who were there?

Dutchy: Learned? That's probably an understatement. I learned so much from the people who were there, the varied jobs that they had, the projects they were down there to do. I did a lot of work with Ann Robb, the archeologist, doing work on some old sealers' huts. I'm a backwoods boy and don't understand much about science, and a lot was above my level. Sometimes they talked more than four feet above my head. But by the time we'd finished with them, they could talk at our level, and we could talk at theirs.

Tim: Did you get away from the main camp at all?

Kevin: We managed to get a few field trips in. One bloke there, Max Downes, who had been to Heard twice before and banded some birds as chicks in 1953, wanted to see if he could find any of those bands. He was hoping to find them on the ground at these nesting areas.

Scott: These were Southern Giant Petrels which are about the size of an albatross, a very large bird, with a five or six feet wing span. They weighed about twenty and twenty-five kilos.

Kevin: We had a look at some of these birds by getting a long stick and lifting it up on its nest to see if it had a band on its leg. We weren't really expecting to find any on living birds. But after about three hours, I found a band! I gave a signal to Max Downes across the other side of the colony, and he came burning across. He thought it was the greatest thing since sliced bread. So, the last part of that day we spent with this bird, taking photos, measuring, doing checks with its eyes and this and that. Eventually we found nineteen banded birds.

Scott: As you lifted up the bird with a stick to see its leg, it would look at you with utter contempt as if to say, 'Disappear, boy, you don't belong here'. Max would find the data from his pack relating to the band number, and say, 'I banded this bird at such and such a day on this site twenty-five years ago'. We'd do a few calculations and work out that this bird was six months older than Kev. Let's be nice to it!

Kevin: It was amazing. Some of these birds, it should be said, didn't like being handled and would try and run away. They have to run into the wind to take off and we had to try and stop them—particularly if they had bands on their legs and Max wanted the number. So it was quite comical to watch them running along across the azorella, which is like a mossy carpet. Max would also be running across trying to block their take-off. Scotty ran across, trying to stop one bird which had almost got to flying speed, and just disappeared! He'd fallen into a gully. As he went down he managed to get his hands on the tail feathers of the bird and went down in a big heap. I was laughing so much I couldn't do much about anything. Max, who was sixty or so years old, came flying down the gully and grabbed the bird in a tackle and got it.

Scott: There was a big scream of 'Oooh, shit' as I hit the bottom of the gully about twelve feet down, but I'd stuffed the bird's aerodynamics by grabbing it as I fell, and that's how Max managed to catch it.

Tim: I guess it beats loading rocks in Sydney Harbour.

The Larcies also helped out with a program to measure and tag elephant seals.

Kevin: Early on we were working with the weaned pups, getting them away from mum and weighing them and tagging them. Then, every couple of weeks, we'd go back and reweigh them, using a tripod and electronic scales. It was a pretty funny kind of thing to do, because Mum didn't want to let them go, and Mum was a lot bigger than we were. But we managed that all right.

Then we had to get some elephant seals after they had had a feed, weigh them and pump their stomachs. I'd never done anything like that in my life. The gear they sent down to do the job wouldn't work, the hose we were supposed to push down their throats, into their stomachs, was too big. We found some right-sized hose on the island and worked out a flushing system, with five or six gallons of water, to make them throw up into another bucket. Meanwhile the seal's lying there spaced right out. He doesn't know what's going on.

Scott: We had one large fellow who didn't come out of the anaesthetic. If you've ever tried to perform cardiac massage on anyone at all, it's a pretty tricky manoeuvre. You ought to try doing it to an 1800 kilo, three-metre-long sleeping bag called an elephant seal! This entails a guy standing on each side driving his knees into the side of this seal, just behind his side flippers. Like dropping your knee into his armpit I suppose. It took us about forty-five minutes. When an elephant seal goes out on you, the eyes go green— just like a traffic light except that it's stop, not go. And this guy went green three times and we brought him back. He finally gave up the ghost, unfortunately. But that was one of the very few we lost.

The Larcies had been on Heard Island—and with the same group of people—for so long that when they returned to Australia they had the same trouble readjusting to outside life that Antarctic winterers have.

Dutchy: I remember the night the ship got in to Hobart. Some other Larcies were there to meet me and it is a tradition to have a drink with friends when we get back. There were just so many people on the wharf, greeting other expeditioners. There were hugs and kisses with everyone I had been on Heard with, but we couldn't actually bring ourselves to say goodbye to them. We were like a pack of penguins on an ice floe; no one wanted to leave! We had had this little group of our own for so long we couldn't face going our own ways. So I went to the hotel and had a shower and disappeared for half an hour. I didn't want to go out with the people who had come to meet me.

Scott: We were away two days short of eight months. I was looking forward to seeing my girl friend again. A friend came to run me around to where she was working and things were very tense, because we didn't know how to approach each other again. It took nearly two or three weeks to settle

*Eat your heart out Eric Bogle . . . the Army Larcies in full cry with
their parody of 'The Band Played Waltzing Matilda'. Bryan Smith
watches thoughtfully (far right), stubby in hand.*

back in. One of the hardest things was driving in Sydney
traffic. After just driving a LARC down a deserted beach
at thirty clicks, to get back on Victoria Road at peak hour
traffic with everything doing eighty to one hundred clicks
was frightening.

Kevin: I had a large adjustment problem. I couldn't handle
crowd scenes. I got back and my sister's children caused
me a hassle because, being young, they made a lot of noise,
and with that and the people who had come around to see
me after I had been away for so long, I couldn't handle it.
I found myself going for walks around the place to calm
down.

The Larcies have their own voyage song, which they performed
with great aplomb one night in Stoppy's Bar and which is
reproduced here with profound apologies to Eric Bogle.

When I was a young man I carried a pack
And I lived the free life of a Larcie.
From Sydney's blue harbour, to the chilly ice pack
I steamed my tin bar-ge all over.
Then in 1989 the country said, 'Son,
It's time you stopped bludging, there is work to be done'.
So they gave me a wool hat and they gave me a grease gun,
And sent me away to the Pole.

And the band played Waltzing Matilda
As *Icebird* pulled away from the quay,
And midst all the tears, the flag-waving and cheers,
We sailed off to Antarctica.

And well I remember that terrible Tuesday—
How the beers stained the sons and the daughters,
And how in that hell they called Stoppy's Bar
We were pissed and full of disorder.
Ulle, she was waiting, she'd stock the bar well,
She rained us with stubbies and all from the shelves
And in ten minutes flat, we'd bloated ourselves,
Nearly threw up right back to the cabin.

And the band played Waltzing Matilda
When we stopped to go to the heads.
Ulle stocked the bar, and when the shutters went up,
We started all over again.

And those that were left, well we tried to survive
In a mad world of booze, cold and icebergs.
And for nearly ten days, I kept myself alive
Though around me the stubbies piled higher.
Then a double Tequila knocked me arse over head,
And when I woke up, in my cabin bed,
I saw what I'd done, and I wished I was dead.
Never felt there were worse things than hangovers.

For I'll go on no more sipping my beer,
All around the wild oceans, far and free.
No more beer kegs, a man needs both legs;
And no more drinking at Stoppy's for me.

Then they gathered the Jafos and Larcies and Boffins,
And sent us down south to Davis,
The riggers, the film crew, the doctors and others,
The brave, sick heroes of *Icebird*.
And when our ship pulled into Mawson Bay
I looked at the decks where the LARCS used to lay,
And thanked Christ there were choppers waiting for me
To carry me into the Station.

And the band played Waltzing Matilda
As they staggered down the rope ladder.
But no Larcie cheered, they just stood there and glared,
As they turned and froze on the ladder.

So every day my cold comrades start
Driving old LARCS and the barges.
And I put on my ventiles and stand on the deck
And watch the parade pass before me.
The Larcies move slowly, their heads stiff and sore,
Hungover men from the long night before.
The expeditioners ask: 'What are they working for?'
I ask myself the same question.

And the band played Waltzing Matilda
As the Larcies respond to the call.
But as year follows year, more Larcies appear.
But no one will give a shit at all.

CHAPTER FOUR

We Enter the Pack Ice • Transvestites Rampage in Stoppy's Bar • Crossing the Antarctic Convergence • Forced Ingestion of Foul Substances • Peter the Bosun Tells His Amazing Arctic Survival Story

JANUARY 11

We are in the pack ice! A fine morning with a scattering of icebergs dotted around the horizon, gleaming and glistening in the sun on a bright blue sea. The pack ice appeared ahead as a thin white line. It is broken pack, and *Icebird* slowed its speed and has no trouble pushing through. There is a great clang as we hit the occasional unbroken floe. The reinforced bow is designed to ride up over the larger ice floes, then the weight of the ship crunches down, cracks the ice and pushes it away on each side. Down on the lower foredeck was a great vantage point, watching these great broken slabs of ice tilting sideways away from the ship—rather like upending great chunks of metre-thick reinforced concrete. The ice is surprisingly stained brown underneath. It is not pollution but algae that is a vital part of the Antarctic food chain.

The *Icebird* is now as steady as a Bass Strait oil platform. I am meeting many of my fellow passengers for the first time as they emerge from their miasma of *mal de mer*. Meal times are crowded again, with two sittings. God, the times are uncivilised. Breakfast isn't too bad from 7.30 to 8.30 am. Lunch is 11.30, and dinner an exceedingly premature 5.30 pm. Clare Robertson describes shipboard life as a blend of comfort and army discipline.

47

The *Icebird* is air conditioned so, unless you go out on deck, you can wear T-shirts, shorts and thongs if you want, and some Antarcticans do. It is quite common to see someone walk from the warmth of the bridge out into the elements on the flying bridge just in shirt and shorts to take a photo. Some hardier souls have actually been sunbaking in a sheltered spot

View from the bow as Icebird's *specially strengthened hull rides up over the larger slabs of pack ice and splits them effortlessly.*

near the funnel—despite the hazard posed by the allegedly depleted Antarctic ozone layer.

I had long coveted one of the Antarctic Division's sheepskin hats, with a flap that covers your ears and fastens under the chin. They are not issued to contemptible round-trippers like me, but Roger Rusling, the Third Mate, has generously donated one of his spares. My rather quaint Mawson-style knitted balaclava has gone back into the kit bag.

JANUARY 12

We had a fancy dress party in 'Stoppy's' Bar, so named because it is Captain Ewald Brune's favourite tavern in Hobart. Some extraordinary get-ups were seen. There is a strong tradition of drag in the Antarctic, it seems. 'Koota', one of the Larcies, appeared as a hugely pregnant maiden with a large balloon wobbling obscenely under his close-fitting evening gown. Three brother Larcies appeared in yellow 'ties and tails' created from cut-down overalls. The formality was offset with briefs worn over their trousers, encasing what mercifully turned out to be bananas. Many voyagers had obviously come prepared. I unwisely went as a Hula Girl. Well, at least I had a ukulele! My grass skirt was a green garbage bag slit into strips, and hair donated by Dennis; surgical gloves suspended from a peaked cap. Two toilet rolls under my singlet completed what was far from a tasteful sight.

Bryan Smith, from *Beyond 2000* (sea-sickness behind him) took a firm line on this kind of thing. 'You're mad', he said. 'I never dress up and I try not to be photographed at parties'. He was quite right! (People are **still** sending unsolicited snaps of me as that ghastly 'Hula Girl'.) We partied on till 5 the following morning. I have a confused recollection of walking out on the flying bridge so dressed. Even more unwanted photographs confirm that I did.

JANUARY 13

Ooof, I have a crippling hangover. Definitely a cooked breakfast morning. Bad timing, because today brought

This unlovely sight was typical of unexpected snaps which were sent to me without mercy, time and time again, by Voyage Sixers.

the Crossing of the Convergence Ceremony. The Antarctic Convergence is where the comparatively mild Southern Ocean meets the super-chilled Antarctic waters. It is the polar equivalent of crossing the equator, although the 'celebrations' are more robust.

All morning the crew delighted in carrying around a vile stew for us to inspect and smell, laced with curry powder, Tabasco and detergent, it was alleged, which we would be forced to consume later. We were told to assemble in the cargo hold, in full ventiles (our cold weather gear). King Neptune (Second Officer Werner Schlieker) and his glamorous Assistant (Stewardess Ulle Feddern) accompanied by other Knights of the Emperor Penguin Court, arrived with due ceremony, tridents, hemp beards and funny hats. Some members of the ship's company were singled out for 'special' treatment! Chris Sattlberger, the only Austrian among the German crew, was one of the unluckiest and had eggs broken on his head and green slime poured over his hair in addition to the indignities accorded to everyone else. The rest of us lined up for a glass of the foul 'brew' (the whole glass had to be drunk, not just sipped), a dipper of ice cubes and water sluiced down the back of our necks and red anti-fouling paint dabbed on our noses before receiving our Certificates of Entry to Antarctica at 66 degrees E longitude. Chris said it took an hour under the shower to get rid of the green slime. Red noses were seen around the ship for days afterwards.

This ceremony is now enshrined in the pantheon of Antarctic ritual on *Icebird*—a rite of passage which has become part of the process of coming to terms with, and getting to, the

Crossing the Antarctic Convergence ceremony. Professor Konrad Muller gets a dollop of ice and water down the back of his neck from 'King Neptune', Second Officer Werner Schliecker.

Continent. There are few real 'journeys' left in the world. Going to Antarctica is a voyage in the classic tradition of appreciating the distances involved, the isolation and the progression along the various stages of the journey—from ocean storms to first iceberg, from pack ice to the first sight of the Antarctic continent itself. There is a nagging realisation that we are a long way from any help if anything should go wrong. It is a thought we consciously put aside as we eat, sleep, talk and carouse in Stoppy's Bar. *Icebird* seems reassuringly safe, functional and secure. It is our home, our haven and our life.

Yet things can go wrong. The wrecking of the *Nella Dan* on Macquarie Island is a recent reality. Our lifeboat drill is a time for much wise-cracking and outward high spirits—a mood not shared by our Bosun, Peter Hadamek. This quietly spoken, slightly built man has survived the sinking of a sister ship to *Icebird* in Arctic waters off the coast of Iceland in 1983. It is directly as a result of that experience that our lifeboats are totally enclosed with fibre-glass canopies, and that *Icebird* carries immersion suits for its crew which will sustain life in the water for up to eight hours. As it would take at least eight days, let alone hours, for another ship to reach us, the question is academic. Without an immersion suit, it is estimated a human being can last only a few minutes in the zero degree waters of Antarctica.

I was told Peter Hadamek managed to survive a sinking and prolonged immersion in Arctic waters, and asked him if he would talk to me on tape about what happened. Peter was reluctant at first on two grounds. First, he said, his English was not good. The second reason I anticipated, following my experience in past years talking to Australian prisoners-of-war about their period of captivity on places like the Thai-Burma Railway and on the Sandakan Death Marches. It was extremely emotionally disturbing to recall traumatic events, even after many years. But, after some encouragement from Niels Grell, the ship's Radio Operator, he agreed to tell me of the events of 1 November, 1983. The *Kampen* was a new ship, only three months old, and was on her way from Holland to Greenland with a cargo of powdered coke.

PH: After three days was coming a very strong storm. So then we check the hatches and we see is water inside.

So what's happened there? Where is the water coming from? And we find out the hatch covers were not waterproof.

We had two heavy cranes on the port side, same as the *Icebird*, and as the water turned the coke powder into a liquid, the wet coke powder kept shifting more and more to the port side. The two cranes listed the ship more and more to the port side. We tried to get the water out, but it was impossible, the seas were too rough. We couldn't go on deck, and we hoped we would get to Greenland before things got more dangerous. The weather was very bad. I had been thirteen years at sea and this was the worst I had experienced. It was over Force 12—more than 100 knots with waves thirteen metres high. A hurricane.

TB: Did the Captain realise that the ship was going down?

PH: That was very strange. We asked the Captain: 'What has happened with the ship and are you going in to the nearest port?' He say no, the ship is safe and we go on to Greenland.

TB: But you knew differently.

PH: Oh, I knew if we went on to Greenland, we would sink. A big container ship came past us and radioed our ship: '*Kampen*, what's happening with you, can we help you? Do you need some help?' Our captain said: 'No, all is clear, we have 190 miles left to Greenland and everything is OK'. But even so, the captain of the container ship gave information to the shore that there was something wrong with the *Kampen*. Then the Coastguard called the Captain, and said: 'Captain, we hear you have some problems, you have water in your ship. Do you need pumps to get the water out?' At this time I was on the bridge on sea watch, so I heard this. And the Captain said: 'Everything is all clear here. There is no problem.'

TB: Had he gone mad mad? What was going on?

PH: Yes, at this time he was mad. He didn't know what was happening with the ship. He didn't seem to understand the problem was so serious. He kept saying that the ship is only three months old, it cannot sink.

TB: Rather like the *Titanic*—it's new, so it can't sink.

PH: Oh yes, we thought it also at first, but when we saw this forty-three degree list, and when the engine stopped, we knew we had big trouble. The coke slurry got in to the

53

engine room and stopped our engines. Then the crew realised the ship was sinking. We have lost power and we are drifting in this terrible storm and high seas in a dead ship.

TB: So the Captain must, surely, by this time have realised there was a problem.

PH: He just said: 'It's OK. The engineers will fix the engine and we will go straight to the nearest port in Iceland.' We were then listing more than forty degrees. This was the first time the captain had spoken to the ship's company.

TB: It's unbelievable.

PH: Yes. It's a terrible story.

TB: How many crew did you have on board?

PH: We had thirteen crew members altogether. The ABs and deck hands had a meeting and agreed that if we could not get in to port in the next few hours, the ship would sink. And we agreed that when it was time for sleep we would not take off our clothes, we would put some cream on our skin, and wait to see what happens.

TB: Were these the only precautions you could take? Were there no immersion suits?

PH: Nothing.

TB: What did you know about the cold? Did you know what you had to do to stop the cold?

PH: We tried to put on as many clothes as we could, and plastered our skin with grease—cold cream. That was all we could do. It was Tuesday when the ship was sinking, and on Tuesday afternoon, it was coffee time. I came into the mess room, starboard side, and there was one metre of water there. The ship was very low. So we went to the bridge and told the captain we had water in our mess room. And he said again: 'That's not a problem. We have 190 miles left'.

TB: He had obviously lost all grip on reality!

PH: Yes. So when we had finished work on that Tuesday, about 7.05 pm, the new watchman said that we should come to the bridge and bring the life raft. The Captain was very white in his face. He didn't seem to be able to speak. He was pacing from one side of the bridge to the other. We asked him if we could get the ship's life boats ready for lowering? 'Do what you want', he said. So we went down to the starboard life boat, but there was too much list on the *Kampen* to launch it.

54

TB: Was that an enclosed life boat like the ones we have on the *Icebird*?

PH: No, just an open boat. So we left that and went to the life raft, and prepared to lower it down to the water with ropes. One man came down from the bridge and said that the Captain had fallen down—there was something wrong with him. We went back to the bridge and asked the Captain what was the matter. He said: 'I am the Captain, I must stay on the bridge, the ship is sinking . . . I don't know why.' And then we asked him if we could launch the life raft. He said again: 'Do whatever you like'. We asked him if he had made an emergency call on the radio. 'Yes', he said. 'Some people, some fishing boats are coming.' Then we felt a little better and we launched the life raft. But it was bad. It didn't fall in the water, but on the next deck down—the aft deck—and inflated itself there. Normally the life raft has two rings. One at the bottom, and the other held up the sides and formed a canopy. But only the bottom ring inflated, so we knew we would have no protection from the waves or the weather.

When the life raft hit the water it drifted out about forty metres, held by a rope. All together we pulled the life raft to within about eight metres of the ship. Then one AB took a rope, jumped into the water and swam to the life raft and held it. Then he shouted to me: 'Peter you come next', because I was not so heavy. I looked behind me at the ship sinking, and then I jumped into the water.

TB: How cold was the water?

PH: Three degrees Celsius.

TB: And you knew enough about that to know that your chances of survival in that water were poor, that you couldn't last very long in that water?

PH: Yes, yes, yes. And when I jumped I went under the water for a few seconds, and felt terrible—I thought I had died in those few seconds. Then I came up, and swam to the life raft. Then the next man came and said that the Captain was not on the ship any more. He had gone. 'What has happened?' we asked. 'He just said: "Do what you can" and jumped overboard.'

And then all the rest of the crew came to swim to the life raft, and the Chief Engineer was not strong enough to hold on to the rope, and we could hear him in the water crying for help, but we couldn't help him, it was impossible. After ten minutes he stopped calling and we knew he was dead. So then we were eleven people in this half of a life raft.

Ten minutes later the *Kampen* started to sink about fifty metres from us. At first all was quiet, but when the ship was about five metres under the surface of the sea, then we heard a big noise and we wondered what it was. It was the 'tween deck hatch covers breaking out and it was very dangerous for us. We could see the floating covers coming towards us. One of them was thirteen tonnes' weight. We were helpless and couldn't do anything, although we cried, 'Help, help, help' but we heard nothing. One cover hit us and punctured a section of the life raft, so now we only had a rubber ring with a little air in it under us. The raft was swamped. The eleven of us were actually sitting in the water with just this rubber ring around us to keep us from floating away in this terrible storm.

Then we heard an aircraft, and we knew something was going on, that somebody would help us. And then, we see very far away on the horizon, a light. But it was an aurora, the northern polar light.

TB: Had the captain made an emergency call on the radio?

PH: Not the captain, but the second officer. But it was on the wrong frequency. He didn't check the channel when he cried, 'Mayday, Mayday, Mayday'. Normally that is done on Channel Sixteen, but he was on Channel Twenty-six. And by very good luck there was somebody standing by on Channel Twenty-Six.

And so we waited and waited, and we were becoming very cold. We tried some singing and huddled together for warmth. But more and more people died. It was too cold. The second officer was next to me and we talked together, and the next second he was gone, dead.

One crew member drank a bottle of vodka before he jumped into the water, and that was not good for him. It made him too hot inside, and he was dead in five minutes. I cried, 'Wolfgang, Wolfgang, what's happened,' but he was dead.

And then we see the fishing boats, three of them coming very fast. Help was coming. But I thought I would die before the fishing boats could get to me.

Our bosun, Peter Hadamek, with magazine accounts of his remarkable Arctic survival story.

TB: Just tell me what it's like to be extremely cold like that. What happens to your body?

PH: We were sitting in the water, shivering. First you lose feeling in your arms and legs so you try and work them to feel them. But that's only for a few seconds, and then the shivering begins again. I could hardly think, my head wouldn't work. I felt very, very tired. I wanted to sleep and felt if I did, everything would be OK. Then I said to myself not to sleep, to hang on. And then the fishing boat came.

Inside myself I said, 'Now it's OK, now I will survive'. And at that same second, I became unconscious. And before I became unconscious—this is not a story—in that one second, all my life flashed through my head. When I was born, when I went to school, my first girlfriend . . . in one second. And in that second, I feel very good. That is not a story or a joke, that is true. Then I became unconscious, and I woke up three hours later in a bunk in the fishing boat.

TB: What happened to you while you were unconscious? They must have told you later.

PH: I was the fourth man to be pulled on to the deck. The first three died because the people on the fishing boat massaged them—it was the wrong thing to do.

Then they radioed and asked for medical advice, and a big helicopter came and lowered two doctors down to the deck of the fishing boat. These were only small vessels, about eighteen metres long. Of course it was very rough, and the first thing that happened was the doctors were sea-sick! I was the next on board and the doctors said not to massage me, I was too cold. So then they took all my clothes off, while I was lying on the deck, in the cold air. But the air was warmer than the water. And they left me naked on the deck for about one minute, and then brought me below decks and left me for five hours. Then I was put in a bunk, and after that, they began to massage me.

TB: How many of you survived?

PH: Six. Seven died.

TB: What do you remember thinking when you woke up?

PH: I live, I live. That is the first thing. Then I feel terrible again. I feel cold and I was angry because I thought I felt my heart failing. But the doctor came and said I was OK and just to wait one hour, and I would feel better. We were eight hours in the fishing boat till we got into port.

TB: How long were you in the water?

PH: I was in the water for exactly one hour. The Chief Officer was the last off the ship, he was in the water for thirty minutes.

TB: Why do you think you survived?

PH: I think the important thing was, when the ship was sinking, all the bunker tanks—the fuel tanks—were leaking. We were black from fuel, it was very thick on our skins, and that helped keep the cold out. I think that was one important thing. I also put grease on my skin before going into the water.

TB: How important was your mental attitude?

PH: Oh yes, I had to fight death. I said to myself I did not want to die, I wanted to live, and see my friends and my daughter and I thought a lot of home. And while we were together in the life raft we sang to try and keep up our spirits.

TB: Do you think that survival experience has changed you in any way?

PH: Yes. Before, I was a man who went to plenty of parties. I drank and people thought I was a funny man. But now I am a quiet man. I do not go to the bar, I stay in my cabin. Everybody who knew me before finds me very quiet. I don't talk much. I don't like this! But I can't help it.

TB: I know that it is difficult to talk about it even now. Do you think about it a lot?

PH: Yes. In this ship, we have lifeboat drill and I am the supervisor for Lifeboat Number Four. And I know what happens in cold water. And when we have lifeboat drill, I can't understand why some of the passengers and the crew come not properly dressed and without their life jackets. I just can't understand it. Before the sinking I didn't care much about lifeboat drill, but now it's different.

TB: Peter . . . you came back to sea?

PH: That was the first question my family asked when I came home. Now you stop! No more going to sea. And I say, why? It is my job. So I had a big accident—you can drive a car, or fly in an aircraft and have an accident. I am going back to sea. Three months later I joined a sister ship to *Kampen*. That is my job.

TB: And now you are in the Antarctic.

PH: Oh, it doesn't matter where. Antarctic, or not, that's my job, I like this job.

TB: Were safety procedures changed after your accident?

PH: After this, all German ships have to carry survival

suits, after January 1984, as a result of the sinking of the *Kampen*.

TB: How long can an immersion suit keep you alive?

PH: These immersion suits can keep you alive eight or ten hours in zero degree water. But who is going to come in eight or ten hours down here? If we sink on this trip I think I will jump overboard naked!

TB: And lifeboats are now covered?

PH: That is good. If we had time to get into our lifeboat on the *Kampen*, I think everyone would have survived.

TB: Getting back to the skipper of the *Kampen*. Before this happened, did you believe he was competent?

PH: He was a good man. I worked for him for three months. He was a very good man. Captain Tompson, a German citizen, married with two children. He was serious, he knew his job.

TB: What happened then?

PH: We don't know.

TB: It seems he lost his grip on reality . . .

PH: Yes, we thought that later when we discussed it. The biggest problem was he waited too long to bring us to the bridge. Two hours before would have given us time to launch the lifeboats.

TB: Looking for reasons why people lived, was age important?

PH: On the *Kampen* all people older than thirty-five died. All the survivors were younger than that.

CHAPTER FIVE

Musing on Whale Slaughter and Japanese Chopstick-Based Research Projects • Iceberg Alley and a Photographic Orgy • Arrival at the Ice Edge • The Lord Chamberlain and the Baroness • Attempted Resuscitation of a Frozen Pig • Appalling Assault on the Ship's Gin Supplies • Coming to Terms With New People • Haggis Hurling at Prince Charles Mountains • Last Tango at Dovers

JANUARY 13 (cont)

Our explosively-operated cabin dunny flushing system has failed. I had to remind my cabin confreres this morning that gentlemen *don't* piss in the sink. Manni, the Second Engineer, is to attend to it later today. Chris Sattlberger will doubtless receive Manni's full report on the affair in the officer's mess over his sauerkraut and pigs' trotters this evening.

We are starting to see more wild life. Some smaller minke whales have been spotted, but no larger whales yet. Even the little minkes are not immune from predatory man. The Japanese are still taking a quota for 'research' purposes—so Tokyo gourmets can carefully 'study' bits of whale meat on the end of their chopsticks in the laboratories of expensive restaurants.

So far the seals are something of a disappointment. Seen from a distance on excrement-stained ice floes, they look more like large garden slugs than the picture book animals we expected.

We are getting close to Mawson Station. The word is that we will be arriving tomorrow. We are already five hours behind Eastern Standard Summer time and in geographical terms under the Persian Gulf. A long way west, and a long way from home: ten days' steaming from Hobart.

At 4 pm I went to the bridge and saw a build-up of big bergs ahead. It looked like—and was—the beginning of 'Iceberg Alley', the approaches to Mawson Station, where grounded icebergs line each side of a deeper channel. These are mostly uncharted waters and the *Icebird* moves carefully along corridors of known safety. This is the route pioneered by the *Kista Dan* on the first approach to Mawson in 1954.

The sun was low in the sky ahead, spotlighting distant bergs on the south-east horizon. Ahead, the outlook was even more stunning. The partly shrouded sun threw down great shafts of light radiating to the ice, as if to portend the Second Coming. Meanwhile on either side of Iceberg Alley were tumbled masses of grounded icebergs—castellated, crenellated, spired and constantly revealing new facets as we crunched through the loose pack ice, undulating ponderously over a long, low swell.

An orgy of photography ensued. Those with long lenses were even able to frame photographically-obliging Adelie penguins lining the edges of some of the floes. A few gawked down at us from the ice slopes of bergs they had managed—somehow— to scale. I tried to describe the scene on tape but Keith Scott agreed with me that it was beyond words. Lines from Coleridge's *The Rime of the Ancient Mariner* kept recurring in my head.

And now there came both mist and snow,
And it grew wondrous cold:
And ice, mast high came floating by
As green as emerald.

The ice was here, the ice was there,
The ice was all around:
It cracked and growled, and roared and howled,
Like noises in a swound!

AUSTRALIAN NATIONAL ANTARCTIC RESEARCH EXPEDITION

SHORE PASS FOR
MAWSON STATION

(VALID FOR FEBRUARY 1989 ONLY)

The bearer of this document is permitted to remain on Mawson Station for no longer than three hours before returning to ICEBIRD. If no helicopters are available when the three hours has elapsed, immersion suits will be issued and overdue pass holders will make their own way back to ICEBIRD over the fast ice.

While on Mawson station, ICEBIRD visitors **must** observe the following conditions:

* Do not speak to any station staff unless authorised to do so by me.

* Do not consume any food or drink that has not been brought with you from ICEBIRD.

* You may urinate in the station toilets, but crapping ashore is forbidden.

* Do not enter any Station buildings except the Mess (and the urinals). The Mess is out of bounds during Station meal times.

I hope you enjoy your brief stay.

....

**DIANA PATTERSON
STATION LEADER**

The bogus pass circulated on Icebird.

I was curious what a 'swound' actually was and looked it up. Archaic English for a swoon, it seems, which I thought was a fairly silent affair. I discovered later that probably Coleridge didn't mean 'swoon' but, rather, used the archaic word for effect. In any case it sounded fine to me, and Clare Robertson, who hardly knew whether to photograph or sketch, was almost swooning under the pressure of 'iceberg overload' again.

JANUARY 14

Awoke to stillness. We have stopped for the first time since leaving Hobart. Our bows are lightly indented into the fast ice that is holding us back from Mawson Station, some thirty-five nautical miles away. It is a superb day, no wind, bright sunshine. A group of ever-curious Adelie penguins has gathered near the bow to ponder

the sight of this curious orange giant that has invaded their fastness.

Fast ice extends out from the shores of the Antarctic continent in an unbroken sheet. During winter it extends for one hundred kilometres or so. But during summer it weakens, breaks up and floats out to sea. The conventional wisdom has it that the fast ice never breaks up and moves away from Mawson Station till Australia Day, or very near the end of January. So why are we here two weeks early? Meanwhile the *Icebird* sits waiting at the ice edge, on charter, reputedly for something like 60 000 DM a day (approximately $44 000 on early 1991 rates).

The weather is absolutely superb. Bright sun, clear skies and glistening ice stretching ahead. Behind us, grounded icebergs line the seascape like miniature mountain ranges. The shapes of their sculptured domes and clefts will become familiar in the two weeks ahead. Paradoxically, this fine weather is the last thing we want at the moment. A big blow with accompanying swell might dislodge the unbroken fast ice that is keeping us from reaching Mawson Station. The Antarctic is never predictable. The old hands call such delays and unavoidable changes to carefully worked out schedules, 'The Antarctic Factor'.

The foredeck has been cleared to allow helicopters to land. Captain Brune wants to recce the ice ahead from the air, and asked for choppers to fly out from Mawson. Des Lugg was duty bound to pass this request on to the new station leader (and first woman to hold such a post on a mainland station), Diana Patterson. It is still early in the morning and Diana (immediately dubbed 'Lady Di' by *Icebirders*) has refused to chivvy the pilots out of bed, saying they need their sleep with the heavy work load ahead of them. As it turned out, the weather was unsuitable for flying, anyway.

There are interesting politics being played here, rather like an English medieval court. Des Lugg is the Lord Chamberlain who comes from the Court in London (Antarctic Division HQ in Hobart). He outranks Diana Patterson, who is the Baron

So near and yet so far away . . . Icebird's foredeck becomes a chopper landing pad for our transport to and from Mawson Station.

(Baroness?) secure in her walled castle. But unless the Baroness lowers the drawbridge, Des and his horsemen and supplies camped outside can't get in. In this case the three helicopters at Mawson are the drawbridge—the only means of exit and entry to the castle—and Lady Di has effective control over them. The pilots are also living with her in Mawson Castle.

Later in the day two helicopters arrive and circle the ship. With much arm waving—particularly by the Head Prefect—they are directed on board. Helicopters always fly in pairs in the Antarctic for safety reasons. Ewald and Des fly off to inspect the ice ahead. The news is not good. Solid fast ice for thirty-five nautical miles. For the moment there is nothing we can do but wait it out.

Voyage Six is the main resupply effort for both Davis and Mawson Stations, with hundreds of thousands of litres of fuel, frozen food, building materials and general stores for the year ahead. We have to get in to Horseshoe Harbour at Mawson Station at some stage to allow heavy containers to be lowered on to barges for transport to shore. Fuel lines have to be connected to the bulk storage tanks. We will also back-load

65

Ever curious Adelie penguins cluster at the ice edge to ponder on Icebird *and all her works.*

some of the accumulated rubbish of the last year and, indeed, the last thirty-five years, which is gradually being removed in these more ecologically aware times. But without the fuel oil the stations cannot get through the next twelve months. Both Mawson and Davis now need to store a million litres of fuel to heat the large two-storey steel structures erected in recent times, as well as the older wooden huts—some dating back to the 1950s. At some stage during the next two months, we have to get in to Mawson and Davis Stations. But the word from Davis Station (600 kilometres further east) is that the fast ice is still attached to the shore there, too. So we wait.

Meanwhile, for the new chums, there is plenty to watch and take in. The Adelie penguins, ever curious, have gathered in groups on the ice to debate the advent of this big orange hunk of metal with strange buzzing devices coming and going from time to time. They waddle along in lines going where, we wonder, and why? They squaaaark at each other and at us as they ponder these strange goings-on. To me they look like a group of liquored-up Freemasons in their dinner jackets, stumbling home in the early hours of the morning after a late-night session at their Lodge.

Clare Robertson, on the other hand, is reminded of women

wearing painfully tight high-heeled shoes: 'Each footstep is torture, sheer hell . . . squaaark!'

Keith Scott noted in his diary:

. . . Just off the stern this morning I watched three Adelie penguins walking about on the ice like old men with gout, inspecting the *Icebird*. The one closest to us leaned back, arching over backwards as if to scratch its belly or gain a more critical view, and the sun shone off its white chest. The birds appear to regard us with some fascination and in between sliding about on their stomachs and holding small conferences on the ice, they spend a lot of time standing by the ship.

It would be good to be allowed off the ship to walk on the ice. Chris Sattlberger and Dave Watts, the photographers, are bursting at their shutters to be allowed on the sea ice to photograph penguins. It is a heaven-sent opportunity as the Adelie rookeries we will be taken to at Davis are on rock, and not as photogenic as the pristine fast ice. But Ewald Brune says no. I suspect there are two reasons for this. Apart from the fact there is a chance the ice could begin to move out with itinerant passengers stranded on it, if he lets one person off the ship, everyone will want to go. So the word is no. Chris Sattlberger is not so easily deterred, and constructs a wondrous remote control device on a tripod, which he plans to lower down to the ice from the bow, and photograph penguins that way. It looks a bit like the craft that American astronauts rode down to the surface of the moon, and there are shouts of 'The Eagle has landed' as his invention lands safely on the ice. It all worked out according to plan. The penguins were intrigued and waddled up to inspect this latest puzzle, while Chris clicked happily away with his remote control cable.

Penguin watching is irresistible. The only time these dinner-jacketed little birds are at risk is when they enter the water at the ice edge. That is where the leopard seals and killer whales lie in wait for a penguin snack. As we are on the ice edge we have ample opportunity to watch how they manage their affairs. First

a group gathers together, squaaarking and waving their flippers energetically. Clearly they are saying to each other: 'OK chaps. Let's go fishing. Now, Rupert, you go first.'

Rupert, generally the smallest of the group, who is being nudged towards the ice edge by the others, looks distinctly unhappy and is clearly protesting, 'I went first last time. What about Clive?' But Rupert can't get back through the scrum. After more shouting and flipper waving he is unceremoniously jostled over the edge.

As soon as he hits the water, a line of penguin heads dips down to assess how he's doing. If the unwilling Rupert isn't snapped up by a leopard seal, there is a palpable easing of tension, and the rest of the mob tumbles joyously in.

Their exit from open water is even more spectacular. The Adelies swim up towards the ice edge from under water and spear out head first, executing a graceful mid-air manoeuvre to land neatly on their feet on the ice—or, if they misjudge, skidding along on their shirt fronts.

A helicopter shuttle service has begun to ferry personnel and some cargo, mainly frozen food, between the ship and Mawson Station. It has not taken long for the well known penchant for practical jokes in Antarctica to surface. The handlers had trouble fitting the carcase of a frozen pig into the cargo compartment of the chopper. After a certain amount of unsuccessful juggling, someone said: 'Oh, put the bloody thing in the co-pilot's seat'. The pig had to be strapped in, of course, and things started to get a bit out of hand. One of the Larcies put a radio headset on the super-chilled porker, and then a peaked cap and sun glasses. I'm told the pilot—on an impulse—then radioed ahead that he had a severe case of hypothermia on board!

Hypothermia is the great bogey of Antarctic survival. Minutes can be critical if someone has fallen into zero degree sea water. The doctor at Mawson, not, I was told later, noted for his love of physical activity during his year down south, was seen

As soon as one unwilling volunteer has made an un-eaten entry the rest of the mob tumbles joyously in. Photograph by Jonathan Kilpatrick.

*The exit from the water is even more spectacular.
Photograph by Jonathan Kilpatrick.*

sprinting for the chopper pad followed by stretcher bearers bearing emergency medical gear. The helicopter landed with all speed, amid flying chips of Mawson granite, revealing the harnessed frozen pig beside the pilot looking even more lifeless than the dead parrot in the Monty Python sketch. Lady Di was reportedly unamused; not because she didn't see the joke, but because she had not been pre-warned.

It was frustrating to be so near Mawson Station, but so far away. We had experienced the same conditions that the *Kista Dan* encountered on her first approach to Mawson Station in 1954. The then Director of ANARE, Dr Phil Law, had chosen several possible sites from aerial photographs of the coast taken by the Americans during Operation High Jump in 1946. There is a shortage of exposed rock in Antarctica and apart from mountain tops sticking up through the ice, there are only a few spots on the coast where the ice sheet has retreated, enabling Antarctic stations to be built on solid rock. As Phil Law pointed out when I interviewed him in Melbourne, that was extremely important.

PL: I looked at these American aerial photographs with a magnifying glass searching for a suitable rock outcrop along the MacRobertson Land coast and there were two that looked potentially suitable as bases. As it turned out finally, one of them was suitable and the other one was not, but the one that was suitable had this horseshoe shape and obviously if we could take a ship into this horseshoe harbour it would be beautifully protected.

The big problem was that there might be a reef connecting the two points of the horseshoe, closing the entrance, and that was something you couldn't tell until you got down there. Another problem was there were a number of islands off the entrance to this possible harbour, so that without an aircraft it would be very difficult to thread our way in to this particular spot.

Auster aircraft were carried on the *Kista Dan* on that first approach to what would become Mawson Station in 1954— which was just as well. The fast ice extended out thirty-five nautical miles from the coast. An Auster aircraft was fitted with skis and lowered onto the ice beside the ship. Phil Law told me later that his pilot Doug Leckie had landed on snow before with skis, but not on sea ice.

PL: We took off in the Auster on skis from beside the *Kista Dan*, flew in and landed just outside Horseshoe Harbour on this polished blue sea ice. There was an iceberg about half a mile ahead and it was in the line of direction of our landing, but we didn't take much notice because we thought we'd stop in another couple of hundred yards. But skis on polished blue ice have practically no friction at all and we went careering on and on and showing no signs of slowing down. This iceberg was looming closer and closer! When we were about a hundred yards off it, Leckie put the plane into a ground loop—he just spun it so we went forward in a series of spinning circles. And the friction of the skis side on, of course, was much greater than the friction running straight ahead. We finished up about thirty or forty yards off the vertical face of this iceberg!

Fortunately the two ends of the horseshoe were separated by reasonably deep water and Australia's first presence on the Antarctic mainland, Mawson Station, was established on one of the prime pieces of ice-free real estate on the coastline of Greater Antarctica.

PL: Mawson is one of the best sites for four thousand miles. Not only is there this lovely enclosed harbour where a ship can just run cables out fore and aft to the shore and hold itself, but it's an amphitheatre, the arms of the horseshoe are elevated, then it comes around the curve of the horseshoe. It is saucer-shaped and slopes up to a high ridge at the back. And in this saucer-shaped hollow we built the station so it got semi-protection from the ridge at the back and it nestled down in this hollow and it looked a lovely little station. And it was on hard polished rock, no sand, no earth, just hard granitic-type rock, polished by glacier action thousands of millions of years ago. And there was good access to the interior, which was also important. The permanent ice cap started just one hundred yards behind the station. And when you got onto that you could go straight inland, with a lot of crevassing for the first ten miles because of the rising slope. But once you were ten or fifteen miles inland, the crevasses stopped and away you went. It was a perfect choice for a station.

From thirty-five nautical miles out—and some thirty-five years later—we could not make out Mawson Station itself. We could see the great curve of the ice sheet, with the stark, rocky ridges of the Masson Range and Mt Henderson sticking up like the back plates of a dinosaur, or the body of a giant lizard, arching down towards the small patch of ice-free coast and outlying islets.

Meanwhile relations between the Baroness and the Lord Chamberlain were, to say the least, cool. The advent of summer scientists returning from field parties had more than doubled the Station's normal population of around twenty-five people, and Lady Di was anxious to off-load as many as possible on to *Icebird* where they would not be eating station food or occupying station beds. Conversely, Des wanted to land the Jafos and Jafas from *Icebird* so they could get on with their respective programs and 'jollies' (as these excursions are known in Antarctic parlance).

Now we have Robert occupying the fourth bunk in our tiny cabin. He is an electrician who has wintered at Mawson and is to go to Davis Station with us on *Icebird* before returning to Australia. He is a pleasant bearded young man in his early twenties, who doesn't spend much time in C3 after sampling The Professor's snoring. There are new faces on board as the geologists, glaciologists, 'diesos' (diesel mechanics) and helicopter support staff and other refugees from the Prince Charles Mountains group (PCMs in polar jargon) cluster around the fresh fruit boxes in the mess, gorging themselves on apples, bananas and some wilting plums. One was seen eating Pavlova and chips—thoughtfully using French fries to convey cream and Kiwi fruit through his beard. They have been on hard tack for three months, while working in a field camp in the PCMs, the extensive group of mountain ranges some 400 to 600 kilometres inland from Mawson.

We are beginning to understand the culture shock that wintering expeditioners must feel when they have to face people from the outside world. Although those of us who left Hobart in *Icebird* have only been together for less than two weeks, there is a sense of resentment and intrusion at these new faces. We are comfortable together, we original *Icebirders*. Why should we have to put ourselves out to talk to or, worse, share our cabins with these interlopers, these outsiders?

The PCM group are even more spooked. Some stand in huddles in the tiny *Icebird* bar with their backs turned to us regulars. Worse, they drink the ship dry of gin in about forty-eight hours. They have been fantasising about gin and tonic for months and now we face a gin-less future.

We circle around each other like strange dogs sniffing each other's posteriors, but quickly build some social bridges. The PCMs men are literally coming down from a high that has nothing to do with gins and tonic. They have lived high in the mountains of one of the most remote and beautiful parts of Antarctica, and I am anxious to talk to some of them on tape before the reality ebbs. They were the party flown in by Dick Smith and Giles Kershaw in the Twin Otter, taking off from the cocoa-marked airstrip beside the *Icebird* three months earlier. The Prince Charles Mountains program was started in the summer of 1968/9, is being conducted over a number of years and includes a comprehensive glaciological and geological survey of the area. Their accommodation, food and fuel had been dragged in by bulldozers the previous winter, in an ambitious traverse led by Lady Di's predecessor, the Station Leader at Mawson in 1988, Phil Barnaart. Known as Dovers Base (after Bob Dovers, a pioneering Antarctic surveyor and first OIC at Mawson Station in 1954), the field headquarters consisted of a cluster of 'apple' huts, a structure originally developed by the PCMs Field Leader Rod Ledingham. An extended apple is called a 'melon', and further extensions are of course a 'zucchini'.

From Dovers Base, two-man teams of a geologist with a field assistant were helicoptered into remote locations and left there for four or five days, until they were picked up (weather permitting) and taken to new areas. Among the PCMs gathered in my cabin for a chat were geologists Doug Thost and Ian Fitzsimons, the 1988 doctor at Mawson, John Gill (doubling as a field assistant in the PCMs), Antarctic Division field training officer Greg Hodge, and field assistant (and mountaineer) Adam Darrough.

Tim Bowden: John Gill, what brought you to Antarctica?

John Gill: You may find this a strange answer, but I felt I owed it to my great-great-great grandfather who was here. He was James Clark Ross who discovered the Ross Sea and was the first man to sail through the Antarctic ice pack. He has been a hero of mine ever since my boyhood when I first heard of him from my maternal grandmother who was his great-granddaughter. I had also read the Mawson and Scott books, as well as *The Worst Journey In The World* by Apsley Cherry-Garrard, and I have been thinking about it ever since I was a child, waiting for an opportunity to spend some time here.

Tim: Was Antarctica as you expected it?

John Gill: No, it overpowered me. I wasn't prepared for the scale of the landscape for a start. I wasn't prepared for the Mawson wind, which is a real killer. I wasn't prepared for the emotional aspects of being here, being away from people that I love, and I didn't realise how long a year was going to be. But Antarctica has overwhelmed me in many ways. It is a far more beautiful place than I expected. There's a tremendous tension in a landscape that is totally forbidding and seems to preclude the possibility of life. Yet you can walk around the side of an iceberg at Auster rookery in mid winter and there are 20 000 magnificent twenty-five to thirty-five kilogram Emperor penguins standing there calmly on the ice looking around them, breeding and thriving in this —50C temperature. It's just an incredible experience.

TB: I read recently that it's been claimed that nobody performs to the full extent of their capabilities in Antarctica, and the longer they stay there the worse it gets.

JG: Yes, I think it's a very harsh and taxing place. I don't think the human body is designed to function to its full physical capabilities in this environment. Personally I've found that. I feel I've aged more since I've been here than I would have if I'd been at home.

Greg Hodge: I know that, out in the field, one of the things that motivates me is the fact that you are extended mentally and physically and you start to find where your own personal boundaries are and you get to know yourself better. Even filling your fuel bottle or taking a photograph can become major mental and physical challenges. You have four or five layers of clothing on and you are struggling sometimes just to move. Your body is working very hard when you are out in the weather, and you become mentally tired because that wind is always blowing.

TB: What about the sheer adventure of it?

Adam Darrough: I guess I'm interested in mountains and wild places and all kinds of extremes. Visiting those places helps you to see yourself and the world as well. It puts life in perspective for me in a fairly important way. If I had to condense my life into five years, if someone said, 'You've got five years of your life to live and nothing else', I don't think I would exclude a moment in the mountains from that five years. You have to perform to your level of efficiency. It mentally stimulates you. There are times when you are down, of course, but there are other times when you are feeling incredibly alive, and you look around and there's just this immense satisfaction in being there.

TB: Are you intimidated by Antarctica?

AD: Well, I think you have to be intimidated. If you do things that have risk, you *should* be intimidated and realise the risks involved—whether you are on a mountain or driving a car fast. I think if you recognise a risk before you go to a place, there are fewer problems coping with those risks because you've accepted them. And ultimately if you have to struggle, you struggle—and if you have to die you die. People don't often die on ANARE activities because there's a large safety net.

TB: People *do* die of course . . .

AD: Yes, and people do suffer in extreme activities. But if you prepare yourself beforehand and accept the risks, well you go there and accept the rewards as well as the risks that come with those rewards. Then there's no bemoaning. I mean if the choppers don't come, if you run out of food and go hungry, well that's the game.

Doug Thost: Sitting in my little two-man tent, high in the Prince Charles Mountains, I remember writing a two-page dialogue in my diary along the lines: *Man just doesn't belong here—there's no niche here for man. He is totally out of place.*

I couldn't help but contrast the PCMs to the coast where Ian Fitzsimons and I were last year. In summer it's the Riviera by comparison. The average temperature is zero, you have fresh water lakes around you, and wild life. There are even lumps of moss up to two or three centimetres high— huge forests by Antarctic standards! And then you go to the Prince Charles Mountains in the middle of nowhere with all those majestic peaks sticking out of glaciers. You might find the occasional spot of lichen on a rock and, if you are very lucky, a deranged snow petrel flying around way off course. There is no life out there at all, and you suddenly realise that the only reason you are alive out there is because of all the logistical support behind you. You've got the right ration packs, clothing and sleeping gear. Even so, when the wind is blowing around forty knots and there's drift blowing in your face, it's −15C with wind chill on top of that bringing it back to −30C, and you find yourself thinking: 'Why don't I go back to the tent and sit there all day'. Or you look at a piece of rock and say to yourself: 'Am I going to struggle out of my great big sledging mitts to write something in my notebook about this piece of rock? Am I going to bother to take a photograph?' And it's so tempting to just say, 'Bugger it'! Even the smallest actions become a super-human challenge.

Ian Fitzsimons: Once Doug and I were stuck in a tent on Mt McCarthy, snowed in, and we were getting low on rations. Of course we could have stretched it a lot further, but the choppers couldn't get in to take us out. It was just us in the tent, and it was the same kind of experience that the Antarctic explorers had fifty years ago. I remember thinking every time I had to pump up my air-bed: 'Well, Mawson didn't do this'. But it's still essentially just you with some food, a little stove and a tent and no way anyone can get to you.

DT: The difference was, of course, that Mawson and Scott knew they were the only people in the middle of the whole place and no one was going to come and rescue them. We had our radio, our daily skeds, and contact with Dovers Base.

When we were blizzed in, there was nothing to do but just wait it out.

There was also time during this forced inactivity for Ian Fitzsimons to write an entire pantomime, titled *Last Tango At Dovers*, later performed at the get-together when all the field parties were brought in to base for the Christmas festivities. Because of the location, all incoming radio messages and telexes were prefixed by the word 'Prince'. Hence a message to Dovers Base leader Rod Ledingham would be addressed to: 'Prince' Ledingham. The theme of the panto was the rotten lot of all field geologists compared with the imagined indulgent life led by 'Prince' Rod Ledingham and his pampered Court, secure at Dovers Base. This was followed by the annual PCMs haggis hurling (Ledingham is a Scot)—in reality condoms filled with porridge.

Ian Fitzsimons (a young English graduate from Cambridge University) also composed a poem:

THE GEOLOGIST'S VOW

No, I shall not falter from camp site to peak;
An ice-axe is anchor and guide to my feet;
Although I may pass over blue ice like glass,
I'll not stop.

And my hand shall not weaken; the hammer it grasps—
Seven pounds that spells splinters that break and fly past.
And the tips of my fingers no cold shall they feel
As I scrawl a description, and rotate the wheel
Of a compass that tells you the lie of the land,
With a needle that points true and rests in my hand.

And I'll stop at each cliff face and write all I can,
Describing each detail, constructing a plan
Of the rocks that confront me and all do their best
To confuse and depress me, my spirit to test.

And the sample I split from the earth's solid core
Shall be thoughtfully chosen, untainted and pure.
And my back shall not bend though the load it sustains
In most circumstances causes aching and pains.

And my mind shall not wander from tasks still to go,
From the samples I'll plunder and seize from the snow
To be ruthlessly ground up, dissected and sliced,
In a room far away from their home in the ice.

And I shall not ask why I battle the wind
That blasts drift through the sky
And freezes my skin.
The beauty I've seen
In the places I've been
Could be why.

Ian Fitzsimons,
Prince Charles Mountains, December '88.

CHAPTER SIX

First Visit to Mawson Station • A Dog's Life • To Rumdoodle or not to Rumdoodle • Icecap Adventures • I Discover a Crevasse the Traditional Way • The Saga of the Wandering Politician • Amazing Happenings In and Out of the Rumdoodle Hut • A Chicken Run In Antarctica • Intrepidness and Bravery

JANUARY 15

I have set foot on Antarctica! The Pollies were in the first helicopter away from *Icebird*, of course, but groups of us were choppered ashore around 8.30 am. Dave Pullinger the pilot obligingly circled the *Icebird* so we could photograph her from the air—the first overview of our floating home since leaving Hobart. Then we flew over the unbroken expanse of ice towards the distant coastline. Mawson Station was a dot on shore until it began to emerge as a jumble of buildings clustered behind the encircling arms of Horseshoe Harbour, still chock-a-block with ice. Chris Sattlberger said it looked like a container terminal into which someone has dropped a bomb. The older wooden huts of the early years, guyed down to the dark granitic rock with wire cables against the blizzards, are dwarfed by the 'Red' and 'Green' Sheds of the new building program. These large metal boxes are grandiose statements of occupation by Australia, and debate still rages fiercely about their usefulness and expense.

We gathered in the Mess Hut for a briefing by the new Station Leader, Diana Patterson, before briefly exploring the Station. The environmental philosopher made a bee-line for a heated outlet pipe dripping undefined steaming substances directly onto the rocks

Following its friction-free landing outside Horseshoe Harbour in 1954, the Auster Doug Leckie piloted is pictured on the sea ice.

leading down to Horseshoe Harbour, and stood there looking pensive.

The Mawson huskies live staked out on a snow drift towards the Western Arm of Horseshoe Harbour. They are losing their winter coats and look a bit patchy and bedraggled. There is an unwritten rule that if you visit the dog line and pat a husky you have to pat them all so that jealousies do not develop. They are descended from Labrador and Greenland stock, bred by the French who intended to use them in Adelie Land. But in 1949 the French ship *Commandant Charcot* was unable to penetrate the pack ice, and the dogs would have had to be taken back to Europe. Australian quarantine laws forbade them from being landed in Australia. But, in typical style, ANARE Director Phil Law got to work on the bureaucracy and did a deal with the Melbourne Zoo on the understanding that the dogs would stay there until ready to be shipped to the Antarctic. They went to Heard Island in 1950 and were transferred to Mawson Station in 1955 where they have lived and bred ever since. Sadly their days in Antarctica are numbered. All nations who are signatories to the Antarctic treaty have agreed that any introduced species must be removed under the terms of the Protocol on the Conservation of Antarctic Flora and Fauna. The dogs must be withdrawn by 1994.

As you approach, they leap and bark and pull at their chains hoping for a friendly pat. Although they have been known to kill each other in terrible fights over a bitch, or status in the team, they never bite humans. Nils Lied, a Norwegian dog handler who worked with them at Mawson in the 1950s, told me he once got a nip when he waded in with his whip to separate a brawling mass of twenty dogs. When the dog responsible realised what he'd done, he ran away from the pack, sat down in the snow and howled piteously. He had done the unforgivable, he had bitten the master!

Certain of us have been chosen for a 'jolly'—an overnight excursion to huts on the ice plateau in the mountains behind Mawson. It is the only night I will be spending away from the *Icebird* in the sixty days of my Antarctic journey. There are huts at Mt Henderson and Rumdoodle. I make a pitch for Rumdoodle just on the name. There is a satirical book on British 19th Century Himalayan climbing called *The Ascent of Rumdoodle*. It was a made-up name. Now I have found one!

Unfortunately every one seemed equally fascinated by the name Rumdoodle. Peter Milton, Socialist Left ALP, and sporting a Russian fur hat from a previous trip to the Antarctic, decided to pull rank. 'I think the Tourism Committee should go to Rumdoodle', he said authoritatively. Someone from our fledgling Rumdoodle group told him that the hut at Mt Henderson had a better view so he changed his mind. What was not mentioned was that the Mt Henderson hut was almost perpetually subject to howling katabatic winds.

The Rumdoodle group climbed into a Hagglunds, a Swedish over-snow military vehicle with rubber tracks, towing a small trailer. Our party consisted of our two Mawson minders, Chris Eavis and Alex Hindle, myself, two Labor pollies—Colin Hollis and Allan Morris—the National Party's Member for Maranoa, Ian Cameron, and our artist Clare Robertson.

One of the advantages of Mawson's location is that it has immediate access to the ice plateau of Antarctica. It is possible to drive straight off the small area of exposed rock on to the ice sheet and up on to the plateau. The rising slopes are heavily crevassed, and the way is marked by forty-four gallon drums with a cane sticking up, each one tipped with a metal disk, so in bad weather you can navigate by radar from one to the other. I was reminded of an experience one of the Antarctic Division's summer field training officers, Greg Hodge, told me about while driving in a similar vehicle in a blizzard.

GH: Three years ago when I was at Casey Station, I was about eighty kilometres inland with a Hagglunds and the wind was blowing at over 100 knots—a decent breeze. There was a lot of drift about, so much so that the front of the vehicle was completely iced up. We were navigating by radar, compass and dead-reckoning techniques. As you come to each bamboo cane marking the route on the plateau, somebody has to get out to identify the metal tag on the cane to make sure you are where you think you are. You can normally use the radar to get to within about twenty paces of these canes. Then, particularly if it is windy, you tie on a rope before you get out and then walk in a big arc to try and locate the cane. We had been doing this all day long, so I was pretty used to operating outside the vehicle in 100 knot winds.

Finally the ice built up on the windscreen and blocked the air intake so much that I had to nip out with an ice-axe to smash the ice off the intake as the engine kept stalling. So I jumped out, but didn't put the rope on. This was because I was only going to the front of the vehicle, not venturing out looking for a cane. As I was busily smashing away at the intake with my ice axe, the blizzard gusted under the vehicle and took my legs out from underneath me. It just blew me away!

I ended up face down on the ground with my fingernails and toes grinding along through the snow and the ice trying to get a purchase. Meanwhile I was just being blown away over polished ice. The drift was so bad that after what would have been three paces I lost touch with the vehicle. I just couldn't see it. And everything started to happen very, very slowly, the realisation that I could no longer see the vehicle, and therefore the chances of getting back to it would diminish as I got further and further away. And I guess I was blown about twenty paces down wind.

TB: And the realisation also, I suppose, that the people inside had no idea what was happening to you.

GH: Yes, they would have assumed I was still around the front smashing off ice. However after about twenty paces my boots managed to get a purchase on a bit of snow, and I lay there for what seemed like an eternity—it must have been about three minutes—and a little lull came in the wind and I managed to scamper back on all fours to the Hagglunds. I was very glad to get back to it, because things could have ended quite differently. It would have taken some time for those in the vehicle to realise I was missing, and by the time they roped up and got outside, I could have been any distance away and the chances of finding me would have been about zero.

TB: And you were the training officer!

GH: Yes, I was supposed to know about these things and teach other people to avoid such dangers. So you can easily forget, and the lesson is that the weather in the Antarctic can be very rough and Mother Nature is very strong. It pays not to assume anything, but treat her with a greal deal of respect.

Sunshine and blue skies were the order of the day for us Rumdoodlers, though, as we bucked and lurched along the marked route from Mawson Station up the ice plateau, through which the exposed bare rocky peaks of the Masson Range and Mt Henderson broke through the ever moving ice sheet. We made a detour to inspect the wreckage of a Russian aircraft—their equivalent of a Dakota DC3—which had been abandoned on the ice in 1965 after being flipped over in a blizzard. Until 1968 it had remained virtually intact, but following the Russian invasion of Czechoslovakia in that year, a bulldozer driver of Czech origin stationed at Mawson, drove his machine up to the Soviet Dakota and drove through it several times to assuage his national fury. It lies today bent and twisted, but looking as though it had been violated only yesterday. Oil lies in pools on the ice, and the metal of the smashed engines shows not one speck of rust after more than twenty years of exposure. It is a reminder that nothing decays or breaks down in the cold, dry sterility of Antarctica's deep freeze environment. On a more mundane level, even husky turds will last virtually for ever. So will human ones. We are under strict instructions to bring ours back from Rumdoodle, and any other rubbish we generate, for incineration or controlled disposal. It is a salutary thought. Will our Antarctic-generated Henry-The-Thirds accompany us back to Australia? The *Icebird* is retaining all our ship-generated wastes in her tanks while we are in Antarctic waters.

As I step out of the Hagglunds on to the ice near the mangled Russian aircraft, I am conscious that I am walking on the Antarctic icecap for the first time. I have not prepared appropriate remarks like Neil Armstrong's lunar homily, 'One small step for mankind', and all that. My first words after a third step are, 'Oh shit!' as my right foot breaks through into a small crevasse and I sink up to my thigh. It is not a life-threatening situation, but as I struggle to pull my leg out, I can hear bits of ice tinkling further down into the blue depths of the 'slot', as the locals refer to crevasses. It is a reminder of the elastic nature of the

This abandoned Russian aircraft was in one piece until 1968 when a crazed Czech drove a bulldozer through it a few times.

moving ice cap, and that the words of the Antarctic Field Manual should be kept in mind when walking on the ice.

Although crevasses are more easily spotted in summer when the surface snow has melted, there is no known method of finding them other than breaking through and discovering the hard way. Des Lugg told us about an elaborate system of sensors the Americans had rigged in front of a big D9 bulldozer some years ago at their McMurdo Station. There is a now famous photograph of the experimental 'dozer with its forward projecting sensors pointing down at an angle of forty-five degrees into the abyss of a large 'slot'.

Australian expeditioners have experimented at various times. In Melbourne, Dr Phil Law told me of one bold effort:

> *PL*: A man named Neville Collins found himself in a very bad crevassed area and devised the method of rigging a couple of long ropes on the controls of his tractor while he walked behind and steered his tractor in this way. He couldn't stop it but he could steer it, and on one occasion it did slump into a crevasse with its tail sort of tucked down in this great hole and the tracks still grinding furiously. But it clawed its way out and went on!
>
> So there was Neville holding the reins but he was separated by this great chasm from his tractor which was beginning to disappear into the distance. He had to run up about a hundred yards to where the crevasse was narrow enough to jump over and then run furiously in his clumsy footwear after the tractor which was still moving ahead steadily at four knots. With his last gasp he was just able to drag himself onto the sledge which the tractor was hauling and lie there panting for ten minutes or so until he had enough strength to run up to the tractor and climb up into the cabin.

I quickly learnt to spot the crumbled look on the surface of the bare ice that covers a 'slot', and take more care. The Russian plane has moved quite a long way since its original accident and it now lies in a heavily crevassed area as the ice carries it slowly and inevitably towards the coast. It is a relief to get back into our red Hagglunds and continue towards the Rumdoodle hut.

The weather is superb, bright sunshine (snow goggles an absolute necessity), little wind, and here we are touring among the rocky peaks (nunataks) of the Masson Range. Snow petrels can be seen whirling around the stark brown pinnacles and tumbled screes, but wild life is scarce. I'm told one touring party once came across the frozen carcass of a disoriented seal which had taken a wrong turning and headed inland. We are to have a quick Cook's tour along the base of the Masson Range before occupying the Rumdoodle Hut, and stop near a spectacular rock face with a mini glacier ending half way up it. There is a rocky moraine at its mouth, ending with a melt-lake of an unusual greeny blue hue.

Without any consultation with our minders, Allan Morris began slipping and sliding down the ice slope towards the steep valley that led up to this melt-lake. His rubber boots could not grip the ripples on the blue, rather greasy ice, and he took a few tumbles as he went down. Chris Eavis and Alex Hindle looked at each other with obvious concern. The forthcoming interview with Station Leader Diana Patterson was obviously running through their minds.

'What? You let one of the politicians head off down an ice slope on his own without crampons, and lost him within *two hours* of leaving Mawson??'

It was too steep to take the Hagglunds down the same slope, so Alex stayed to keep an eye on Allan while we toured off to the spur of rock that has been named Rumdoodle. Suitable photographs taken (Allan Morris was a speck in the distance at this stage), we drove further along the contour of the slope, hoping to get down to the valley by another route and come back closer to the wandering politician.

On the valley floor we had the added bonus of a spectacular ice cliff with striated bands of mud and rock, and stood on an ice-covered melt-lake holding our Antarctic Field Manuals towards the camera (we were supposed to carry them at all times) as evidence for the Antarctic Division's Senior Medical Officer, Dr Peter Gormly, before making contact again with Allan Morris. Relieved looks flashed between our two minders.

The Rumdoodle hut is a small green structure anchored by cables to a rocky scree at the base of a nunatak. Clare Robertson found out in the course of conversation in the evening that it is the third hut to be placed there. The first blew away and the second rather mysteriously exploded—perhaps during a sudden change in air pressure.

As it was likely this was to be my only night of the trip 'on the ice', I had included a bottle of excellent French cognac in my kit and we had a brew of coffee and a warming libation before going out for a walk along the valley floor about 9 pm as the low sun sent long shadows from an apricot coloured sky.

I was puzzled by a phenomenon as we walked along. Every so often there are perfectly round portholes of clear ice in the opaque glacier ice, like shafts of clear glass going down into the depths. I can think of no obvious explanation for this. At various points on the valley floor there are large boulders sitting on the ice which have obviously rolled down from the brown stony cliffs of the Masson Range. I found out later that the two phenomena are connected. The smaller stones can be warmed right through by the summer sun, and sink slowly into the ice, turning as they go. The result are the clear tubes I had noticed. The larger rocks, too big to be warmed through, sit permanently on the ice. They, too, like everything else on the moving ice cap, will eventually be carried down to the sea.

How lucky to have fluked Rumdoodle! Almost no wind (unlike the poor storm-bound wretches at Mt Henderson), magnificent scenery, and ice ridges and slopes for grown-ups to toboggan down. Distinguished Honourable Members are seen sliding helplessly down icy slopes on their backs, feet and arms waving in the air, hooting with mirth. They are joined by Antarctic veterans, a journalist and an artist, all let loose in this most spectacular Antarctic playground.

There is not room in the hut for everyone to sleep, and a polar pyramid tent must be pitched outside and guyed down with pegs and snow blocks. Colin Hollis and Ian Cameron volunteer to sleep in the tent on the ice in their sleeping bags. I've done enough camping out in my time not to be too jealous.

The hut at Rumdoodle. Note polar tent, pitched at left, in which hardy politicians slept on ice.

Our amiable minders cook an evening meal from dried rations with a use-by date of 1984. There is no risk of any bacteria in our freeze-dried stew, rice and chocolate. Later I enjoy some melon jam at Mawson that was recovered from a supply dump laid down in 1954. It tasted fresh and delicious. Clare Robertson told me she was so conscious of not leaving behind any waste that might be permanently preserved that she swallowed the foam generated by her evening teeth-cleaning!

Following a determined assault on my bottle of cognac, conversation ranged far and wide—from morale problems being experienced by Antarctic Division personnel to the latest excesses of the building program. Ian Cameron, the only conservative politician present, was in full cry.

His line was that allocating Government money to the Antarctic Division was rather like 'giving it to blackfellers— they just pissed it against the wall'. As to the accommodation module on the *Icebird*—'the Antarctic Division would do better to leave it on the wharf instead of filling it with the bludgers, wankers, artists, writers, ferret-strokers, philosophers and Division free-loaders all costing the tax payer a poultice'.

I was silly enough to respond, and said that it was all very well him behaving like John Clarke impersonating a Neanderthal National Party back-bencher, but if he was including himself among the bludgers and wankers, it might just be that if he stopped spouting such bone-headed crap and took some notice of his surroundings he might learn something about the Australian Antarctic operations first hand that might make him better informed in Canberra than before he set out. I said he'd obviously made up his mind on all the major issues before he left so there wasn't much point him being there anyway. Clare Robertson was sitting wide-eyed on her bunk, looking from one of us to the other as if watching a Davis Cup singles rally. Clearly it was time everyone went to bed, and we did. It turned out in the morning that the cognac bottle was empty! Obviously it must have been knocked over accidentally in the night . . .

During the night the Rumdoodle Hut was shaken by some healthy blasts of katabatic wind, but the brave souls in the tent were not disturbed and Colin Hollis came in to the hut at 7 am to make coffee for the stay-a-bunks. Within an hour the cheerful roar of an approaching Hagglunds was heard, and the Mt Henderson party arrived with stories of their windy night. We also had time to run up to see where they had overnighted—a smaller hut, admittedly spectacularly situated, with a panoramic view down to the coast. They had actually climbed Mt Henderson and were suitably proud of themselves.

JANUARY 16

We were back at Mawson Station by 11.30 am and, consistent with Lady Di's policy of husbanding station resources and keeping as many of the visitors on board the *Icebird* as possible, we were choppered back to the ship in time for lunch. Even Sandra Fahey, the Antarctic wife who had won the lottery to spend some time with her husband, Brendan, an electrician at Mawson, was helicoptered back to sleep on board the ship, too—to the obvious surprise of Des Lugg. Clearly diplomatic relations between ship and shore are under some strain.

During our absence from the ship, some efforts were made to explore a route through more open water to the west. The only trouble with that was the waters were uncharted. Ewald described how the ship came within metres of a rocky spike that soared up without warning from the ocean floor. He showed the depth sounding print-out to us in the mess and it was quite dramatic! The kind of steep nunatak mountains we camped beside in the Masson Range at Rumdoodle are also to be found under water, off shore. It is simply too dangerous to move outside the known channels. There is nothing to be done for the moment but wait.

A nice surprise. Happened to be standing at the bar when Captain Ewald handed me a yellow slip of paper saying there would be a 'Chicken Run' at 8.30 pm and to be on deck wearing full ventiles and life-jacket. What happened was unexpected and superb. The *Chicken* is the *Icebird*'s half-cabin launch, which also has a modest ice-breaking capacity. It is the captain's pleasure to sometimes take selected guests on tours in the waters around the ship. Most of those on board on this occasion were the ship's crew, and some of the Australian staff—Evan the steward from Newcastle and Tasmanian Tania, the stewardess from the passenger's mess. Ewald does things in style. We were handed a mug of hot spiced *glühwein* by the attractive blond stewardess Ulle Feddern as soon as we clambered down the Jacob's ladder hung over the port side of *Icebird*.

This particular 'jolly' was organised so that Chris Sattlberger could get some photographs of the *Icebird* from the water. Suddenly, to my astonishment, we saw *Icebird* go astern from her position on the edge of the fast ice, and set off at full speed to the east. Had there been a mutiny? Were we to be abandoned with the Skipper to fend for ourselves—an Antarctic re-run of Bligh abandoned in the long-boat from the *Bounty*?

There is nothing like the absolute power wielded by a captain! Ewald had arranged for the ship to crash through the ice floes between the ship and where the *Chicken* was positioned so Chris could photograph her in action. It was fascinating to watch *Icebird*'s bows ride up over the larger floes, and a great

By courtesy of Captain Ewald Brune—a Chicken run off the ice edge at Mawson. Photograph by Keith Scott.

crack run forward as though a giant zip fastener had been ripped open. Then as the weight of the ship broke through, great slabs of ice were stood on end, and collapsed sideways in a welter of spray and broken ice. It was so spectacular I let my *glühwein* get cold.

JANUARY 17

Weather still superb—which means no change in the ice conditions. The politics of ship and shore remain vexed. The *Beyond 2000* television crew managed to stay overnight at Mawson Station but were not made particularly welcome by Lady Di. Scott Davis, the sound man, had to sleep on the floor and they were not given towels. It is not good PR. It reminds me of the attitude the Australian Army had to journalists in the early stages of the Australian Vietnam commitment in 1965. Creighton Burns dubbed it the 'Feel Free To Fruit Off' Philosophy. There is much muttering and mumbling on the ship from those with jobs to do on shore, and from people who were on shore, but who have been transferred to the *Icebird* and now have nothing to do. Heard

about one joyous bit of Antarctic madness today. Not having to worry too much about their personal appearance during a year down south, six Mawson expeditioners had 'Mohawk' style haircuts, except that each sprouted a different letter of the alphabet. When they stood in a row and bent down, their partly shaven heads spelled M A W S O N!

Played Scrabble during the afternoon with Keith Scott, with the Head Prefect observing. Had a personal best for some time of 466. Keith picked up lousy letters and let me on to all the triple scoring words.

There was talk in the mess about the difficulty of attracting top scientists to actually winter in the Antarctic, instead of just swanning down in the summer 'window' period. There is some resentment of this annual influx from those who have wintered, because the summer scientists get whisked around by helicopters taking advantage of the twenty-four-hour daylight. One of the despised summer scientists said that there wasn't any point in staying down for the winter because all there was to do was have 'boffins wiping the arses of the machines during the winter'.

I thought I had my sleep patterns in hand, but it is disorienting to have sunshine at midnight. Actually the sun dips under the mountains behind Mawson at that time and stays just below the horizon for about two hours.

I have been making some live broadcast contributions to Ian McNamara's *Australia All Over* program on ABC Radio, through the INMARSAT ship's satellite communications system. It is an act of some dedication. Because of the time difference with Eastern Australia, I have to broadcast at 1.30 am! I have tried staying awake following a late session at Stoppy's Bar, but found it did not actually enhance the creative process, even though I felt I was cheerful enough. The safest procedure was to go to bed early and set the alarm for 1 am and try to sound more chirpy than I felt. Broadcasting from the ship's bridge at that time was a surreal experience. Even the penguins were asleep in the semi-darkness with the sun briefly below the horizon, their heads slumped on their breasts or half tucked under their flippers against a background of blood-red sky reflected on the ice.

The daily mixture of comfort and mild adventure caused Chris Sattlberger to dub me 'Your Intrepidness'. I responded by calling him 'Your Bravery'. I fear this form of address will outlast the voyage.

CHAPTER SEVEN

Voyage Six Ice Edge Megawank • Thaw It and Burn It; French Chef Accused of Culinary Vandalism • Ship's Stability in Doubt • Misinformation Perturbs Politicians • Unseemly Party Trick Observed • What Is a 'Pricket' of Larcies? • Penny's Paranoia Puzzles and Perplexes • The Captain's Birthday Party; Vegemite Not Served • Search for a Missing Vessel Fails

There are signs of stir-craziness among the overcrowded denizens occupying *Icebird* at the ice edge off Mawson Station. We are bursting at the seams on board because of the summer scientists, most of whom have returned from the Prince Charles Mountains and who have been effectively banished from Mawson Station by Lady Di. The novelty of shipboard life even in the Antarctic is palling—I note sourly in my diary that it's like a combination of a third-class boarding house and being in gaol. Doug Thost, one of the PCM geologists, has designed a drink coaster inscribed: V6 ICE EDGE MEGAWANK. Chris Sattlberger (His Bravery) told me there is hard evidence for this. Manni is complaining over the evening meal in the Officers Mess about excess quantities of pubic hair clogging his beloved filters.

Roger, our French chef, is not the most popular man on board. His Bravery has an assignment to construct a photographic record of Voyage 6 for the *Icebird*'s German owners. Half-crazed with boredom of life on the ice edge, he decided to take some happy snaps in the galley to pass the time.

CS: I entered the galley around noon and found both Roger and his off-sider boiling immense amounts of lamb chops in a gravy that seemed to be pumped up straight from the engine room sump oil basin. The reply I got from Roger when

94

Our much discussed chef, Roger Milliet.

I mentioned the ridiculous amount of fat was, 'But you don't know the Australians! Of course this is dreadful. In France, nobody would eat like this! But here—this is the way they like it!'

It was Roger's so-called curry that pushed me over the diplomatic edge. I like a curry and headed eagerly to the mess for the evening meal when I heard it was on. The lumps of grey gristly meat and tasteless gravy that glugged on to my plate were devoid of even the most rudimentary spices. Even the rice was inedible—gritty and half raw. I was still brooding about this culinary abomination later in the evening when the hapless Roger bustled past where I was sitting in the mess.

>*Tim*: Roger, that curry you served us tonight . . .
>*Roger*: Ah yes, the curry, did you like it?
>*Tim*: I would have thought that any Frenchman with an ounce of culinary pride would have slashed his wrists before serving up tasteless bilge like that even to a dog. It was vile. There were no spices—not even any curry powder. It was tasteless gunk. And the rice was raw as well!

Roger: It is very difficult to cook for the Australians. They like the meat and the potatoes. They do not like the subtle flavours . . .

Tim: Just try us Roger, just try us!

(At this moment our Voyage Leader, Des Lugg, happened to walk past. He has the amazing knack of always being on hand when anything of significance, particularly a breach of good order and military discipline, is happening.)

Des: Any complaints about the food should be passed through me, please!

Roger seized the moment and disappeared.

Despite the basically boring diet, there is plenty of food and we eat largely to pass the time. His Bravery reported that he has tipped the scales at an all-time high of ninety-eight kilograms. There are a number of birthdays, of course, and on these occasions Roger appears after the evening meal triumphantly bearing a thawed Black Forest cake with candles blazing. As his culinary philosophy is to thaw food and burn it, a defrosted cake should have a sporting chance of being half-way reasonable. Alas, the entire store of frozen Black Forest cakes has somehow become impregnated with diesel fuel. It is a wonder the candles don't cause an explosion.

Despite the dismal standard of the cuisine, Captain Ewald Brune is becoming concerned at the amount of food and drink leaving his commissariat. The following notice appeared on the information board.

IMPORTANT MESSAGE FROM THE CAPTAIN

As many of you will have noticed, we are having stability problems with *Icebird*. I have been unable to correct the slight list to port that has developed during the last two weeks by the usual methods of pumping ballast tanks. The problem has been traced to B & C decks on the Module. In order to stabilise the ship at the beginning of this voyage, I based my calculations on an average weight of 75 kilos per passenger. Since the beginning of Voyage Six, these estimations have been grossly exceeded.

Consider the following facts:

* Twenty-five tonnes of food have been consumed on this voyage so far— more than on any previous voyage.
* Thirty-five tonnes of drinks have been drunk.
* The difference in height between the cover of Hatch No 3 and the sea deck is now ten metres.
* The total weight to be considered (25 +35x10) is 600 metre tonnes.

As previous expeditioners will know, following seas and a lightened ship cause *Icebird* to roll heavily on the homeward voyage. I must know how much extra weight is being carried on the bodies of passengers in the module on B & C Decks before we sail for Davis.

Therefore, tomorrow morning, all Module passengers will present themselves to the ship's doctor, Kevin Donovan, in the surgery, to be weighed. (B Deck at 10 am, C Deck at 11 am.) Only by so doing can I assure the stability and safety of the ship after cargo discharge.

Options available to me are:

1 If C Deck passengers are much more heavy than B Deck voyagers, I can move them to B Deck and vice versa.
2 Or I can put most of the overweight passengers into the C Hatch area with sleeping bags.

Ewald Brune
CAPTAIN

Even the Captain was getting bored. But a significant number of passengers did turn up to be weighed!

The Philosopher has taken to prowling around the decks of the ship in his yellow ventiles, and Mawson-style balaclava. He spends more time out in the elements than in the ship's air-conditioning, watching the penguins watching us. Like many on board he is growing a beard, and his grey stubble and staring eyes behind his glasses give him a wild and faintly alarming appearance. 'Lawrence of Antarctica' is an amiable enough bloke to talk to, although I am still puzzled by his presence on *Icebird* and what he is actually doing. He is to give a talk soon in the mess as part of our program of lectures by various on-board experts, so maybe we will have a better idea. He must be under some personal tension. His cabin mates report that he talks—or rather swears loudly—in his sleep.

The atmosphere on board is screaming out for a good practical joke and Geoff Taylor (who runs an engineering firm in Hobart that services the *Icebird* when she is in port there) sought me out. The ship has a news service that comes in by telex

The Philosopher in pensive mood.

on the INMARSAT satellite every forty-eight hours or so. With five federal MPs on board, Geoff thinks that a phony news item, detailing the surprising development that the Australian Treasurer Paul Keating had resigned and gone to work with the World Bank, might cause some interesting reactions. One of the Antarctic Division's radio operators could key in the story on the telex to match up with the legitimate news items, but Geoff had a problem. He wasn't sure if he could word the bodgie message with the right journalistic flavour to make it credible.

'Just leave it with me', I heard myself saying. I devised the appropriate report and Canberra Times journalist Keith Scott, who was in the know, hung around on the bridge where the telexed news service was left for interested passengers to read.

Labor's Colin Hollis was the first politician to read it. He swung around to Keith.

    CH: Bloody Keating's resigned!
    KS: That can't be right.
    CH: It's right, all right. Look, here's the AAP report! This is not good news for Labor, comrade.

```
    CANBERRA - THE SUDDEN RESIGNATION OF THE TREASURER PAUL KEATING
TO TAKE UP A SENIOR POSITION WITH THE WORLD BANK HAS THROWN THE
AUSTRALIAN LABOR PARTY INTO TURMOLL.
    THE PRIME MINISTER MR. HAWKE SAID IN CANBERRA THAT HE WOULD
ANNOUNCE A MAJOR CABINET RESHUFFLE WITHIN 24 HOURS.
    THE VALUE OF THE AUSTRALIAN DOLLAR DROPPED 5.6 CENTS AGAINST THE
US DOLLAR IMMEDIATELY NEWS OF MR. KEATING'S RESIGNATION REACHED
NEW YORK.
    DEFENDING THE MOVE, THE PRIME MINISTER SAID THE AUSTRALIAN ECONOMY
WAS IN EXCELLENT HEALTH, AND HE APPLAUDED MR. KEATING'S DESIRE
TO FURTHER HIS CAREER WELL BEFORE ANY FEDERAL ELECTION.
    LABOR PARTY FACTIONS ARE LOBBYING INTENSLY, AND THE FRONT RUNNER
FOR THE TREASURY BENCH IS BELIEVED TO BE THE MINISTER FOR FINANCE
SENATOR PETER WALSH.
    THE LEADER OF THE OPPOSITION MR JOHN HOWARD SAID THAT THE
HAWKE GOVERNMENT WAS SELF DESTRUCTING IN MAGNIFICENT STYLE AND
THE COALITION'S VICTORY AT THE NEXT ELECTION WAS NOW ASSURED.


    MOSCOW - A STRONG EARTHQUAKE SHOOK MOUNTAINOUSTADZHIKISTAN IN
SOVIET CENTRAL ASIA EARLY TODAY, DESTROYING BUILDINGS AND CAUSING
AN ESTIMATED 1400 DEATHS, THE OFFICIAL TASS NEWS AGENCY SAID.
    THE ASSOCIATED PRESS REPORTED THE TREMOR STRUCK THE SOUTHWESTERN
PART OF THE REPUBLIC, LOCATED NORTH OF AFGHANISTAN AND BORDERING
CHINA, AT 2:02AM MOSCOW TIME (100Z AEDT MONDAY).
    IT REGISTERED 6.0 ON THE RICHTER SCALE, ACCORDING TO THE US
GEOLOGICAL SURVEY IN WASHINGTON, AND SEVEN ON THE 12-POINT SOVIET
SCALE.
    THE QUAKE CAUSED 'DESTRUCTION AND CASUALTIES', TASS SAID.
    ITS EPICENTRE WAS 50 KILOMETRES SOUTHWEST OF THE REPUBLIC'S
CAPITAL OF DUSHANBE AT THE VILLAGE OF SHARORA, THE AGENCY SAID.
    IT WAS THE STRONGEST QUAKE TO HIT THE SOVIET UNION SINCE THE
DEVASTATING DECEMBER 7 SHOCK THAT HIT NORTHERN ARMENIA, 2,100
KILOMETRES TO THE WEST.
    THAT QUAKE DESTROYED MANY NEW APARTMENT BUILDINGS AND KILLED AN
ESTIMATED 25,000 PEOPLE.
```

The infamous Telex.

Colin then took off down the four flights of stairs, through the crew's quarters and up into the Module to tell the other federal members, Allan Morris, Peter Milton, Bob Chynoweth and the National Party's Ian Cameron. Through the closed door of the cabin Cameron's guffaws could be clearly heard. 'Har har—you bastards are stuffed now. Har har har.'

After some time the clearly shaken MPs emerged and went to the Mess for lunch.

I had one detail badly wrong. It is not possible to have a Treasurer from the Senate, so my conjecture about Senator Peter Walsh becoming Treasurer was a bad blue. I found out from Colin Hollis later that MPs are so used to journalists getting things wrong that this did not arouse the slightest suspicion. Another thing I didn't know was that Bob Chynoweth was the chairman of an important Labor Caucus committee which would have to meet in the process of electing new ministers in the event of a reshuffle.

Keith Scott unashamedly sat himself near Socialist Left faction member Peter Milton and eavesdropped during lunch. Milton said he would have put himself forward for a ministry if he had been in Canberra. 'If we had all been right-wingers they would have found some way of getting us out of here', he was heard to say. 'I wonder if the Russians would fly us back?'

One of the ground rules of the scam was that the practical joke be contained on the *Icebird*. This was an edict laid down by Des Lugg who had been informed after the deed had been done. Des had gone a distinctly whiter shade of pale behind his pepper-and-salt stubble of beard. I had the feeling that he felt he had enough problems on his hands without this little number! The ship's radio operator was told that if any of the politicians attempted to ring out on the INMARSAT satellite system they were to be informed that the story was a fake.

Some thirty-six hours later (!) Bob Chynoweth went to the bridge to make a call to Australia. Unfortunately, Nils, the radio operator, hadn't worked out who were politicians and who weren't, so Bob wasn't told. I fantasised later what the effect of the news of Paul Keating's entirely fictitious move to the World Bank might have been if the news had reached Bob Hawke via Bob Chynoweth's call. In view of the somewhat patchy nature of their relationship, perhaps it might have changed the course of Australian political history in 1989.

By the time the bubble burst the whole ship's company was on to it. I don't know why, but the finger of suspicion seemed to be pointing in my direction. There is no justice in this world! After all, I hadn't thought of the idea, just been its instrument. In view of a rumour that Peter Milton—who was on the Parliamentary Committee that dealt with ASIO—intended to have me investigated on my return to Australia—never substantiated—I decided to get in first, and told the story to Ian McNamara on ABC Radio's *Australia All Over*.

Most of the pollies took it well, although they were clearly not delighted at being the last on board to know. Ian Cameron fell about hugely all the way through.

There are so many wild rumours circulating around the ship on almost any issue you could name, that people have taken to mouthing mock public address announcements. 'This is Rumour Control, Rumour Control . . . ' followed by the latest furphy.

One of the geologists, Doug Thost, who has just come back from the Prince Charles Mountains, told me about an appalling experience he had in Antarctica the previous year.

> *DT*: I spent twenty-six days in a two-man tent with a Japanese colleague, conducting a geological survey of a remote group of islands 130 kilometres south-west of Davis Station. Yoichi had brought a small cassette-player with him, and only three tapes.
>
> The first was of a Japanese comedian who, Yoichi assured me, was very funny. He must have been *very* funny, because every time Yoichi played the tape—and he never tired of playing it—he would shriek with laughter in the same places. The second tape was *The Sound of Music* sound track, and the third was *The Best of Abba*.
>
> I will say no more!

This year Doug had brought his own Walkman and his own tapes—with headphones.

Bryan Smith has told me of a grotesque party trick performed by the Larcies late one evening in Stoppy's Bar. One of them stretched a surgical glove over his head and nose, creating a seal, and began to blow it up like a balloon. Such is the strength and elasticity of a surgical glove, that the whole thing swells up into a gigantic cockscomb with obscenely waving sausage-like fingers. When it gets impossibly swollen—about half a metre high—it explodes, showering observers with accumulated saliva.

Bryan has also advised that it is unwise to leave cameras or tape recorders unattended in the bar. The late-night Larcies have a habit of grabbing a strange camera, exposing themselves,

Larcie Captain Phil Clark performs an amazing feat with a surgical glove, pictured here only seconds before it exploded.

and snapping a close-up. They do this almost by reflex action. Some drunks also broke into my tape recorder that I had unwisely taken to the bar and left an unwanted contribution, but fortunately had not erased anything important.

Bryan Smith and I decided to run a competition to select some suitable collective nouns to describe the Larcies. There is considerable enthusiasm from *Icebirders*.

'BEYOND REASON' COMPETITION FOR LARCIE
COLLECTIVE NOUNS

The judging panel of Bryan Smith and Tim Bowden considered over seventy entries. Judging was done after the collective nouns had been listed *without* the names of the contributors.

The judges' criteria were: 1 Appropriateness
                             2 Originality
                             3 Humour

There was splendid variety and ingenuity in the entries received, although one rather spiteful anonymous contribution has been handed over to the Larcies for handwriting analysis and appropriate response.

The eighteen finalists are listed below, and the winner will be announced at 6 pm during dinner in the mess tonight.

Laxative Grunt Guzzle Swelling Throb Wank Lair Letch Elite Sixpack Erection Liability Giggle Sleaze Larrikin Pricket Penetration Tumble

The winner was the passengers' stewardess, Tania Hinden, from Tasmania, who collected the bottle of French champagne donated by Bryan Smith with her 'Liability' of Larcies suggestion.

A certain paranoia is abroad in the ship. Penny Greenslade is an entomologist doing continuing research into the limited number of creepy crawlies in Antarctica. Peter Milton found an article featuring two of her discoveries, the Antarctic Springtail, and another mite rejoicing in the name of Gamasellus racovitzai (if my notes on this matter are accurate). John Hackwell, a talented author and illustrator, drew up a cartoon featuring Penny's two bugs and a third—the Paranoia cameronius, or Moron-oa cameronius—which seemed to have

The author at the mercy of a 'liability' of Larcies.

103

a surprising resemblance to the Member for Maranoa, Ian Cameron. 'The cameronius has a swelled cranium, common with the Queensland species'.

Penny, who was unaware of the existence of a copy of her article on the *Icebird*, other than one she possessed, became convinced that someone had rifled through her personal possessions to provide John Hackwell with the material for his cartoon. She seemed to be terribly upset and conducted interviews with the principal suspects (including Peter Milton and me) in her darkened cabin, using a concealed tape recorder. It was all rather tedious really.

JANUARY 19

The Skipper's birthday. Naturally there was a party in Stoppy's Bar, and a scratch band, The Bergbusters, was formed with guitar, my ukulele and various percussion instruments. I managed to glean some extra information about the life and times of Captain Brune, including some of his past polar mishaps. I already knew of his hopes to captain a still-to-be-built ice breaking passenger liner on the growing Antarctic tourist trade. He is also extremely puzzled by Australians' deep attachment to the gastronomic delights of Vegemite, and regards this traditional Australian fare with a particularly vehement fear and loathing!

ODE TO CAPTAIN EWALD BRUNE ON THE OCCASION OF HIS BIRTHDAY OFF MAWSON STATION 19/1/89. (Tune: Vilikens and his Dinah)

By Tim Bowden

Now this is a song about our Captain Brune,
Whose birthday today has created this tune.
But the way things are going with *Icebird* we fear,
We'll still be off Mawson at this time next year.

Chorus: Dinky-di, dinky-di,
We'll still be off Mawson at this time next year.

Now while Captain Ewald sits it out in the ice,
He's thinking of plans that are sexy and nice.
'To hell with ANARE—tourism's the go.
I'll get a new ship and my fortunes will grow.'

Chorus: Dinky-di, dinky-di,

He'll get a new ship and his fortunes will grow.

'Farewell to all Jafos and boffins and bums.

With a girl on each knee I'll be doing my sums.

There'll be music and dancing and whoopee each night—

No choppers or Larcies or foul Vegemite.'

Chorus: Dinky-di, dinky-di,

No choppers or Larcies or foul Vegemite.

'Five Parliamentarians now on this ship,

The journos and writers enjoying this trip,

Philosophers, artists, historians galore

Had better assist . . . or they won't get ashore!'

Chorus: Dinky-di, dinky-di,

They'd better assist or they won't get ashore.

But Captain, dear Captain, let's look at your past

To see if your dreams of the future can last.

Will tourists be told of the ship *Gotland Two*;

Crushed in the ice—fare thee well and adieu.

Chorus: Dinky-di, dinky-di,

She was crushed in the ice—fare thee well and adieu.

In the '85 season *Icebird* hit a rock,

The drive shaft next year put your ship in dry dock.

The very *next* year—on good information—

You collected a rock off our own Davis Station.

Chorus: Dinky-di, dinky-di,

You collected a rock off our own Davis Station.

So Captain, dear Captain, wherever you are,

At 'Sunday Morning Service' or at Stoppy's Bar,

Remember your motto, where'er you may be,

Put your trust in the future, and, 'Let's wait and see'.

Chorus: Dinky-di, dinky-di,

Put your trust in the future and 'Let's wait and see'.

Ewald accepted this with good grace, and The Bergbusters played on with a bracket of singalong Australian songs including the inevitable *Waltzing Matilda, Click Go The Shears* and the *Pub With No Beer.*

'Rumour Control' is active again.

• There is a Russian icebreaker due to visit the area which will smash us a route into Mawson.
• We will go on to Davis Station without waiting.
• If we can't get in, Mawson Station will have to be closed down.

I have a sneaking suspicion that Kevin Donovan, the ship's doctor, is seeding the misinformation. He has a wicked sense of humour, and is an Antarctic veteran. He wintered at Davis Station in 1975 and Mawson in 1986.

I am playing more games of Scrabble than I ever have in my whole life. The videots are glued to the screen. 'The Blues Brothers', 'Conan', and 'Top Gun' grind on endlessly in the main mess. Trivial Pursuit and Backgammon are non-stop in tandem in the smaller smokers' mess nearby.

The medical experiments continue relentlessly. I have had an allergy test on my arm, and the results are negative. Like everyone else, I am only allergic to the continuing lack of action.

CHAPTER EIGHT

Bored Politicians on Ice • Pride and Prejudice • Chilli and Rice Bubble Sandwiches • Inventing Antarctic Myths; Ginger Beer Plant Terror • Dings and Cinderella • How Women Came to Antarctica • Whizzers and the Art of Long Distance Communication • International Antarctica • Mysterious Gremlins Sabotage Electronic Equipment

JANUARY 17

(Story filed for ABC News)

Five Australian Parliamentarians made history yesterday by conducting the first ever committee meeting in Antarctica at Mawson Station.

A sub-committee of the House of Representatives Standing Committee on the Environment, Recreation and the Arts preceded their inquiry into tourism in the Antarctic by having some first-hand experience on the ice plateau behind Australia's Mawson base.

Chairman Peter Milton, Bob Chynoweth, Allan Morris and Ian Cameron (and fellow MP Colin Hollis) camped out at Mt Henderson and Rumdoodle in huts and Antarctic tents under the midnight sun of the Antarctic summer.

Peter Milton told the ABC's Tim Bowden, who went with the party, that the movement of the ice cap and the excessive winds at Mawson made regular flights to and from such a location a doubtful proposition. However the fact that tourists were already visiting Antarctica on cruise ships from other countries indicated that tourism of some kind was inevitable and several proposals had been put to the Environment

Committee from interested Australian tourist operators.

Peter Milton said the committee favoured some modest ship-based tourism at first, closely monitored by the Government to see that the environment was protected.

The question of search and rescue operations would have to be considered in the event of any emergency. Peter Milton said his own view was that Antarctica should be a world park. He did not support large-scale tourism, but the fact that Australia claimed forty-two per cent of the Continent made it important that more Australians visited and were aware of Antarctica.

The politicians, like everyone else, are getting bored languishing off the ice edge at Mawson. Their 'first ever on the Antarctic' committee meeting was symptomatic of that. The Tourism Committee has a 'minder' from Canberra, a rather sour little man who made it perfectly clear to Keith Scott and me that he had a low opinion of all journalists and journalism in general. Later on in the voyage it became clear that the politicians he served vied with journalists in his contempt priorities. There were strong overtones of 'Yes Minister' in his clearly expressed opinions that coping with the idiosyncrasies of politicians made the job of running the country (through dedicated public servants like himself) extremely difficult.

The Minder was looking after the four pollies on the Tourism Committee. Colin Hollis, who represented the Public Works Committee and was keen to have a look at aspects of the controversial Antarctic building program, didn't have a minder, although his committee carries more clout. The Minder appeared to take a narrow view of his responsibilities to the Tourism Committee, and Colin largely had to fend for himself. I had the strong impression Colin would make mention of this on this return to Canberra.

JANUARY 18

Got a guernsey to go ashore and choppered away at 10 am. Appreciated the chance to explore more of Mawson Station. The communications via ANARESAT

Photographed circa 1956, these wooden huts were still in use in the late 1980s.
Antarctic Division photograph by John Bechervaise.

are also cheaper than the *Icebird*'s international INMARSAT system. We have to take our own lunches from the ship. Some of the Larcies have obviously been helping out. Clare Robertson reported her white bread sanger filled with rice-bubbles and chilli sauce!

Some of the earliest wooden huts erected are still in use. There are 'blizz lines' strung between the huts so that expeditioners can feel their way from hut to hut during winter blizzards. Some of the huts have trapdoors in the roof so those inside can get out that way if they are snowed in. The brew hut (for the all important station-home-brewed beer) has its ceiling and walls papered with Playboy nudes circa the 1960s. All the older huts are guyed down to the rocks with steel cables to avoid being blown into Horseshoe Harbour by blizzards or strong katabatic winds.

Another historic structure is Law Hut, the original sanitary system still in use despite the heated pipes and flush toilets of the new Red Shed. There is a pleasant scent of pine when you enter Law Hut. The crappers are situated over a number of forty-four gallon drums, each with a ready-to-go fire and its own chimney. The trick is to make sure you don't commit the unspeakably anti-social act of piddling into the drum when performing other more serious business. From time to time a drum is fired, helping to keep Law Hut warm, and incinerating that which might otherwise have to be taken back to Australia under new strict environmental guide lines! In earlier years, the firing of the crappers used to be known as 'lighting the Brownies' camp fire'. I'm told Phil Law is delighted that this building bears his name.

The mess and recreation club are still housed in one of the original wooden structures, although due to move to the towering Red Shed when it is finished. Behind the bar of the rec club is an amazing collection of 35 mm feature films, dating back to the black and white days. Videos have taken over in the 1980s and 1990s, but the still serviceable projector is occasionally used to screen old favourites. In the pioneering years Phil Law was adamant that each base should have a reasonable number of films and a good library. Popular films were screened again and again—and sometimes backwards for variety. The sound would be turned down as expeditioners supplied their own dialogue. Some of the classics, like *Pride and Prejudice*, took on a cult status on some stations.

Phil Law swears that when he arrived on a relieving expedition to Macquarie Island one year, the entire Station had taken on the manners and verbal affectations of Jane Austen's genteel early 19th century England. Tom Manefield, who wintered on Macquarie Island in 1949, told me in an interview that he thought he had seen the film *Pride and Prejudice* at least 100 times in his life, and most of those screenings were on Macquarie.

TM: For the last two or three months we were there we were so bored with all the other films, but we never got bored with *Pride and Prejudice* so we played it almost every night and would enact it, and we would turn the sound down and all do the different roles. I was always wanting to be

'The gentleman dapper stepped into the crapper . . . '
Historic Law Hut, still a preferred waste disposal point despite flush
toilets available in the new accommodation.

Lady Catherine de Bourgh 'taking a turn around the room'.
I rarely wanted to be Darcy. I was more often cast in the
female roles like Miss Elizabeth. Another role I absolutely
adored was being Mr Collins chasing the ducks down the
park. Well, we would enact this as the whole thing went
on. I know in the take-over session with the following party
we played *Pride and Prejudice* a few times and they thought
we were all berserk and ready for a psychiatric institution.
In fact, a lot of our life became full of the manners of the
early nineteenth century—you know, satires like that wonderful moment of humour where Mr Bennet says:

Dear Elizabeth, your mother tells me that you will not marry
Mr Collins and she says to you that if you don't she will never
speak to you again. What a dilemma; I shall never speak to
you again if you do.

Incoming expeditioners found the ritual behaviour of the
incumbents a complete puzzle until they developed their own
idiosyncrasies in the course of their own year south. Antarctica

111

was completely devoid of myths and rituals when the first Australians arrived at Mawson, and they had to create their own. John Bechervaise was the Officer In Charge of Mawson Station for its second year of existence in 1955 and again in 1959:

JB: People invented gods they could laugh at. For example, our expeditioners developed a sort of animistic attitude towards the blizzard. 'She's on again the bastard, here she comes again!'

There was one little man who had taken down a ginger beer plant and he came into the mess and said, 'She's working, the ginger beer plant is working'. From that moment the ginger beer plant became a sort of presence behind everything. Men would come into the mess in mock terror having being pursued down the slopes by the ginger beer plant—this sort of thing.

EXCERPT FROM MAWSON STATION LOG FRIDAY 17 JULY 1959
Today's events have been mainly attributed to 'The Ginger Beer Plant', a stalker through the silent huts of the station. On the mess blackboard this morning, Chris, Night Watchman, had written: 'The Plant's got me . . . help . . . it's tak . . . ' (The trailing writing was particularly effective.) It all helps, as they say, to pass the time.

Today's Aphorism (Grahame Budd): 'If the Ginger-Beer plant hadn't existed, we should have to have invented it'.

JB: Fellows would say, 'Oh, I met a beaut sheila down the Western Arm, opened up a nice little milk-bar down round there. She's absolutely beaut and she's willing, too', and this sort of thing would go on for weeks. 'Did you see her?' 'Oh yes, she was there. Sends her love to you . . . ', all sort of make-believe things like that would happen. In a sort of a way they were creating myths.

One very early Australian Antarctic tradition was the Saturday night 'ding', and John Bechervaise also saw the birth of that particular ritual.

JB: We always had a Saturday night ding and at that ding we always had beer only. Most people drank as much as they wanted to that night, unless they were on duty. The man on duty never drank at all. I never knew anybody to betray that trust of being completely in charge of the station. And, occasionally, it was necessary for the person who was on night duty to look after one or two people on their way to their sleeping bunks and that sort of thing—that might happen occasionally. But the Saturday night ding was an excellent opportunity for people to speak to me or to each other and get things off their chests. A person could come up and say almost anything he liked to his OIC and this was accepted and very often you got some sort of problem at the very beginning that way.

On Sunday night we had an open forum after dinner. We always had wine on Sunday night for dinner—we had sufficient wine to go right through the year, claret or moselle or riesling—and then at the open forum people could stand up and say what they liked or make any suggestion they wished or make any kind of complaints they wished. This open forum I thought was very satisfactory—particularly as it followed the ding of the Saturday night when people had already had their tongues a bit loosened.

You tried to have certain principles which were stated at the very beginning but, on the other hand, you also tried to have as few absolute rules as possible. And I think that's where, to an extent, an OIC should be able to invite a man up to his sanctum and perhaps give him a brandy or something, and have a chat and get things cleared up in that way, and I think that still happens.

The mid-winter dinner has always been an established polar ritual going back to the days of Shackleton and Scott, and in the 1950s, the Australians added the occasional performance of a bawdy pantomime, Cinderella. Des Lugg told me of the elaborate preparations for the staging of Cinderella including the painstaking filling and testing of meteorological balloons with substances to most effectively simulate the reality of breast tissue for Cinders and the Ugly Sisters. There is usually a certain amount of re-writing to incorporate contemporary events, but the basic script is, well, basic. Here Cinderella is sobbing because she can't go to the Prince's Ball. Enter the Fairy Queen:

> *Fairy Queen*: Now what's the matter Cinders dear?
> Come, come, shed not another tear.
> *Cinders*: O Fairy Queen it's nothing much at all,
> I cannot go to the Prince's Ball.
> (Sobs on Fairy Queen's shoulder).
> *Fairy Queen*: The Prince's Ball? What's wrong with that?
> Or did someone feed it to the cat?
> *Cinders*: You've got me wrong by some mischance,
> It's in a hall, not in his pants.
> *Fairy Queen*: A dress, I'll fix that in a tick,
> With a couple of wanks of my magic stick.
> And that's not all, so please don't weep,
> I've light blue slippers and a jeep.

And so on. Cinderella is still performed on some bases in the 1990s, but the *Boy's Own* club of Antarctica was ended in 1976 when the first woman expeditioner wintered on Macquarie Island. Since then increasing numbers of women have visited and wintered in Antarctica and in 1989 Diana Patterson was appointed as the first woman Station Leader on the continent. As it happened, our Voyage Leader, Dr Des Lugg, was a key player in the events that led to the first woman joining an Australian Antarctic expedition.

> *DL*: It's very interesting that the question of women for some years had been effectively avoided. Then it came to the International Women's Year—and that was quite by accident. But I had a small part to play in this in that recruiting doctors was very difficult and the only way I could see a future in getting enough doctors was to actually recruit women. I can remember it was 1975 and Clyde Cameron was our Minister and a group of us went to the Minister's office in Parliament House—just before the Whitlam Government was dismissed—and discussed what we were going to do and canvassed all sorts of issues. And then finally I said, 'Well, Minister, I do have an application from a woman'. All the eyes of the bureaucrats fell on me indicating,

'You have committed the unpardonable!' But I felt duty-bound to tell the Minister that a woman had applied. He said, 'Well, would you take her?'

I said, 'Well yes, a most interesting woman has applied who has done a lot as a surgeon and I think would be quite suitable as the first woman to winter on Macquarie Island'. He said, 'Done!', and agreed. So the Minister had made the decision and that was fine.

And then the press had a field day saying it was tokenism because of International Women's Year. But, really, it was going to happen at some stage and it happened then, and since then we've put a small number of women in but I think all of those women that have gone have been the best in their chosen field and have competed very well with men, and it has changed the expeditions.

Many of the early women expeditioners were doctors and my wife, Ros Bowden, interviewed three of them—Louise Holliday, Gillian Deakin and Lyn Williams—for a program she prepared for the ABC on the role of women in the Antarctic.

LH: I got to Davis Station and some people weren't really happy to see a woman down there because it somehow emasculated all their excitement and feeling that only men could do this job. But I understood that old ideas die hard and some of these guys felt fairly threatened and I did my best to be friendly, and after the first few weeks things settled down and, really, I got on just as one of the expeditioners.

GD: I think people spend a lot of time thinking, 'How are you going to cope with the year?'. I mean, it is an extraordinary place and it is difficult at times to live there, simply because it's a very simple society and there's no kind of buffer zone where you can go. If you're having difficulties at work you can't walk away, come home and talk to someone else about it, because the same people you're having difficulties with are at the dinner table and will be there at breakfast the next morning and so on. So there are pressures down there and there are situations that arise that are quite stressful at times. But I went down there with the idea that if there were any problems that the men were having regarding me, that was their problem. I had to remember that; it wasn't my problem and it only became my problem if I made it so. I decided before I went down to consider it in that light.

LW: I think when you arrive people treat you as a woman. By the end of the year they treat you as you are or as you warrant or deserve. The prejudice aspect is largely gone by the end of the year.

GD: I went down there as an expeditioner, and I didn't go down there as a woman. The fact that I *was* a woman obviously affected some of my activities and the fact that I was a doctor down there determined how I behaved as well. But, generally, the fact that I was a woman rarely became an issue. The day-to-day living down there was irrelevant to what sex you were.

One of the most enduring objections quoted by those opposed to women going to Antarctica was the old 'toilets' argument. How would women 'manage' in a blizzard on a field trip? This was tackled in an admirably practical manner by Dr Gillian Deakin.

GD: I found a little device called a Sanifem, and I recommend it. Any woman in the outdoors should purchase one of these, it makes life very easy. It's a shaped funnel with a long tube that fits nicely between the legs and serves the purpose very well. Using that meant that I never had to take off any clothing at all for a pee. You had to direct the funnel carefully though!

There is no doubt that the presence of women on the Antarctic stations has modified some 'traditional' behaviour—even the sacred Cinderella pantomime, staged at the mid-winter dinner.

GD: I helped to write the mid-winter play. We broke with tradition and we incurred a lot of flack from the old traditionalists. Many people on our station felt that although it was a fine tradition set by Mawson back in the 'thirties, Antarctica had come of age and we could move on from a fairly puerile production, dare I say.

So we wrote a play which was Antarctic political satire. We had a very appreciative audience and it was topped by a superb meal cooked by our French chef, Roger, who produced a seven course meal that went on for several hours and was accompanied by fine wines. By the end of that evening everyone was saying, 'I've always wanted to tell you what a great mate you've been' and, 'what I like about you is . . . ', and it was a great evening, a really fantastic evening.

Managed to make a phone call to Ros from the Communications Hut. The satellite dish at Mawson is covered by a geodesic dome to protect it from wind and ice. The rate from Antarctica on the ANARESAT is pegged to Australian domestic STD rates—much cheaper than the *Icebird*'s INMARSAT at $16 a minute!

Satellites have transformed the whole communications system to and from Antarctica. Sun spots and auroral activity used to black out the old Morse-keyed messages for days on end. To minimise cable traffic from Antarctica to Australia, the Antarctic Division developed a message code of groups of four and five letters, known as a WYSSA by expeditioners. (WYSSA is the code for 'All my love darling'.) Although the telephone is the preferred link these days, a booklet 'Communicating with Antarctica' is still issued by the Antarctic Division listing the codes for two-way communication. Some examples of 'whizzers' are:

WYTOY   I think about you all the time and hope you are getting along all right.
YIKLA   This is the life!
YIKPO   This place gives you a pain at times.
YARAJ   Have met with an accident.
YAPGA   Grandfather hasn't been very well.
YITUB   I am not sure whether men training dogs or dogs training men.
YOGIP   Please send details of bank account.
YOMAS   I was not serious when I referred to . . .
WUYGT   Elephant seals are breeding.
YAYIR   Fine snow has penetrated through small crevices in the buildings.
WYMIP   Are you all right am worried about you?
YIHKE   I have grown a beard which is generally admired.

This code did not always hit the right emotional buttons for those at home. One Antarctic wife I spoke to in Melbourne, Trish Clemence, admitted to being profoundly irritated by the formality and impersonal nature of incoming whizzers. Her husband, a RAAF pilot, Peter Clemence, sailed south for Mawson in December 1956 for a fifteen months' stint at Mawson Station. They had been married for only seven weeks and two weeks after Peter left she realised she was pregnant! The Clemences are still together, but Antarctic service obviously puts severe strains on personal relationships.

However, working on the basis that most problems fix themselves up one way or another in time, the WYSSA system did keep the wintering expeditioners insulated to some extent from the day-to-day worries of home. No more. I was told that the yearly phone bills for some winterers have topped the $3,000 mark. As one of the drawcards for Antarctic service is the opportunity to save money, the communications haemorrhage is a factor to be reckoned with.

Some of the cryptic messages received in the whizzer era indicated a certain disenchantment from the home front. The OIC of Davis Station noted in his official log of 7 March, 1969:

. . . My wife sent a whizzer today saying that my finances were unstable but she had bought a Jaguar. Thank goodness for the impractical, attractive feminine race who do things that the average male would shrink at even thinking of!

The communications hut is working at full blast at this time of the year. Radio Operator Bob Orchard said the four operators haven't had a day off since the shipping season started. They work in a funny mixture of high and low tech. There is a long line of chattering tele-printers transferring weather information between Antarctic stations and out to Australia or South Africa, and long racks of relatively ancient transmitting and receiving gear stretching from floor to ceiling, gradually being replaced by computerised equipment that would fit in a handy-sized suitcase.

The Mawson radio hut is in constant communication with the Japanese, Russian, French and German Antarctic stations,

Radio operator Bob Orchard tending the ever-chattering teleprinters relaying weather information at Mawson Station.

as well as all the Australian stations and Australia. Much of the weather data is punched through on teleprinter, using radio signals bounced off the ionosphere, in the time honoured way. Eventually this will be taken over by satellite, but not yet. Sun spots and flares can knock out these teleprinter links for days at a time. The ANARESAT system gives direct satellite communication with Australia. You can fax Antarctica these days!

The radio operators are constantly 'talking' to their Russian, French, Japanese and German counterparts on the teleprinter circuits—and to Pretoria in South Africa. I joined Bob Orchard in the communications centre:

B: Here comes Eric from Pretoria! He sometimes prints in Afrikaans, but he's just typed 'Good morning' so it's English today.
T: You've got some phrases up on the wall in Afrikaans.
B: I think it's more difficult than Japanese.
T: The English translations are: 'Good morning, how are things, cheerio, all the best, nice work, my pleasure Sir, really

very nice, have a nice sleep and enjoy the evening, slow but sure, poor but randy, good shot, you naughty child, pretty girl, love, many thanks for all your trouble, merry Christmas and a happy new year.'

B: The two Japanese operators, Taka and Ryaki, at Syowa speak really good English. They are due to leave now, their winter is over. But we have a lot of communications with them and they have some of their quaint phrases. When Taka opens up the day's sked you don't expect a bloke to say: 'I like you'!

T: You must get to know each other quite well from a distance, I suppose.

B: Yes, we do. The Japanese ship *Shirase* is down here at the moment and Taka is returning to Japan on it, and it's calling into Mawson. It was due early in February, but they have had an accident at the Japanese station. One of their vehicles has gone down a crevasse, and the ship has gone around to collect the people who were injured and that has delayed the departure of the ship. But he'll be calling in, and we're keen to see him.

T: What sort of things do you talk about on the circuits?

B: Usually communications. Our time is very limited for collecting this information and getting it to move, so as far as socialising is concerned we need special skeds. Then we talk about station life, and that's about it.

T: What about emergencies?

B: If anything happens to our expeditioners in Antarctica, which has happened at all our bases in the past, we can't get assistance from Australia. We always need people like the Russians who can come to our assistance and will do so, no matter what time of the year it is. We are disappointed in the way our Government does things. Our Director says things like, 'The hand of friendship reaches across Antarctica again', a cheap way of dodging responsibilities, I think. And if the Russians can land an aeroplane at their Progress Base, just along the coast from Davis, so could an Aussie pilot. When those Japanese I mentioned a few moments ago were hurt, they have a ship that can go to their aid, a Japanese ice breaker owned by the Japanese Government. We lack a lot. We claim the greatest amount of territory. We have a scientific program, there's not doubt about that, and we're building some magnificent Taj Mahals down here. But do we really need it? We need means of getting to and from here quickly—as you realise yourself, stuck on the *Icebird*.

T: Are we piggy-backing on the other international operators down here? Do we ever help them?

B: We give them a few drums of kerosene now and then for their aircraft. Perhaps that's being a little bit cynical. Our Prince Charles Mountains people flew Russian parties around the various places they wanted to go to in the mountains. The Russians weren't expecting it and our guys were there, and that's all part of the deal down here. To help one another. When their aeroplanes were flying through here a couple of months ago, we supplied them with fuel. OK, that's Russian aeroplanes. Where are the Australian aeroplanes?

T: We had an emergency at Davis a few days ago, those two chaps injured there. Obviously this would have been a key communication point during that exercise.

B: Mawson became involved getting in contact with the Russians. We do have a pretty good relationship with them, we work them several times a day so there was no trouble making contact. We explained the circumstances to them, that assistance was needed—of course this came from head office—and the met fellers were hauled out of bed, balloon flights were done, forecasts done, and the Russians were on their way. It didn't take long at all. The Russians eventually flew them out to South America.

In a small ante room—almost a porch—at the communications centre I found Trevor Lloyd and Peter Newman in the make-and-mend section of the Mawson electronic industry. They were shaking their heads over the 'Antarctic Factor' as it affected incoming electronic equipment. There is an extraordinary high incidence of faults in equipment straight out of the box. When I walked by they were regarding $15,000 worth of brand new testing equipment with evident distaste:

Trevor: One of the jobs we have to do is to test two-way receivers. When you are testing them you have to test their sensitivity, and one of the problems is varying the actual signal generator level. This is one of the problems with this tester.

Peter: We use a receiver generator test to set up the radio links we are trying to work, and the very levels that we are trying to test are the ones that are intermittent. So we can't accurately set up equipment down here.

At the moment we are trying to get around the problem. We don't even have a handbook to help us fix it. There is only one boat left in the season. Either we get a handbook and try and fix it here, or they try and send down another unit so we can swap them over. That's just one of the problems we have to put up with. We don't have the staff to check them at head office in Kingston, Tasmania, so we have to rely on the manufacturers to send the gear down to us in reasonable shape.

Trevor: There's a stock standard power supply, off the shelf, which we've got four or five of here and which you can buy for around $100 from any electrical supplier. Yesterday I tested one, and found that the transformer, which is the core of the whole thing, had short circuited. Now that should not have happened. There's no reason why shipping down here in a well packed container should affect that. It is one of the many examples that I have come across so far. Five out of five radios in one box were unserviceable— brand new radios.

Tim: Five out of five!

Trevor: Five out of five with major faults which will take a long time to fix. If we were back in Australia we could go back to the company which supplied them and say 'fix it'. But down here, what can you do? You fix it yourself, and this means you can't get on with the work you are supposed to be doing, which is setting up a communications system. We spend a lot of time back-tracking to get the equipment up to scratch before we start. And that is wasting our time down here.

Tim: These things haven't been dropped from a great height or anything like that, have they?

Peter: No, this test set was packed very well in an instrument case.

Trevor: Even simple things like cable ties—you go to use them, they snap in half. You go to use banana plugs, ordinary standard plugs, and I found that in a box of 100, the red ones all broke in half and the black ones were fine. The plastic becomes brittle and breaks. We are paying the price for faulty workmanship at the manufacturing level, and no acceptance testing at Kingston.

Tim: First mend the testing equipment, and then start fixing the other gear!

Trevor: That's a fair summary I think.

JANUARY 20

We are at sea again! This was most unexpected, but a welcome break from going slowly potty waiting at the ice edge. Two helicopters have been recalled from Mawson Station and are lashed to the fore-deck. A German ship, the *Wilhaditurm*, an oil rig tender some sixty-five metres long and under charter to the University of California, is reportedly in our area, but has not been in radio contact with its owners for five days. We have been asked to search for her. It is a private expedition and there is no trained radio operator on board.

JANUARY 21

We are steaming slowly through broken pack ice. Around midday the sea mist lifted and the sun broke through. The plan was to send up our helicopters to see if they could spot the *Wilhaditurm*. This was done, but they saw nothing. I think everyone is thinking the same thing—if something had happened to the ship there would be little chance of survival.

JANUARY 22

We are back at our old spot at the ice edge again. There was no sign of the *Wilhaditurm*, and no radio communication either. It is all most odd.

I was told later that in fact the *Wilhaditurm* had been in the area at the time, but for some reason had maintained radio silence for a week. There was speculation that she had been engaged in some seismic work connected with oil exploration—hence the radio silence.

Our neighbours in cabin C2, 'Beyond Help', have thrown a party. They have a most ingenious method of keeping beer cool. It is placed in a mesh bag and simply hung out the porthole in Nature's Antarctic refrigerator. The idea has caught on, and there are festoons of beer cans to be seen dangling from many of the module portholes.

CHAPTER NINE

Nearly Nipped by the Ice • Awesome Forces Of Nature Observed • Vegemite Revenge on German Crew • Lord Cameron and 'The Order of the Great Dag' • An Antarctic Barbecue • Larcies Lower Bad Taste to New Depths; Iron Man Contest Endured • Wintering with Emperor Penguins; Feminism Uplifted to Ultimate Heights • Huddles and Mavericks • 'Chicknapping' a Death Sentence • Further Reflections on 'The Worst Journey in the World'

JANUARY 26   AUSTRALIA DAY!

I was blissfully unaware, but apparently we were in an awkward situation early today. *Icebird* has an ice-strengthened bow, but cannot withstand heavy pressure from the side. We were breaking ice, which means charging into the fast ice until we grind to a halt, then retreating to charge again on a slightly different angle. Sometimes the ship gets temporarily jammed and the cranes have to be swung over the side (on occasions dangling the launch *Chicken* for extra leverage) to rock the vessel to free her. During one of these jammings, the fast ice nearby started to move out, and we were in some danger of being caught from the side. We reversed away and returned to the ice edge to wait.

The sight of pack ice on the move is awesome. Imagine unbroken slabs of metre-thick ice, several square kilometres wide, moving along at two or three knots and hitting the solid bulk of a grounded iceberg. It is like the irresistible force meeting the immovable object. With *Icebird* safely in open water, it was fascinating to watch. As the moving ice sheet hit the berg,

Icebird attempting to break the fast ice en route to Mawson Station. Note the distinctive patterns in the ice caused by charging at different angles to create space in the solid ice sheet.

it ran up its flank, toppling back with a great crash and showers of ice and spray. Then it just kept coming, as the iceberg refused to move—an amazing spectacle as tonnes and tonnes of ice just kept rearing up in great slabs, and crashing back. A reminder also of the enormous forces ready to crush the *Icebird* if we were caught in the wrong situation.

One of the emerging rituals of polar travel is the January 26 Australia Day Ceremony when the Australians have a chance to get their own back on the Germans who forced them to ingest that vile Tabasco-laced stew and inflicted other indignities during the 'Crossing the Antarctic Convergence' shenanigans. The politicians took a prominent role with Ian Cameron clearly relishing the role as the Governor General. Or, to give him his full title, His Eminence Governor General of this Antarctic Territory Lord Ian Milton Dixon Cameron of Maranoa, KCMG, MGB, KGB (and most probably CIA), VD & Scar.

The pollies' Minder displayed a natural talent in helping to construct appropriately pompous prose for the Australia Day

Ceremony, which took place on the helicopter flight deck— in the open air! I was to be the GG's Clerk and read out the citations and announcements. Lord Cameron assumed his Vice Regal role with aplomb, with decorations, sword and cocked hat. As it turned out, we were more than a little over-scripted. My ungloved hands turned into ice and couldn't turn the pages.

Those singled out for special attention had to eat some Australian 'delicacies' manufactured by the Larcies—Nutella and Vegemite sandwiches spread centimetres thick, and meat pies concealing all manner of evil intrusions (including the inevitable Vegemite) and chilli on a bed of green peas. Garth Varcoe, the sole New Zealander on board, was one of those singled out:

Clerk: Garth Varcoe, from the Land of the Short Flat Vowel, stand forward.

GG: I was going to ask you what was the capital of New Zealand, but everyone knows, including yourself, that it is $2,500. I'll ask you instead: For what single act is Captain Cook most revered by New Zealanders?

[Varcoe was given no time to answer.]

Australia Day shenanigans. I am the Governor General's clerk, at left, next to GG Lord Cameron who clearly relished his Vice Regal role.

GG: Your time is up. Captain Cook is most revered by New Zealanders for pioneering the route from Auckland to Bondi!

You are hereby awarded the Order of the Great Dag.

I won't go on. The German crew had to drink an appalling beverage fomented by the Larcies containing (among other things) beer, Vegemite (of course), custard, Tabasco and chilli sauce.

Roger the cook had been given the day off and we were to have an Australia Day barbecue on the aft deck. That was all very well, but by lunch time the weather had closed in and it was starting to snow! Still, the galley was shut and that was that. We turned out in our Antarctic gear to queue for singed chops and snags cooked over a half forty-four gallon drum. I mean, how Australian can you get!

One of the field assistants from the Prince Charles Mountains, Adam Darrough, peered out a porthole to assess the queue for the barbie, and emerged from the heated interior of *Icebird* standing nonchalantly waiting in shorts, T-shirt and thongs. Unfortunately for him the cooked food ran out and fresh supplies had to be cremated. Unable to lose face by retreating to the warmth whence he had come, he stood there bravely turning visibly bluer by the minute. Then, having endured about ten minutes of snow and frigid breeze, Adam (who is an accomplished rock climber and Alpinist) sat seemingly unconcerned on the ship's rail and ate his singed snags!

During the afternoon the Larcies had organised an Iron Man Contest with a further series of revolting gastronomic abominations to endure.

I was in the press team with Keith Scott, Bryan Smith and his camera crew Mal Ludgate and Scotty Davis. The tasks to be performed were:

1 Drink a bottle of beer straight down, and turn round a certain number of times holding a broomstick. (That was definitely the pick of the tasks.)
2 A bowl of rice-bubbles and honey to be licked from a plate without hands or implements.
3 Eat six biscuits thickly coated with . . . Vegemite!
4 An unrolled condom partially filled with evaporated milk had to be drunk, and then blown up until it burst.

5 A bowl of custard containing five raisins was placed on the floor, and the task was to locate the five raisins by mouth (no hands or spoons) and spit them out on the ground.

On Bryan's advice I concealed a pencil and burst the condom while blowing it up—but the press team was disqualified, much to Keith Scott's chagrin. The sight of the politicians participating brought great joy to all bystanders. Cameron was disgusting and spat most of his condom of milk over me. During the finals he became a bit more expert and sprayed it over the photographers. The use of condoms seems to prevail in most Larcie sports. When I suggest to Phil Clark (one of the Larcie officers) that they had lifted bad taste to new heights, he was most indignant and said it was all good clean fun compared to the Royal Military College at Duntroon when they had to eat a can of dog food as well and the condoms had tomato sauce in them.

The evening was marked by a command performance by the Bergbusters Band in Stoppy's Bar, with an Australian singalong. I wore my finger nails down to the quick playing the ukulele.

VOYAGE SIX DRINKING SONG—SUNG BY THE BERGBUSTERS ON *ICEBIRD* ON THE OCCASION OF AUSTRALIA DAY 1989

(With apologies to Ted Egan)

Chorus

There are lots of Bloody Good Drinkers
In the Polar Territory,
From Hobart to Macquarie
They're always on a spree;
Down to Mawson Station
From Davis to Ca-sey—
There are lots of Bloody Good Drinkers
In the Polar Territory.

In Stoppy's Bar on *Icebird*
A rigger dropped down dead.

I wondered why he died smiling
Till the Larcie beside me said:
'He was in with mob of good drinkers
And the others are all put out.
He'd just knocked down a stubby,
And it was his bloody turn to shout!'

Chorus

We had a wake the other day
When a boffin mate of mine
Slipped and fell with a helluva yell
Into a bloody great vat of wine.
Now you may not believe this,
But the story's going around.
He made three trips to the dunny
Before the bastard drowned.

Chorus

So try to hold your grog down
Until the Polar dawn,
And if you find your level rising,
Have a technicolour yawn,
Maintain our reputation
For all the world to see—
That we've got some Bloody Good Drinkers
In the Polar Territory.
Chorus

JANUARY 27

Oof. Was woken at 9 am by Dennis (who alleged I was snoring) and fell back in my bunk with a low moan till 10.30. I was supposed to send a broadcast to Sydney, but due to the enthusiastic singing of the night before, I had no voice! Most embarrassing.

The weather has become windy and rough, which could be good news if the ice starts to move. Rumour Control has it that we are to berth at Mawson within twenty-four or thirty-six hours. How often have we heard that one in the past two weeks?

The *Icebird* University continues. A Tasmanian, Ron Fehlberg, gave a talk on Tasmanian national parks and showed slides of Cradle Mountain, Frenchman's Cap and the South West area. The sight of that lush vegetation seemed most strange in our present circumstances. We have also had lectures from glaciologist Ian Allison, biologist Don Adamson, photographer Dave Watts and the environmental philosopher, Lawrence Johnson. Unfortunately I am still no better informed on what The Philosopher is doing on Voyage Six, because I fell asleep shortly after he began his talk.

The Philosopher and I are hardly speaking following an extremely anguished game of four-handed Scrabble. Barry Batts, Keith Scott and I have been having regular games after lunch. Lawrence asked to take part, so we had a four-hander. Never again! He took a minimum of twenty minutes over each of his moves. It got so tedious that Barry, Keith and I took to having constitutionals on the deck between turns. Finally it became clear that no-one could clear their letters—which meant that the winner would be declared once the total value of the letters left had been subtracted from the individual scores. The Philosopher had two tiles left, and 'passed' on the last round, effectively indicating that he could not move. We all passed (desperate to end the marathon game apart) and Lawrence asked again if we had all finished. He then triumphantly put down the two letters Io—one of the moons of Jupiter. I had great pleasure in telling him it was invalid as proper nouns were not allowed in Scrabble!

I won, too. I'm sure all this means we are going increasingly stir crazy. Our Scrabble group swore a solemn oath that we wouldn't play with The Philosopher again on the voyage. I have had fair success in Scrabble so far, but have met my nemesis in the Head Prefect, Ian Hay. He has an excellent vocabulary, great tactical skill and a ruthless instinct for the jugular in his word placement. We have only managed two games so far, and are one-all. Unfortunately his job as Deputy Voyage Leader leaves him little time for word games.

**I have had a fascinating interview with Graham Rob-
ertson, a biologist who has spent the winter camped
near a breeding colony of Emperor penguins out on the
sea ice. He has been studying their breeding habits and
feeding ecology. To do this he equipped some of the
penguins with computers stuck to their backs and then
recovered them after these amazing creatures had
walked seventy kilometres to open water over the sea
ice and back again. All in the dead of winter, too, with
temperatures sometimes down to −50C with wind chill.**

This experiment has wonderful links with Antarctic history.
In the winter of 1911, before Scott set out on his disastrous
bid for the South Pole, it was decided to send an expedition
to Cape Crozier to try and recover some fertilised eggs from
an Emperor penguin breeding colony which was known to be
there. It was thought that the Emperor embryos could be the
missing link to the evolutionary puzzle of how birds developed
from reptiles—apart from the extraordinary fact that these
birds somehow managed to incubate and hatch their eggs on
the sea ice in the depths of the polar winter. Apsley Cherry-
Garrard's description of that winter journey in his book *The
Worst Journey In The World* is a polar classic. His companions,
Wilson and Bowers, would later perish with Scott. That the
three of them did not die on the Cape Crozier journey is a
tribute to the triumph of the human spirit against impossible
odds. During one blizzard their tent blew away, effectively
condemning them to death. But they stumbled over it some
hours later, snagged in some ice. As Cherry-Garrard put it,
'Our lives had been taken away and given back to us'.

The going had been hard enough before that. The three men
had to haul sledges in pitch darkness for a round trip of some
150 kilometres, and the cold was unimaginable.

We had our breakfast, struggled into our foot-gear, and squared up
inside the tent, which was comparatively warm. Once outside, I raised
my head to look round and found I could not move it back. My clothing
had frozen hard as I stood—for perhaps fifteen seconds. For four
hours I had to pull the sledge with my head stuck up, and from
that time we all took care to bend down into a pulling position before
being frozen in.

There was no respite from the cold, even in their tent at night.

The long shivering fits following close one after the other all the time as we lay in our dreadful sleeping bags—hour after hour and night after night in those temperatures—were as monotonous as could be. Later we got frost-bitten even as we lay in our sleeping-bags. Things are getting pretty bad when you get frost-bitten in your bag.

When I met Graham Robertson, he was very conscious of the history behind his scientific project with the Emperor penguins, particularly the Cape Crozier expedition described by Cherry-Garrard.

> *GR*: It's always crossed my mind when people write historical accounts of particular journeys, with the hardships they experienced, that they might indulge in what you might term 'retrospective falsification'! Perhaps several years might have elapsed between when they wrote the article or the book, and when they actually made the journey. But when people publish actual temperatures like −60 degrees C that Cherry-Garrard was talking about, that is something I can definitely relate to because we put up with −40C and −50C when wind chill factors are considered. Minus 60C is just extraordinary!
>
> And these people didn't have portable Apple huts. We could hop in an Apple or the heated Hagglunds vehicle and shelter from the wind, and go back to our sleeping hut. But these guys were out for three weeks straight, in a tent, sled hauling in total darkness as well. And—from my perspective in having been through an Antarctic winter—I find it almost impossible to conceive that extra notch of hardship.

Cherry-Garrard was the right man at the right place and time to describe the rigours of *The Worst Journey in the World*. His great contribution to polar history and to literature was to write superbly about the events he shared in Antarctica with Scott's party.

The blizzard raged with monstrous fury; the winds of the world were there, and they had all gone mad. We had bad winds at Cape Evans this year, and we had far worse the next winter when the open water was at our doors. But I have never felt or seen a wind like this. I wondered why it did not carry away the earth.

The awful level of their personal suffering can be gained from this short passage on the return journey from Cape Crozier bearing their frozen Emperor penguin eggs.

There was no unnecessary conversation; I don't know why our tongues never got frozen, but all my teeth, the nerves of which had been killed, split to pieces. We had been going perhaps three hours since lunch.

'How are your feet, Cherry?' from Bill.

'Very cold'.

'That's all right; so are mine.'

We didn't worry to ask Birdie; he never had a frost-bitten foot from start to finish.

Half-an-hour later as we marched, Bill would ask the same question.

I tell him that all feeling has gone; Bill still has some feeling in one of his but the other is lost. He settled we had better camp; another ghastly night ahead.

That the Emperor penguin should choose—or even be able— to incubate an egg and feed its young in the polar mid-winter is an extraordinary tribute to its adaptability to Antarctic conditions. The Emperor is the largest of the sixteen species of penguin, and also the heaviest. It stands 1.15 metres tall, and weighs up to forty kilograms. This makes it twice as heavy as the next largest species of penguin, the King.

From the ship we had seen some Emperors standing on ice floes. The smaller Adelies barely came up to their chests. Even from a distance they had a marvellous dignity. Graham Robertson told me how they had linked their breeding cycle to the annual summer break-out of the fast ice from the Antarctic coastline—part of their remarkable adaptation to local conditions. Yet everything about these splendid birds demands description by superlatives. Indeed, feminists may well marvel at the roles adopted by male and female in the chick-rearing process. Immediately after laying her egg in mid-May, the female passes it over to the male to nurture in his brood pouch—a patch of naked skin on his lower belly that keeps the egg at his body temperature. He then lowers an

Male Emperor penguins huddling on the sea ice for communal warmth at Auster rookery.

Both male and female Emperor penguins have a brood pouch for their chicks.
Photographs by Graham Robertson.

abdominal fold over the egg, which is somewhat precariously balanced on his crampon-style claws. For the next sixty-five days he lives off his own body fat, balancing the egg on his feet, while his good lady shuffles off over seventy kilometres of sea ice to the open sea to feed (laughing and chortling?), while her male partner drops in weight from forty kilograms to about twenty kilograms before she returns to help feed and, indeed, take over the brooding of the hatched chick.

During her absence the colony of incubating males (brooding over their role models?) huddle together on the sea ice to gain collective warmth to resist the blizzards and winter cold of Antarctica. They are the only species of penguin to do this. All other penguins breed in summer, nest on terra firma, and guard their territory jealously, even if it is only a small circle of stones, as the Adelies do. But the Emperors put aside all territorial rights for group survival. Dr John Gill, who volunteered for duty as one of Graham Robertson's field assistants, recalls his feelings of disbelief in first seeing a huddle of Emperors.

JG: Auster is a scene of amazing desolation. The bergs, grounded bergs, are like a vast ruined city and in the winter twilight they glow an unearthly and beautiful blue colour. They are embedded in this great plain of sea ice which is grey and swept clean by the wind, except for silver tails of snow drift which trail off to the horizon. Even late in the morning in winter the sky is so dark that you can still see the stars. It always seems to be blowing a minor sort of gale, and it's an incredible feeling, moving through this scene of enormous desolation and greyness and whiteness and blueness, suddenly to round a berg and there are tens of thousands of these wonderful robust, regal-looking birds, standing there as though they are perfectly at home. Which, of course, they are.

In order for Graham Robertson to study the feeding habits of the Emperor penguin, he had to camp with the Emperor colony of some 11 000 pairs at Auster Rookery, fifty-five kilometres north east of Mawson Station. He attached data loggers to the backs of selected birds before they began their seventy kilometre march over the fast sea ice to the open sea to feed.

He then had to find these birds in amongst the huge huddles of Emperors (which he did by homing in on a small radio transmitter also fixed to the penguins' backs) and transfer the coded information to a field computer. He flushed the stomachs of some returning birds to weigh and analyse what they had eaten. One of his photographs shows a cluster of Emperor penguins about to be examined, standing in some Australian-designed portable steel sheep yards on the sea ice, while some of their confreres look at them from the outside with evident amazement. Graham Robertson's own sense of wonderment at the behaviour and survival tactics of the Emperor penguins remained high during the whole of the winter he spent with them.

GR: I remember one day in early July when we visited Auster Emperor penguin colony to conduct the winter count of the incubating males. At that time of the year the sun doesn't actually rise, so the whole colony was bathed in a very dim twilight, amongst towering grounded icebergs. During the winter incubation period there are only males in attendance at the colony and, because it is so cold, all the males pack in very tightly to share each other's warmth. On this particular day there were about three huddles of several thousand birds each, I guess. My companion and I approached one of these huddles to within about fifteen or twenty metres, which is the closest safe distance you can approach a group of Emperors without disturbing them. A bird on the upwind edge of the huddle, with its back towards us, and leaning forward into the other birds to share their warmth, looked around and gave us what I call that distinct Emperor sideways stare—that is, back on to us, body slouched forward over the egg on its feet, its head turned at right angles to its body, and staring at us for any movement that might cause it alarm. Perhaps it was a little confused about humans being in Antarctica during winter. We looked totally out of context there.

A month previously the males and females had been through their usual courtship procedure, and the female had laid the egg and passed it to the male and then headed out across seventy kilometres of frozen sea to reach open water where she would feed for the sixty-five-day incubation period.

So, effectively, the male fasts for the full incubation span. In fact, even more extraordinarily, the full winter fast for the male Emperor penguins is about 110 or 115 days, because the incubation period is preceded by about forty days of courtship and pairing off during which time they don't have a single meal. And at the end of that time when the egg hatches, the males have lost about forty per cent of their body weight—they haven't had a meal in 115 days. And then they have to turn around in the dark and walk seventy kilometres across the sea ice to reach open water before they can go fishing. It is quite an extraordinary exercise.

Anyway, I remember distinctly this group of males we were looking at and a particular male on the leading edge of this huddle. I looked across at my field assistant and I noticed that he, just like me, was wearing ten kilograms of Antarctic clothing, special clothing designed just so we could stay alive in this environment. And I also looked at his face and saw it was flushed red against the cold—it was about −35C with wind chill—and that is right on the cutting edge of life, you feel this in your bones. I also noticed that the skin around his eyes was furrowed and tight, ageing him temporarily by about ten years or so, just the effect of cold on the human body. And I could sense by his movements that his feet and hands were getting cold and soon I knew he would want to go back to the vehicle and have some hot drinks and perhaps go back to the field hut.

Then I looked back at the male bird which was still staring at us, and I realised, perhaps more clearly than ever before, the distinct peculiarity of this species of penguin which enables it to cope and breed in this environment. Certainly it is obvious that it is breeding in the middle of an Antarctic winter which is extraordinary enough. But there are things within the bird that casual observations don't allow you to appreciate. The fact that it can carry within its body weight about forty per cent fat, which it mobilises through this 115 day fast. Also its feathers keep out most of the winter cold. These feathers are more like scales than feathers. They are four layers thick and they provide about eighty-five per cent of the Emperor penguin's insulation. Emperors also have very small feet and small flippers compared to the size of the body. This is for heat conservation.

138

We turned and walked slowly back to the vehicle, and as we walked I glanced over my shoulder and looked at the male we'd been watching. Once we had retreated to a safe distance, this bird broke my gaze and placed its head once more within the warmth and confines of the birds around it. And in doing that, it ceased being the single bird we had marvelled at and became once again just a single cell of this much greater organism—the huddle itself, which gives you the impression of being a living thing in its own right.

Counting the penguins to try and get a reasonably accurate idea of how many were actually breeding at Auster and Taylor rookeries was extremely difficult. Graham and his field assistants tried every possible method from the kind of crowd guesstimation that goes on at football matches to photography from a camera suspended from a meteorological balloon above the huddle. He found that the various methods varied wildly. Counts by eye varied from 4300 to 22 950 at Auster alone! But photographs revealed a more realistic 10 900 breeding pairs at Auster. Graham believes that previous estimates of the number of Emperor penguins at Auster could be at least fifty per cent out.

I was also fascinated to find out how the returning Emperor partner located his or her mate amongst these huge huddles. And they do it by imprinting each other's calls in their memories.

GR: So when the female returns at hatching time to relieve the male of the newly hatched chick, she's got to find that male in the midst of thousands of others, distributed seemingly randomly amongst the colony, in the dark. And they find them by their call. The female walks in and parks herself by a huddle of males and then trumpets—calls out at the top of her voice. If she gets no response, she moves to another huddle and calls again. Sooner or later the male will hear her and pull his head from the centre of the pack and trumpet back. Then he will break from the huddle, waddle over to the female and they will be reunited. That is quite a remarkable adaptation, particularly when you hear the din of a colony, when these birds are all calling at once at the tops of their voices. Each call is unique. They don't jam each other's signals.

The parents also have to locate the chick when they return from the sea with food. So in the first few weeks of chick brooding when the chick is being carried around on its mother's feet, they sing to each other repeatedly so that each may remember the other's call. There is constant activity and sound going on in those first few weeks after hatching. When the male returns after three weeks at sea, the female gives the chick to the male for the last two weeks of chick brooding, and the male and the chick imprint on each other as well. After seven or eight weeks of brooding the chick gains its independence and is left with others in a creche on the sea ice. And for the four months after that, until they fledge, the mother and father are free to walk the 100 kilometres from the colony to open water to catch food for the chick. And on these feeding trips they might be away for three to four weeks at a time, and all the while the chick is back at the colony fasting on its own. The parents locate the chick when they return to the colony by calling. They can remember each other's calls amongst thousands and thousands of others that to our ears all sound the same.

Because the male has to fast for so long he sometimes fails to make it back across seventy kilometres of sea ice to open water and food. So there tend to be more females than males in the colonies. This leads to a situation where numbers of females, without partners, hover around the edges of the colonies desperate to move in on courting couples to break up the action or, later, to try and steal an egg, or 'chick-nap' a newly hatched Emperor. Graham Robertson called them 'mavericks' and observed their behaviour.

GR: So you find that trios form: there'll be a bona fide couple and a maverick roaming around in the wings as well. Every time the male and female want to get together in a romantic way, the maverick is there to interrupt them. They usually get a belt with the flippers. But the mavericks are also fairly important, in terms of the disturbance they create at hatching time, because they have a great desire to brood something. So they roam the outskirts of the colony just looking for spare chicks. Chicks, just by chance, spill out on the sea ice—sometimes the parents are a little bit clumsy in tending them—and you have a group of mavericks, four or five of them, racing in from twenty metres away, all trying to scoop up this spare chick. And they'll form a kind of rugby scrum over the chick and they'll be rucking it with their feet and scooping it with their bills to try and get it onto their feet for the brooding rights.

You also see frozen eggs that have been abandoned two months previously. They freeze on the sea ice and then they break—the internal contents expand—and the mavericks will pick these frozen eggs up and attempt to brood them. It must be a shock to have a frozen egg sitting in your brood pouch if your body temperature is 38C, so they don't hold them there for very long. They are just constantly looking for something to brood.

Interestingly, the same phenomenon was observed by Cherry-Garrard, Wilson and Bowers during their 1911 expedition to Cape Crozier.

Those who previously discovered the Emperors with their chicks saw the penguins nursing dead and frozen chicks if they were unable to obtain a live one. They also found frozen eggs which they must have incubated after they had been frozen. Now we found that these birds were so anxious to sit on something that some of those which had no eggs were sitting on ice! Several times Bill and Birdie picked up eggs to find them lumps of ice, rounded and about the right size, dirty and hard. Once a bird dropped an ice nest egg as they watched, and again a bird returned and tucked another into itself, immediately forsaking it for a real one, however, when one was offered.

Unfortunately there is a sad ending for a chick or an egg acquired by a maverick.

GR: If mavericks steal chicks and attempt to brood them, the chicks don't survive because the mavericks don't have a partner to help with the feeding. So, unfortunately, after the bird gets tired of brooding the chick, because it can't feed it, as its stomach is empty and it needs to go to sea to feed itself, it just abandons it on the sea ice where it usually gets snapped up by another maverick. But ultimately these chicks perish.

John Gill told me that despite all the uncomfortable procedures that Graham Robertson and his field assistants were submitting the Emperor penguins to, they never retaliated in any way.

JG: They are very benign birds. They're curious, they like to come over and have a look at you. But the gentleness of their natures impressed me. You can do all sorts of things— terrible things—to Emperors: catch them, turn them upside down, pump out their stomachs. And even though they have quite a lethal-looking bill which I am sure could do quite a lot of damage, none of us suffered any damage at the hands of these marvellous birds. They can almost knock you over with a flipper and they could do quite serious damage with their bills. But they showed no aggression towards us at all.

The field results showed that when the Emperors reached the open sea, they dived to very great depths to feed. Dives below 300 metres were commonplace and one bird, as Graham Robertson put it, 'plunged into the twilight zone' at 458 metres, the deepest dive known for any bird. Why they need to go that deep is not completely explained. Graham did find that Emperors' stomachs contained small stones which might have to be gathered from the actual sea bed.

With more commercial fishing of Antarctic waters likely, Graham Robertson's research will be important in calculating how much fish, squid and krill can be harvested commercially before the penguin population is affected.

Meanwhile, the Emperor penguin remains the unacknowledged paragon of the liberated male, caring unto death itself, which sadly often overtakes these nurturing fathers if their ladies are a bit late back from cavorting and living it up in the krill-rich waters of the Southern Ocean.

But what happened to the frozen Emperor penguin eggs obtained with so much human tenacity and suffering by Cherry-Garrard, Wilson and Bowers in the winter of 1911? When the only surviving member of the Cape Crozier party,

Apsley Cherry-Garrard, arrived back in England, he personally took the eggs to the Natural History Museum in Kensington.

I had written to say I would bring the eggs at this time. Present: myself, Cherry-Garrard, with First or Doorstep Custodian of the Sacred Eggs. I did not take a verbatim report of his welcome, but the spirit of it may be dramatised as follows:

First Custodian: Who are you? What do you want? This ain't an egg shop. What call have you to come meddling with our eggs? Do you want me to put the police on to you? Is it the crocodile's egg you're after? I don't know nothing about no eggs. You'd best speak to Mr Brown; it's him that varnishes the eggs.

I resort to Mr Brown, who ushers me into the presence of the Chief Custodian, a man of scientific aspect, with two manners: one, affably courteous for a Person of Importance (I guess a Naturalist Rothschild at least) with whom he is conversing, and the other, extraordinarily offensive even for an official man of science, for myself.

I announce myself with becoming modesty as the bearer of the penguins' eggs, and proffer them. The Chief Custodian takes them into custody without a word of thanks, and turns to the Person of Importance to discuss them. I wait. The temperature of my blood rises. The conversation proceeds for what seems to me a considerable period. Suddenly the Chief Custodian notices my presence and seems to resent it.

Chief Custodian: You needn't wait.

Heroic Explorer: I would like to have a receipt for the eggs if you please.

Chief Custodian: It is not necessary; it is all right. You needn't wait.

Heroic Explorer: I should like to have a receipt.

As if that wasn't bad enough, things actually got worse. The professor who was supposed to examine the eggs died. But eventually a report was written, and I hope that Cherry-Garrard took some cold comfort from its final sentence.

If the conclusions arrived at with the help of the Emperor Penguin embryos about the origin of feathers are justified, the worst journey in the world in the interest of science was not made in vain.

CHAPTER TEN

We Depart Mawson Station • A Photographic Frenzy • We Hit a Rock; Disaster Averted • The Chicken Trip of a Lifetime • Davis Station's Garden Fixed • Why Do Elephant Seals Poop in Each Other's Faces? • Walking on a Lunar Landscape • Russian Jackboots and Chinese Hats • A Cruel Hoax Perpetrated • More Piss and Friendship

JANUARY 30

We are on the move again! Iceberg Alley is looking quite familiar as it is the fourth time we have been through it since arriving at Mawson. Our ice breaking has had little effect on the fast ice. Des Lugg says we will try for Davis Station, 650 kilometres east. The fast ice is still attached to the coast there, too, but it is thought we have a better chance of getting in. We will have to come back to Mawson Station later, as we are carrying the major fuel supply for the coming winter.

I had a fantastic experience this morning when I came down to breakfast. Tania Hinden, our stewardess, had Vangelis's *Antarctica* playing on her tape recorder in the serving area of the mess. Outside, in brilliant sunshine, fantastic ice sculptures of broken pack ice glided past the porthole. The music and spectacle blended in a splendid coincidence and just swept me along with a tremendous feeling of exhilaration. I was not the only passenger to be enthralled by it. All this before breakfast, too.

The photographers went into a frenzy later in the morning as we passed a striated iceberg that looked rather like a warped version of St Paul's Cathedral dome. A group of penguins had climbed half-way up the dome and the reason for their ascent became clearer as we sailed by. A pod of killer whales was swimming and blowing in a small patch of open water at the base of this berg, doubtless hoping some would slip off. Adam Darrough quipped that the penguins as well as the berg were in danger of being zapped by excess Kodachrome radiation.

FEBRUARY 1

Woken by the loud-speaker announcement that we were nearing Davis Station. It was worth getting up for. The approaches to the anchorage are studded with grounded icebergs. Against the whiteness of the bergs, the brown rocks of the coastline look as if a chunk of Sturt's Stony Desert has been transplanted to Antarctica. The Vestfold Hills region is one of the largest ice-free areas in Antarctica. It is a most unexpected sight.

Ewald had told me that the approaches to Davis were quite hazardous. He had run aground on an uncharted rock there a couple of seasons ago. As we neared the Station (which looked as though it had been built at Coober Pedy) the familiar jumble of old and new buildings could be seen, with the grandiose new steel structures dwarfing the old wooden 'donga' line. Davis is known as 'The Riviera of the South' because of its benign summer climate, and there were clear sunny skies and little wind as we nosed cautiously towards our anchorage. There was still a kilometre of fast ice between ship and shore, but open water to the west. Two small rocky islets signalled the point we could not go beyond, because of shoals and shallow water.

Ewald thought he had a sporting chance of using *Icebird* to break the ice out and away from the landing area at Davis, and he almost did it. Never had I enjoyed more the privilege of being allowed on the bridge. Clearly the precise positioning of the *Icebird* was vital to the operation. The Captain was conning the ship from the starboard side flying bridge, while Horst, the First Mate, was dashing from the chart table to the satellite navigation system and shouting co-ordinates to his skipper.

The ice breaking had spectacular results. As the bow charged into the fast ice, great cracks radiated out. As we watched, enormous slabs of ice slowly drifted away to open water. On one occasion we opened up an old tidal crack and saw a split unfold like a giant zip fastener, running over to a rocky islet off our starboard bow and continuing all the way to the mainland.

I had the strong impression that Ewald was having the time of his life playing God with his ship and literally moving, if not mountains, great plains of fast ice. It seemed that with one more charge we might actually clear the landing area, but there was a bang and a shudder, so strong that it caused me to stagger on my feet, and the bow rode up in the air and *Icebird* listed to starboard. We were high and dry on a rock.

I was surprised they didn't take off the forward power for what seemed a long ten seconds. Horst was not actually at the controls when we hit because he was checking the satellite navigator for our position. Ewald walked in from the flying bridge and almost casually moved the throttle into full reverse. But this had no discernible effect on our situation. He then had a quick conference with Horst over the chart table and studied a diagram of ballast tanks and cargo areas on the back bulkhead of the bridge.

Geoff Taylor, who ran the engineering firm in Hobart which looked after *Icebird*'s repairs and maintenance, was also on the bridge and he had a long face. He said that if the double-skinned hull was holed we would not be able to break any more ice and would have to return to Australia for repairs.

The air of studied calm adopted by Ewald and his First Officer immediately after we became snagged on the rock changed noticeably as soon as the Captain consulted his tide charts. I was told later that we were a few hours off the highest tide of the month. Urgent German was barked into the bridge telephone. While ballast was being pumped aft, the ship's cranes were swung out over the side, one of them dangling the ever-useful *Chicken* in an effort to rock *Icebird* and help in the disengagement process. Barry Batts (who speaks

German) told me later that shortly after we hit the conversation was along the lines of, 'Let's try this', and 'Let's try that'. After the state of the tide was known, the instructions to the crane driver were more along the lines of 'Get a bloody move on mate!'

The Chicken is swung over the side to help tilt Icebird *as Skipper Ewald Brune tries to free his ship from the uncharted rock off Davis Station.*

Werner, the Third Mate, got on board the *Chicken* as it was lowered over the side. For reasons I could not immediately understand, he took the little ice-breaking tender down past the stern of *Icebird*. I thought he had decided to abandon us to our fate, or perhaps wanted to take photographs. When I put this to Ewald later he said, 'Both'!

Rumour Control was, like the *Icebird*, running on full throttle. As the second vessel chartered by the Antarctic Division, *Lady Franklin*, was in the vicinity, perhaps it would have to tow us off. Our Voyage Leader Des Lugg was not on board at the time but having a rare visit ashore—to the station where he had wintered in 1963. He looked off shore to see *Icebird* with her cranes swung over the side and not moving at all; he did not have to be told what had happened.

After about an hour of this varied activity, *Icebird* slid off the rock (to a certain amount of collective relief) and we dropped anchor, just off the edge of the kilometre of fast ice between us and the shore that had stubbornly refused to yield to Ewald's ice-breaking. The good news was that there was no significant damage. The hull had not been holed, just dented. 'It was', said Nils the Radio Officer, 'like putting a dent in the family car. You expect that kind of thing down here.'

Ewald had given me the nod for a *Chicken* run around the Davis Station coast at 9 pm, and I presumed we weren't going because of all the previous excitement. I was wrong. We left at 9.30 pm and it turned out to be a fantastic experience. *Chicken* first called into the Adelie penguin colony on Magnetic Island. We clunked on a submerged rock as we came close to the rocky shore. It was that sort of day.

I thought the Adelies were not at all fussed by our presence although they kept up a continual squawking. Their chicks had almost lost their baby fluff but were still there. The penguins seem to spend most of their time guarding the little rings of stones that mark their nest areas. This is necessary because of the regular stone-thieving that goes on, with much squawking and waving of flippers. The trick is then to pinch a stone from someone else's nest. And so on.

148

*An Adelie penguin guarding a nest on the Magnetic Island rookery.
Note the ring of stones.*

What followed was the ultimate photo opportunity as
we cruised slowly among the grounded icebergs near
Davis Station while the sun dipped down towards the
horizon. There was not a breath of wind and the reflections of the bergs in the translucent water were
perfect. Some of their ice cliffs glowed pink and red
in the setting sun. To say that a photographic frenzy
ensued is an understatement. Heavy breathing and the
rattle and crash of expensive shutters were the only
sounds to be heard on the slowly moving *Chicken*. I
burned up my two last films and was so carried away
that I opened the back of my camera before re-winding.
Chris Sattlberger lent me another film. He said that for
a professional photographer to do that under those
circumstances was an act of great charity and
friendship. I could only agree.

Our artist, Clare Robertson, noted in her diary:

...I would be hard pressed to think of any more
exquisite experience in my lifetime than that dreamlike

149

sunset sail around the skirts of the icebergs in the clear, still, golden evening. The sun set with a tall sun pillar, soaring vertical behind a mask of icebergs on the horizon; the water is as smooth as the polished and glowing interior of a sea shell. The icebergs seem lit blue from within and reflect pink, apricot and gold from the setting sun. Tiny filigree pieces of fretted clear ice slide past, our wake curling the dark water and making them dance. Sometimes we drift silently along corridors lined with glowing castles and spires, waxy walls of fissured ice, fringes of silvery icicles catching the light. It is too lovely for words.

Captain Ewald Brune had seen it all before and he chuckled delightedly at our wonderment, a piratical blond-bearded figure behind the wheel in his red anorak and peaked cap. All that beauty and some hot spiced *glühwein* as well. I was perhaps overstating things a bit when I told him that after that particular 'jolly', I had not lived in vain!

FEBRUARY 2
Ashore at Davis Station by chopper at 8.30 am. It's a bit like a Mt Isa mining camp with a few icebergs in the background. The Station Leader, Simon Young, welcomed us and took us on a tour of his domain. His boss, the Station Manager Rob Easther, is also at Davis for part of the summer season, although he will return to Hobart before winter. Simon's office is still called the OICERY just as it was before the bureaucracy changed his title from Officer In Charge. The main storage shed is an incredible, high tech affair, with great moving stacks sliding along at the touch of a button, while red lights flash and sirens hoot. Despite the fact that Davis Station lies on the fringes of the Antarctic ice cap which locks up an estimated seventy per cent of the world's storage of fresh water, it is one of the Station's most precious commodities. The fire system in the storage shed is not water-based, but squirts out halon gas. If the alarm goes off you have 100 seconds to get out of the building—or you die!

150

The toilet system is rather daunting, too. The original models were called 'destroylets', fired by propane gas. The trick is to urinate first and then attend to the main business. Dr Kevin Donovan, who wintered at Davis in 1974, said that if you didn't manage to separate the two functions a terrible blast of urine-laden steam burst from the device, much to the displeasure of the expeditioner in the next cubicle. Then there was a terrible roar and a different kind of stench as fire attacked your Henry The Thirds. It was difficult, said Kevin, to be at all discreet about toilet habits at Davis.

All water has to be quarried from the ice cap and transported for fifteen kilometres over the lunar landscape of the Vestfold Hills. Unlike Mawson Station, which still uses its old wooden mess building, the Davis winterers are accommodated in one of the new buildings. The 'club' area has a big picture window which faces out to sea, with a temperature gauge like a wall clock which indicated that the outside temperature was −5C. The former indoor garden in the lobby was a desert of empty pots and tubs; the strict environmental guidelines of the Antarctic Treaty now forbid any introduced fauna or flora. In the past, expeditioners appreciated a little greenery, and even vegetables used to be grown indoors. I came across a rather sad entry from the Station Log written by the OIC at Davis in 1969.

Tragic news in the garden. Inadvertently, while Paul Watts (diesel mechanic) was draining the hot water service tank into various receptacles, urging us to put it to good use, among the filled vessels was the slop bucket from the dark room. I carried this lethal load to the garden and gave the plants a good dose of developer and fixer.

Initially I thought the dilution and subsequent watering would reduce the acidity and had hoped that the fixer and developer would neutralise each other, but it was otherwise, and slowly the plants have wilted including a couple of lettuce ready for the table. It will be necessary to discard the tank contents and start again from scratch.

After the rather restricted ice-free area around Mawson Station, it was a pleasure to be able to move around more freely in the bare rock environs of Davis. A group of us decided to go for a walk along the coast to an elephant seal wallow, in the company of Rod Ledingham, who had just returned from leading

Elephant seals near Davis Station, moulting and, as usual, pooping in each other's faces.

the Prince Charles Mountains field party for the current summer season. As it happened, we didn't have to walk far to see elephant seals. A group of four had installed themselves in a temporary wallow among the Davis huts, bellowing ill-temperedly if people went too close. 'Wallow' is an accurate description. These huge slug-shaped creatures have the un-attractive habit of lying top to tail and crapping in each other's faces. Their eyes glow a dull red when they lift up their wrinkled heads to roar at visitors who come too close.

We were walking in a desert, over shattered shards of rocks where nothing grows—except perhaps a patch of extremely hardy lichen or a rare tuft of moss. Some stones have green algae underneath them, the Antarctic equivalent of scrub land. The rocks glitter in the strong sunlight with frost-shattered flakes and crystals and extrusions of blood-red garnet. Some of the hills are striped with dark ribbons of basalt. Further inland, in this stormy wasteland, are lakes ranging from pure fresh water to heavy concentrations of brine. It would be possible to construct an all-weather rock airstrip here, big enough to accommodate Boeing 747s. There were moves to build an airstrip in the Vestfold Hills in the 1960s, but nothing was done. Increased awareness of environmental damage now makes such a strip less likely. Already one hopeful entrepreneur has put up a plan to build a hotel in this area, serviced by direct flights from Australia. The tourist pressures on Antarctica are building.

Before we reached the gross huddle of elephant seals, we found a pretty little Weddell seal, with spotted grey fur, sunning itself on the rocky beach. Rod Ledingham explained that you have to crouch down to approach seals, as they become worried by tall beings looming over them. I crawled up and scratched the basking seal on the tummy, and it wiggled its flipper in sensual appreciation.

I found a deceased Antarctic fish on top of a rock, with characteristic large bony head and narrow body. How could it have got there?

While we were on our walk, the politicians had been flown 160 kilometres further west to the Larsemann Hills, another substantial ice-free area where the Russians have a base; the Chinese are establishing theirs nearby. Australia is represented by Law Base—a small cluster of huts only occupied during the summer season. We were there first, as it happens, but neither the

I crawled up and scratched the tummy of a basking Weddell seal.

Russians nor the Chinese take much notice of our forty-two-per-cent-of-Antarctica claim. Apparently Ian Cameron was desperately keen to get some Russian souvenirs. While the four Labor politicians (led by Socialist Left MP Peter Milton) hobnobbed with the Russian welcoming party, Cameron, the only conservative representative, stayed outside trading some bottles of Scotch he had stuffed into his ventiles with the Russian workers. 'You like Scotch—me like your hat' type of thing. He reportedly scored a hat and some black, high-topped Russian boots, styled like jackboots. 'How appropriate', said one of my companions unkindly when he heard of it. Cameron took it all with his habitual good humour.

By the time they got to the Chinese base, the quest for souvenirs had become even more intense. Peter Milton already had a Russian hat scored on a previous Antarctic visit, so he was keen to acquire a Chinese equivalent. But whereas the Russian hats were the splendid fur ones you see Mikhail Gorbachev sporting on TV, the Chinese had rather modest peaked caps with ear flaps. Nevertheless they had rarity value. After all the interpreted niceties had been dispensed with, Peter Milton reportedly asked about a Chinese hat.

The Chinese explained that they had a problem about this because each man was issued with a hat, and there weren't any spares. Would something else be suitable? Apparently Peter Milton said he was still very keen on a hat.

There was more discussion in Chinese. Then the interpreter said that perhaps they could send one back to the *Icebird* at some later time.

Now, as it happened, one of *Icebird*'s officers did have a Chinese cap from the previous voyage. When word of Peter Milton's quest got back to the ship, a different officer wore the cap each day for the next three days. This got too much for Peter Milton who fronted Des Lugg to find out if his Chinese hat had arrived. I'm told that Des exploded and spelt out in no uncertain terms how he viewed the disastrous diplomacy of it all.

Back in the Davis mess, after our walk, I heard of a wonderful practical joke perpetrated the year before on the incoming OIC (everyone still calls them that despite the official change of title to Station Leader). A radio operator, Allen Rooke, had been stationed at Law Base for several months while the Davis wintering party was in the process of being changed over during the normal summer shipping season. During the time at Law Base, Rooke and the two Australians with him had seen a lot of the Russians who were establishing their Progress Base. They often dropped in for an Australian beer and some tucker. They were very fond of Australian biscuits, Allen told me later. A good deal of gear was traded, too. The Russians liked our boots and various articles of Antarctic issue clothing, and Allen was able to trade a complete set of Russian clothes, full leather suit and black fur hat complete with an Aeroflot badge. In fact, he had everything but the boots.

History does not record who thought up the scam, but the idea was mooted that Allen should pretend to be the 2IC of the Russian base on an official visit to Davis to meet the incoming Australian OIC. Such visits were fairly routine, and, indeed, even necessary under the Antarctic Treaty. As it happened, Allen had a bit of an ear for languages and had picked up a respectable amount of Russian over the two months he had been stationed at the Larsemann Hills. In fact, the Russian OIC, Anatoly, had been scheduled to make such a visit but had to cancel because his resupply ship was due at any time.

Law Base is about 100 nautical miles from Davis Station and the Australians radioed that Viktor, the 2IC, would like to come instead and would the Davis people accord him the usual hospitality. The name was to have been Igor, but for some odd reason Allen broke up every time anyone called him Igor. So he became Viktor.

It was agreed that an Australian helicopter (piloted by Pip Turner) would provide Viktor's transport, and he set off. He had to borrow Pip's black flying boots at the last moment to complete his ensemble. Pip Turner circled the Station a few times as though he was giving his Russian guest a full view of the Australian operation, and landed on the chopper pad.

A beaming Australian OIC advanced to shake his hand and welcome him to Davis. Viktor, it became apparent, did not speak a great deal of English, but appeared to understand it reasonably well. They drove down to the mess for a cup of coffee. This was a dangerous time for the scam, because many of those still on the base knew Allen Rooke, and would know nothing of Viktor.

'This was the hairiest moment', Allen recalled later. 'I was introduced to one guy whom I'd just worked with for sixteen months! His eyes revolved wildly in his head, he stammered greetings, and backed away until he had sussed things out. Then he hugged me and said he hadn't seen me since our Russian ship called at Mawson Station two years before.'

After coffee, the OIC and the official photographer took Viktor on a tour of the station he'd worked at for the past year. By that time Rumour Control was well at work, and word had flashed around the base that a scam was under way. Expeditioners helpless with mirth were collapsing out of sight behind buildings as the OIC explained the fire control systems in the storage shed, and toured the living quarters with his Russian guest. Viktor was presented with an Australian sheepskin Antarctic hat and an Antarctic Division tie and invited back to the OIC's quarters for a Quiet Little Drink.

They were joined by a selection of Australian guests; some were aware of what was going on and some were not. As it happened, Allen Rooke was not a drinker in the Russian style—he had had no alcohol for about six months. But the more beer he drank, the more confident he felt in his new role. When the OIC produced several bottles of extremely good Scotch whisky, his broken English and Russian patois achieved new heights of comradely believability.

It was decided Viktor would stay the night, and appropriate radio messages were sent back to Law Base for relay back to the Russians at Progress Base confirming this.

By now Viktor was in very fine form indeed or—as Allen himself put it later—'I was bloody drunk, that's what I was'. On this particular evening, everybody made a point of turning up for the evening meal and a special table was laid for the official party, complete with carafes of wine. The OIC stood up and made a speech during which he welcomed Viktor to Davis and stressed the importance of international cooperation and friendship in Antarctica and, indeed, the world. Viktor felt his moment had come. He lurched to his feet and in broad Australian thanked the OIC for his hospitality—particularly his Scotch whisky. The mess erupted with the mirth that had

156

been suppressed for so long. The OIC went quiet and, said Allen, 'looked at me with red eyes'.

'He didn't speak to me for two days. Eventually I got my hands on a bottle of the same brand of Scotch that he'd plied me with, and presented it to him in the mess. That fixed things up, and he even helped me write my annual report.'

The Russians thought it was pretty funny, too, when they heard about it. Antarctic post-war history is laced with stories of Russian/Australian hospitality, although when Russia first set up its base in 1957 at Mirny, 600 kilometres east of Davis Station, East-West relations were tense, and the Cold War could well have translated itself to Antarctica. But it never did, and Australian/Russian relations have always been extremely cordial there. In fact, it was the Russians who flew the two injured Australians from Davis out to South America while we were voyaging south in *Icebird* in the summer of 1989. ANARE's first Director, Phil Law, told me of one particularly friendly encounter with the Russians in the early 1960s at Mirny.

PL: Their parties were always pretty desperate from a drinking point of view because the Russians drink with a different purpose from ourselves, they literally drink to get drunk. To us it's a bit of a disgrace to finish up under the table, but to the Russians it's an honour and, of course, they drink vodka and we're not generally used to such heavy spirits. So we had a certain problem handling this hard liquor with the Russians and I, as Leader, had to be particularly careful how I went about things because I had to preserve appearances. I had to remain standing on my feet, try to talk sense and make sure I kept my eye on what was going on and that nothing untoward happened. So I was being pretty careful. I wasn't exactly emptying my drinks into the aspidistras but I was sipping them cautiously, rather than tossing them off in the Russian style. However, it was still heavy going.

I must mention that the Americans had an observer there for the first couple of years and it was most informative for me to be able to talk to him about his experiences and how the Russians did things, so that I didn't put my foot into it in some way. On this occasion, we had a lot of drinks over a beautiful lunch ashore. I played the piano accordion, they sang Russian songs—luckily I knew some of the songs from the Russian choirs that I'd heard. Then after a lot of grog they took us out into the cold for a bit of a tour of the station. When you hit the cold after a heavy session of drinking it's pretty desperate, but we survived that. Then, half way through, they brought us back in for afternoon tea. And for afternoon tea, instead of the vodka and beer that we'd had before, they turned on sweet champagne— which is terribly sickly stuff—with very good Russian cognac. So after libations of this we went out again to do further investigations and I did about half of the ration of the afternoon when I began to feel pretty crook. I went to the American observer and said, 'Look, I feel terrible. Can I go and put my head down somewhere?' 'Yes', he said, 'I know exactly how you feel, I've been through it so often, come into my hut'. And he took me into his hut and laid me down on his bed and put a bucket beside me in case I was sick and I passed out for a couple of hours.

Then I awoke and I realised that we'd invited the Russians back to our ship for dinner, so I walked half a mile back across the snow and ice to our ship where it was tethered against the ice edge and went on board and supervised the preparations for the big dinner for the Russians. I wasn't looking forward to this dinner very much after all the alcohol we'd had but I decided we could probably handle the Russians in a different fashion. The Russians came down about seven o'clock for dinner and it was noticeable that their two leaders were late coming—they'd obviously had their heads down like I had. But instead of giving them the sort of liquor routine that they were used to, spirits and beer, we turned on the English system. We gave them sherry and then white wine, red wine and finally champagne—and, boy, did we lay them out. So honours were even at the end of the day.

Well, next day on the ship after we'd left Mirny, I had a debriefing session with the boys. We wanted to record as much as we could of the Russian station, how they were doing things, what sort of equipment they had, what sort of vehicles, what sort of radio sets. So we got all our experts down and we were sitting around the table in the mess room saloon and discussing all this and I said, 'Now, two things

I'm most interested in. First they had a little vehicle called the "Penguin" and I wanted to have a ride in it and I didn't get a chance, I'd like you to tell me about it'.

They looked at me and said, 'But you did have a ride in it'. I said, 'No I didn't'. They said, 'Yes, you went down to the power house in it'.

'No,' I said, 'The power house was another place I'd like to have had a look at. But I had to go and put my head down, so I didn't get a chance'.

They said, 'Yes you went to the power house and, as a matter of fact, you not only went there but you had your note book out and you carefully wrote down all the details that they told you about their diesel generators and things'.

I said, 'I did not', and pulled my notebook out. There were three pages of hieroglyphics that I've never been able to translate up to this day. Apparently I was valiantly trying to show I was quite normal and asking questions and writing it all down in the book and all these squiggles were the result.

On another occasion Phil Law and a bevy of Australian expeditioners were again battling with Russian hospitality, involving numerous 'bottoms up' toasts to appropriate national icons.

PL: If you toast thirty or forty different people with vodka you don't last very long. This time we went through the usual routine. We'd toast the President of the USSR and they'd toast the Queen of England, and then the Prime Minister of Australia, the Premier of USSR, the Russian expedition and then the Australian expedition. Then you'd work your way down to minor things.

One of our fellows was a bit of a joker and the BBC's Goon Show was very popular at that time. I think there was a saying or something relating to 'rhubarb'.

TB: If people were talking in parliament, they'd say 'rhubarb, rhubarb, rhubarb, rhubarb' to imitate the debate . . .

PL: Anyway, this chap got up with a perfectly straight face and raised his glass and said, 'Rhubarb'. And all the Russians stood up solemnly and everyone said, 'Rhubarb', and they downed their vodka. And then another Australian stood up solemnly and said, 'More Rhubarb', and everyone got up and solemnly drank a toast to 'More Rhubarb'.

And then another very drunk Australian, who'd completely had all this nonsense of toasting, stood up and raised his glass and said, 'More Piss'. I was horribly embarrassed and wondered what to do. But the Russians became very excited about this and jumped to their feet and shouted: 'Da! More Piss. Piss and Friendship'!

It makes you proud to be Australian, really.

CHAPTER ELEVEN

Oil on Icy Waters • Russian Bulldozers and Chinese Dogs • Hazards of Antarctic Flying • Difficulties of Faxing Engine Spare Parts Explained • Making Do in Antarctica; Seals' Teeth Dentures and Running Tractors on Butter • The Ice Breaks Out at Last • Politicians and Public Servants Head Priority List for Early Voyage Home • An Account of Shagging on Heard Island

(TO ABC RADIO NEWS EXBOWDEN *ICEBIRD* SUNDAY FEBRUARY 5)

The Antarctic Division's resupply ship *Icebird* has managed to refuel Davis Station despite unseasonably persistent sea ice between the ship and the shore.

Tim Bowden on board *Icebird* said 450 000 litres of fuel were pumped ashore through a 1200 metre line laid over the sea ice. Enough frozen food has been helicoptered ashore from *Icebird* to last Davis Station's thirty expeditioners through the coming winter even if it is not possible to discharge the heavier cargo by barges and amphibious vehicles.

The fuel line at Davis is kept rolled up on a big drum, rather like a garden hose reel on a grand scale. A helicopter took a line from ship to shore, and the hose was pulled over a kilometre of sea ice to start pumping. Unfortunately the hose leaked, and a puddle of oil was clearly seen on the ice, much to the chagrin of Antarctic Division personnel and the expressed concern of the environmental philosopher and other conservation-minded souls on board.

FEBRUARY 3

A day trip to Law Base by helicopter—and what a day! I shared a helicopter with Rob Easther, the Davis

Interviewing Andy McTaggart at Law Base, in the Larsemann Hills not far from the Russian and Chinese stations.

Station Manager, and the Head Prefect. Leigh Hornsby, our pilot, had permission to fly along the lip of the Sorsdal Glacier, one of the most spectacular sets of ice cliffs on the coast of greater Antarctica. 'The Riviera of the South' lived up to its reputation as we flew over the brown rocks, fiords and lakes of the Vestfold Hills and began our traverse along the front of the Sorsdal Glacier, with the second helicopter following behind us. An amazing bird's-eye view of the great ice walls, blue ice caves and crevasses. And, of course, the whole of this enormous mass of ice is being pushed slowly out to sea, eventually to break off and float away as great icebergs.

We gained height as we approached the Larsemann Hills— another rocky area where the Antarctic ice cap for some reason has retreated. It is quite clear that attitudes to the environment vary considerably from country to country. The Russians have used heavy rock-moving equipment to bulldoze a road from their Progress Base to the edge of the ice sheet, where they have an ice airstrip. The landscape is heavily scarred by this activity.

The Chinese have set up their base closer to where their supply ship can berth, and have rows of what look like red bulk containers on a site they have also bulldozed. The structures would not win any architectural awards, but they do the job, and the Chinese achieved it all in one season.

My brother journalist Keith Scott (flying behind in the second chopper) and I were not going to be able to visit the Russians or the Chinese who are extremely busy with their building programs. Our polar politicians had that privilege the day before. We were bound for Australia's modest operation in the Larsemann Hills, Law Base, only occupied in the summer months.

Law Base is one hut and a cluster of Apples, set in a superb location looking down a stony valley to an iceberg-strewn sea. As it happened, my helicopter companion Rob Easther chose the spot and established Law Base in 1986.

RE: It's just such a spectacular place that I must admit that was my major priority in deciding to put the base here.

Antarctic, or Sturt's Stony Desert? The author turns his back against flying stones and dust from the helicopter rotors during aerial unloading of frozen food at Davis Station. Photograph by Chris Sattlberger.

Behind us is a little lake that has quite an acceptable water supply, so that all fits together well, and it is only about three kilometres up to the plateau and, down the other way, a couple of kilometres to the sea. So we've actually got a good link between the sea and the plateau for resupply options.

TB: The lake behind is now officially known as Lake Easther—named after your good self!

RE: I originally proposed it be called Sarah Tarn because I came down to Antarctica and my daughter was born about five weeks after I left. I had not seen her for the whole year I was at Davis—all I had seen was a faxed photograph, so I was keen to name something after her. But the Antarctic Names Committee decided that was not to be.

TB: It's a great thing, though, still to be finding bits of new country which you can actually put names to.

RE: Some people get right into that—but you have to be quick around here. In the last couple of years the features we are looking at now have been named by the subsequent parties that have come here. It becomes quite a game and good fun. But although ANARE people have been visiting this area over the past thirty years, not much was named. Now that we have a presence here, a lot of people are looking to name some of the features.

TB: What is of interest to scientists here?

RE: There are 200 lakes in this ice-free region. Some of the freshest water in the world has been found in these hills. The geologists are interested in the rocks here, and there is also some vegetation tucked away—some mosses and lichens growing in the area.

TB: I notice that there are no vehicles at Law Base—unlike the Russians and Chinese. Is that a deliberate policy?

RE: Yes, the only vehicles that do come here do so in winter, and there are snow drifts right up to the huts so they can be kept on the snow. But it is such beautiful walking country that there is no need for vehicles—apart from helicopters. We go to great pains not to have vehicles travelling over the surfaces here.

TB: This is a contrast to what the Russians are doing.

RE: I can't help remembering back to when we carted these huts here during the winter. We had to drag our sleds across the rocks and soil to reach this spot, and we were so concerned that we were leaving an imprint of our presence that after we'd finished I had the group of expeditioners go round and dust off the rocks and smooth over the soil so there was no sign of our tracked vehicles ever having been here. To come back a couple of years later and find Russian heavy-tracked vehicles roaring around all over the place was a shock. They even drove through Sarah Tarn which was quite mortifying!

TB: It really is an extraordinary situation having the Russians, Chinese and Australians working and living so close together. How does it work out?

RE: There are never any problems working these things out down in Antarctica, and I suppose that is really the essence of the origins of the Antarctic Treaty. It is a unique situation, and all of us work cooperatively together here. There are no international boundaries in the activities that go on. The Soviets recently flew two of our injured expeditioners out to South America and in part repayment we are supporting a party of four Soviet scientists in the Vestfold Hills. We have equipped them fully with camping gear and supplied them with food. They are very happy about that. The same thing has happened here with the Chinese. It is amazing to talk to expeditioners of other nations. They have the same sorts of priorities and concerns and enthusiasm for the place—it's quite a magical, unreal world in that sense I guess.

TB: Some of the other nations' attitudes to the pristine nature of Antarctica are not quite as they should be. The Russians are roaring around the place in heavy vehicles. Are the Chinese transgressing in any way?

RE: To our surprise, the other day a couple of our expeditioners came across three dogs roaming around here which quite appals us. According to the Antarctic Treaty we are not supposed to introduce any species into Antarctica, and we are concerned about that. They are not working dogs, just roaming about the hills. We are looking for ways to politely suggest they might be put back on the ship or sent home, or disposed of in some way. We are concerned that they would obviously molest penguins and perhaps annoy seal pups, or even kill Weddell seal pups.

TB: What can be done about other nations' more brutal approach to the landscape?

RE: We have established environmental management guide-lines for this area, ways in which we dispose of rubbish, not having vehicles in the area and, I think, just by our example we have already impressed some of the expeditioners here from other nations. They think this is the neatest, tidiest and most simple little base that they have ever seen. So, perhaps just by example, we are doing something positive. I'd love to get our environmental management guide-lines translated into Chinese and Russian and just drop them in at some point. I think this will probably happen in due course through diplomatic channels, through the management of the Antarctic Treaty.

We flew back to Davis Station at a much higher altitude, after having flown over the Russians' ice airstrip on the plateau. The wind had dropped, and it was still a cloudless day. It was fascinating to look down on the broken pack ice, which looked like a sprinkling of giant white confetti on the dark blue ocean.

Flying has played a vital part in Australian exploration and scientific work in Antarctica, and as I looked down on the broken pack ice I was reminded of an incident Phil Law had described to me. In the late 1950s fixed wing Auster aircraft were being used to photograph and map the coastline of Oates Land:

PL: We couldn't get the ship closer than sixty miles to the coast because of heavy pack ice and there was no way of getting over it. If it had been smooth fast ice, we could have sent a land party across, but with broken-up pack ice jammed tight that was impossible. Eventually we ran into a big pool of open water that was about a mile long and our little aircraft at that time was an Auster aircraft which is about the size of a Tiger Moth, very small. But this Auster could be mounted on wheels, floats or skis, so we changed the undercarriage to put the floats on, and hoisted it out into this pool of water. The coast was about sixty miles off and this thing had a range of about a hundred and eighty miles all together, so I said: 'We'll do an equilateral triangle—that is, we'll fly sixty miles into the coast, sixty more taking photographs and then sixty miles back to the ship'.

Now, when you take off from a remote spot, you take note of the position of distinctive icebergs or something to act as markers when you get back because the ship is not very visible. On this occasion we didn't bother because there was this one mile stretch of open water. It was the only pool in hundreds of miles of pack ice, so we just hired off down south, and we did our sixty miles to the coast and then we flew sixty miles along the coast. I remember winding the window down and holding this great clumsy Air Force F24 camera, which is hand-held; you had to crank a handle to turn on each frame. My hands were freezing off holding this out, but at least I was getting a continuous run of photos of this sixty miles of coast.

But when we started back on the third leg of the triangle, we couldn't find the ship! We had radio contact but no radio compass because this aircraft was too small to fit these refined things into. We couldn't even see the big lake of open water we had taken off from. And we said on the radio, 'What's happened? Where are you?'

The Captain said, 'Sorry but that open water that was here has all gone, the pack ice has closed in'. So I said, 'Well can you make some smoke that we might be able to see?' But a diesel engine can't make much smoke, it's not like an old coal-burning ship, so they tried to produce a bit of smoke, but we couldn't see anything.

To give an idea of how difficult it is to find a ship, just imagine a room with its floor covered with confetti—the broken pack ice—and a plane which is a fly on the ceiling looking down. The ship is about a tenth the size of one piece of confetti. So that's a rough idea of how difficult it was to find it. And both the ship and the ice were white! In later years we made sure they were painted red, but that wasn't much help at that stage.

We were beginning to run short of petrol by now and we also realised that we couldn't land on broken-up pack ice with floats. Secondly, even if we did survive a crash landing the ship couldn't possibly find us. They wouldn't know whether to turn to go north, south, east or west, and if we

The giant confetti of loose pack ice seen from the air during the journey from Davis Station to Law Base.

couldn't find the ship from the air, how could they find a little plane from the surface? So by this time things were getting desperate.

Then I had an idea which to this day I think was one of my brighter efforts. I called over the radio for all the binoculars on board to be issued out, and to divide the sky into sectors and give each man a sector to scan with binoculars. And some bloke scanned his sector of the sky and found us as a little spot, and they talked us back to the ship.

But our problem didn't stop there, because we still had to land, and there was no water to land on. This was solved by the ship steaming full speed ahead, and the churning of the propeller washed the pack back immediately behind the ship and left a pond about thirty or forty yards long. Luckily in a float plane the drag of the floats acts like very severe braking and you stop extremely quickly, but it needed a very good pilot with a lot of courage to land in that forty yards of water, because it really meant you had to aim the plane right up the tail of the ship and put it down exactly on the edge of that ice. Doug Leckie did just that and finished with the propeller still rotating, just practically touching the stern of the ship.

Phil Law reckoned that experience was every bit as hazardous as anything he had read in the older polar exploration literature!

Flying in the heated cabin of a modern helicopter seemed ludicrously luxurious by comparison. As we neared the Davis chopper pads we could see the other helicopters from the Station ferrying frozen food from *Icebird* in wire cages suspended beneath each aircraft. After a sandwich in the mess it was suggested that some of us more privileged types might like to help with a bit of unloading. Having been carefully drilled on *Icebird* about the correct procedures for approaching helicopters, the unloading procedures were something of an eye-opener. Actually I couldn't keep my eyes open for very long because of the clouds of grit and dust whipped up by the rotor blades.

As a chopper came in with a full wire cage of frozen food, it would clunk it down, and disengage the carrying hook. Then it would fly over to an empty cage, while some brave soul clipped it on and gave a thumbs up to the pilot. Off he'd go back to the ship to replenish. It was a rather confusing situation, with constant prop wash, engine noise and shouting. After several hours of this I noticed something out of the corner of my bloodshot eye (due to the flying grit). What I saw was the skid of a descending chopper about a metre from my head. So much for the sixty-metre safety rule! I decided I'd done my bit and headed back to the mess for a coffee.

It was interesting to talk to the Station Leader, Simon Young, about the logistics of resupplying an Antarctic Station. Clearly, if something was forgotten there was no way of sending a repeat order. The advent of modern communication techniques like the fax has helped in swapping plans and diagrams. 'You can't fax a spare part, though', said Simon. On the other hand, some things could be over-supplied. Hardly anyone shaves in Antarctica and Simon believes his high tech store has enough disposable razors to last Davis Station into the twenty-third century.

Making do is an established Antarctic tradition. Des Lugg makes the point that the Antarctic is no different today from when Scott or Mawson were there initially, or when ANARE

A heavily crevassed section of the Sorsdal Glacier, about to 'calve' into the surrounding sea.

began. There might be better technology today, but that doesn't change the environment. It still isn't possible to fly in and out at will to evacuate people. A successful Antarctic expeditioner has to be able to do things outside his or her speciality.

DL: Some years ago one expeditioner lost his contact lenses and broke his spare pair of glasses. He got a relative—it almost caused a diplomatic incident, actually—to try and get the Americans to fly spare glasses in. That was impossible. But by using the ophthalmologist's prescription which I managed to get, some advice from the Division (which was then in Melbourne) and with the help of the diesel mechanic on the Station, we ground lenses out of perspex to the right formula. They were thick and ugly, but their owner was able to see properly, and carry out the rest of his program.

Similarly, someone broke a tooth and we were lacking spare false teeth that year. Now in those days we were killing seals for dog food, and a seal's tooth was cut to fabricate that spare tooth. There are many such stories. We put on a water reticulation service and some of the pumps broke down, but there were a number of old Hoover washing machines here. They were cannibalised, and we had little pumps running everywhere. But they did the job.

One year toothpaste supplies weren't ordered for one of our stations. So I got an urgent call to ANARE headquarters in Melbourne. What can we do? I rang up a few firms. Some were reluctant to give me a recipe, but one firm finally agreed to provide a list of the basic ingredients which I knew were on the Station. The doctor mixed up a bit of peppermint oil and a few other things, and they had toothpaste. It wasn't in tubes, but it worked well.

Repairs in the field are another area of making do. We only had one solitary Snow Track vehicle at Davis in 1963, and a Ferguson tractor. We got permission to try and get overland from Davis to Mawson. We had to blast rock to get up onto the Vestfold Hills from the sea ice, and establish a depot 100 miles inland on the ice plateau. On our way back from this forward supply depot we noticed an oil leak in the engine. The driver/mechanic was our chef, actually, and he fiddled around for some time and said: 'The gasket's gone and we don't have a spare. And if I take the head off the engine, we don't have enough oil to replace it all even if I could make a gasket. So what I suggest is we drive around the clock and go for it.'

I did a quick calculation that we had a certain amount of butter and other food oils, and that if we melted them down, we could supplement the amount of oil. So we drove non-stop, and when the oil warning light came on we would leap out, fill up the sump with the butter and vegetable oil, and press on. And so we got back to our first depot near Davis where we were able to get more oil supplies.

In an effort to cut back on the amount of rubbish that has to be back-loaded to Australia in these more ecologically aware times, Davis Station has a high combustion sealed incinerator which burns rubbish efficiently without smoke. Unfortunately, on one occasion it was fired incorrectly and the bricks inside melted down. This led, inevitably, to the incinerator being called Chernobyl!

This, said Station Leader Simon Young, led to a diplomatic

problem when the incinerator was referred to as Chernobyl in front of some Russian visitors. 'Fortunately, they did have a sense of humour.'

Back on *Icebird* the latest from Rumour Control is that they are going to attempt to cut the lingering fast ice between ship and shore with a chain saw! One of the Larcies swore a solemn oath that this had actually been tried. One rumour now confirmed is that the *Lady Franklin*, the other chartered Antarctic supply ship, is to rendezvous with *Icebird* at Davis and take on board those with urgent reasons to be back in Australia. We are now running about three weeks behind schedule. There is much lobbying and speculation on who will go.

FEBRUARY 6

The *Lady Franklin* arrived about 11 am and moored alongside *Icebird* top to tail like resting elephant seals— the only difference being more satisfactory sanitary arrangements. Unlike the seals, we take all our poop home with us. The *Lady Franklin* is an older ship than *Icebird* and the extra berths needed have been created by placing accommodation modules below decks in the cargo space. She is a Canadian ship, and the word was that although the below-decks sleeping arrangements were noisy and claustrophobic and not helpful to those who tended to sea-sickness, the husband and wife team looking after the galley were noted for their gourmet cooking—for those able to avail themselves of it.

No sooner had the two ships begun to pump fuel and exchange various items of cargo than the fast ice began to break away from the shore. This is an example of 'The Antarctic Factor' at work. There happened to be a plethora of barges and LARCS buzzing about in the open water as well. Great organised chaos ensued as *Icebird* and *Lady Franklin* hastily uncoupled and moved further out to sea, while the barges—motorised pontoons really—manoeuvred to dodge the moving sheets of ice. Fortunately the leaking fuel line had been reeled back to shore by this stage. Some hours later the ships were able to resume their fraternal embrace and swapping of people and goods.

A farewell party at night in Stoppy's Bar. Not surprisingly the pollies were top of the priority list for an early return to Hobart. Bryan Smith and the *Beyond 2000* team were also leaving, because of overseas commitments. Colin Hollis asked me why I wasn't important enough to transfer to the *Lady Franklin*. Aware that my audience was largely composed of Antarctic Division office-based personnel who were south on a 'familiarisation' tour and drawing public service allowances accordingly, I unwisely said: 'Because after politicians, the next order of priority for the Division are the office-whackers who are burning up all the overtime'. There was a howl of rage and I was picked up and came within a whisker of having my head dunked in a nearby toilet.

The *Lady Franklin* sailed the next morning and I had mixed feelings as she sounded her siren and headed out through the grounded icebergs towards the open ocean and Australia. I knew that my family in Sydney, Ros and the boys, would be expecting me to be on board, as would the ABC! But with only a limited number of berths on the *Lady Franklin* and a great many of *Icebird*'s passengers with varying degrees of personal and professional crises awaiting them in Australia, I could not really make out a case that my departure was vital. I was also conscious that we were going back to Mawson Station and there would be more opportunities to experience and record there in perhaps less hectic circumstances than before. Despite all that, I was surprised at the depth of the melancholy that swept over me as I stood at the rail and watched my former shipmates sail for home.

My spirits lifted momentarily when I recalled a chance meeting with Dr Peter Gormly, the Division's Medical Director (who had given us our original lecture about the hazards of hypothermia in the Antarctica) on the *Lady Franklin*. They had come via Heard Island, where various scientific programs were being carried out. One involved taking blood samples from cormorants as well as studying their breeding situation and attempting to take a census. 'The common cormorant, or shag, lays its eggs in a paper bag', wrote Ogden Nash rather whimsically.

Most scientists with projects on Heard Island have to go ashore on a daily basis, weather permitting. Peter Gormly said his *sang froid* was destroyed one evening on the *Lady Franklin* when a woman biologist working on the cormorant program came to him and said: 'Peter, if we are going shagging tomorrow, will you knock me up early?'

Collapse of middle-aged medical party, eyeballed by an unamused scientist.

CHAPTER TWELVE

We Adjust to a Half-Empty Ship • The Phenomena of Big Eye and Long Eye • The Psychology of Wintering Explored • Antarctica as a Marriage Hazard • An Account of a 'Bad-Taste' Party • Are Women a Civilising Influence Down South? • Splendours of the Fram Bank Experienced • Hazards of Examining Historic Wastes Revealed • A Story of Eggs, Pancakes and Penguins

FEBRUARY 8

We awoke to a ship that seemed, by comparison to what had been before, like the *Marie Celeste*. With forty souls now on their way back to Australia in the *Lady Franklin* we have lots of space. Dennis and I decide to move in to the vacant 'Beyond Help' Cabin C2 next door and leave The Professor to snore alone. My precious foam ear plugs are starting to deteriorate. There is a slight awkwardness about the move. After all, we have spent five weeks cooped up together in C3. The Professor seems reasonably relaxed about the decision and we agree to continue our pleasant habit of meeting for a pre-dinner Scotch in good old C3.

Barbara (Babs) Graham was on corridor-cleaning duty and began trilling excerpts from *The Sound of Music* and *Oklahoma* with concert-style projection while she swept. Worried faces appeared round cabin doors, and there was some disquiet that this habit might persist. I was given the delicate diplomatic task of indicating to Barbara that her cabin bathroom might be a more appropriate concert venue. She seemed hurt. Communal living is a finely tuned affair.

Those who have had more experience than I have said that the Voyage Six on *Icebird* has been, by and large, a congenial journey. That has certainly been my impression. Several

175

voyagers have not been particularly popular, but any abrasive moments have been absorbed and reacted to fairly good-humouredly by the group. In any case, we know we are on board for a maximum of two months. There is only a fleeting parallel with the situation faced by the much smaller groups of wintering expeditioners who must adjust to each other and work out their community behaviour for a whole year.

I've been talking with the ship's doctor, Kevin Donovan, a cheerful Naval officer who has a short tubby frame more than faintly reminiscent of an over-sized penguin. He has been on a number of summer voyages but has also wintered twice on the Antarctic continent, at Davis in 1975 (a group of fourteen) and Mawson in 1986 (a group of twenty-eight) and well remembers how difficult it was to face up to the thought of meeting people from the outside world when the first ship of the summer season was due:

KD: I suppose the first inkling of isolation having an effect was people starting to talk about whether we should all run away and hide somewhere for a joke, so that the newcomers would come into an empty base. That sense of wanting to run away and hide was in everyone a little bit. You are wary of meeting new people; you feel, I suppose, offended that someone is coming in. You have forgotten what you were like when you arrived. You feel comfortable with everyone that you know, you are aware of their habits, their likes and dislikes, and it is extremely easy to live with them by that stage. New people coming in have different likes and dislikes, and you don't know what they are. You are going to have to use unused social skills to find out.

In Antarctica they have two types of eye, Big Eye and Long Eye. Big Eye is the nickname for the so-called wintering—or summer—insomnia, where there is twenty-four-hour daylight or darkness. As summer approaches it becomes lighter for longer, and the circadian rhythm gets upset to the point where the expeditioners have difficulty sleeping. The same thing happens with the long darkness in winter. Whenever anyone has this kind of sleep disturbance, it is known as having Big Eye.

Long Eye was defined to me as 'A ten-foot stare in a forty-foot room', where the expeditioners look straight past or straight through people when they talk to them. It seems to be something to do with isolation. People who have been in some sort of psychological trauma display it. I occasionally imagine I see it in people who come off shipwrecks or have survived an earthquake. The news cameras are pointing straight at their faces, but they look straight past and walk

Hands across the spectacularly striated rock near Davis Station. Author (left) Dr Kevin Donovan (right).

on in complete disregard of what the people around them are doing. If you talk to winterers when you arrive on the first ship in, they don't look straight at you, they look through you. It's very unnerving. I suppose being conscious of it I tried not to do it when I got home, but it was still noticed that whenever I talked to people I'd be looking seemingly straight through them, not at them.

Former Radio Operator Doug Twigg believes that you can assess what kind of a year it has been on a base almost before you set foot ashore, and even before actually talking to anyone. 'There's an atmosphere. Some years you walk into a station there and the station is really jumping—everybody is running around and helping one another and work is getting done. Other times you walk onto a station there and there's a sullen atmosphere. It's not long before all the dirty washing starts to get aired and you hear what's been going on.'

Psychological testing of wintering expeditioners is now routine. But it was not always so. Phil Law told me of some of the problems experienced in the late 1940s and early 1950s.

PL: On several occasions we had psychological problems of a major level where we've had to do something at a station. On one occasion a man became mentally deranged at Wilkes Station, he had to be flown out by the Russians. It was a terrible business where he had to be kept in a make-shift padded cell for a couple of months or more with only the medical officer being allowed to open the door and go in. On an earlier occasion we had a man in trouble at Macquarie Island, we had to divert a New Zealand frigate to pick him up and bring him back to Australia.

I used to be impressed with the enthusiasm turned on for me—the sort of man who would say, 'Look, I will do any job. I don't care what job it is so long as you take me'. I thought that was a wonderful sign of enthusiasm. But Antarctica is so isolated that many things in life are removed from your environment.

Really, all you have down there is your job. If you don't like that job or you're not good at it, your chance of success is heavily reduced. So the most important thing when picking an Antarctic person is that he should love his job, because he's got to be at it fourteen or sixteen hours a day for the whole year. And if he's good at it, then he gets the respect of the other men regardless of his personality, and that's a plus.

Clare Robertson had an interesting talk with a Davis winterer who told her about the pecking order that inevitably occurs among the small group on the Station. 'Tubby', a South African, told her that someone is always at the lowest rung of the ladder, the butt of every joke. Only half in jest, Tubby suggested that the Division should actually advertise for someone to take on this role.

Sometimes the forming of groups and sub-groups in wintering parties can be disastrous. In his book *Sitting On Penguins* Stephen Murray-Smith told of a situation at Casey in the mid 'eighties when a group of construction workers effectively assumed 'ocker' control of the base, after the Station Leader had lost control of the situation. They commandeered the best accommodation, declared their own 'public holidays', and organised 'Let's see who can get drunk quickest' parties on home brew. The building program was set back some months because the trouble-makers had to be pulled out on an earlier voyage than planned. Such gross 'Mutiny on the Bounty' situations are extremely rare.

With that in mind, I asked Dr Kevin Donovan what made a good expeditioner.

KD: Difficult question. I suppose he's got to go south, he has to leave everyone he knows in Australia, join a group of people who are strangers, and get on with them for twelve months in rather limited or close living conditions. The old saying was that Antarctic expeditioners had to be gentlemen—with the emphasis on the gentle, that they had to have consideration for other people. That is knowing when not to make a noise, knowing when you are expected to make a noise, being able to fit in with a lot of people—different personalities—and steer a course that doesn't allow your own personality to get smothered by the group.

TB: How important is the role of the OIC or Station Leader in maintaining harmony, or is that something that just evolves naturally as a kind of group dynamic?

KD: The leader has a difficult course. He can either lead by dictatorial despotism, or he can lead by example or by using management skills as such. Lem Macey, who wintered many times since 1948, was a most experienced leader. I met him in 1976, after he had been the OIC at Mawson in 1975. He said his method was to stand back for a bit at the beginning of the year and see which way the group was running, then go out and say: 'Well, follow me'—seeing that they were going in that direction anyway. I'm not sure how much of that was in jest or reality. He was certainly well respected by the people who had served under him.

TB: You must have situations where people polarise into cliques, and other years when they don't. What's your experience of this?

KD: One of the advantages of being at Davis was having only fourteen people. There weren't enough in our group to form a clique. The four meteorological people were the single biggest occupational group. In other bases there might be more radio operators than any other work area, and that group has become a clique and not fitted in to the wider group.

TB: Can anything be done about this? Should it be nipped in the bud? Do you as the doctor take responsibility for the psychological health of the community as well?

KD: The doctor is more concerned with the psychological health of the individual. If you see someone getting depressed or upset or not mixing, then certainly that comes under the medical sphere. I suppose the prevention of clique formation or the prevention of groups of people becoming either dominant or different from the other groups is more a management problem, and that is the concern of the OIC.

TB: In the case of somebody who is obviously becoming depressed, what do you do?

KD: Well, I always try and find out why. It could be bad news from home, it could be he is not happy in the situation he's in. Most of the people I've counselled have been concerned with something that was happening back home. The big problem with being in Antarctica is that once the last ship goes, there is no way you are going to get back to Australia. So that whatever happens at home, if a relative dies, or your partner runs off with someone else, there is no way you

180

are going to be able to influence what the outcome is going to be. If your wife gets a boyfriend in Australia you can always deal with it in some way, thump him on the nose or grab your wife and go off on a holiday or something. When it happens while you're down south, there is absolutely nothing you can do. All you can do really is worry about it, or regret the outcome.

TB: I suppose some people come down to Antarctica to escape from personal relationships.

KD: Certainly in my Mawson year a couple of the marriages were on their last legs, and the men concerned came down knowing that when they got back the divorce would be through and everything would be back to square one again. Certainly some came south without any inkling that their marriages were likely to break up, and they were the ones that felt it the most when it happened. But it seems to me that the most common way this happens is not for the expeditioner to be told during the year, but to find out the day they get back.

TB: I wonder if anyone has ever studied the rate of relationship or marriage breakdown in Antarctic wintering personnel?

KD: I don't think it's ever been documented. It certainly seems high. At Mawson in 1986 two marriages broke up unexpectedly. Two were expected in that they were shaky when the men came down, and one broke up shortly after getting back. So, considering the small number of married personnel that go down there, that is certainly a high rate of break up.

TB: The Antarctic is a marriage hazard?

KD: Wintering is a marriage hazard. I suppose you should qualify that by saying separation is a marriage hazard.

Before sailing south on *Icebird* I'd heard a taped interview with Dr Don Dowie who wintered at Mawson in the winter of 1957 and who talked about the delicate business of coping with people's particular idiosyncrasies, some of which can be disproportionately annoying and irritating.

DD: When you're cheek by jowl for a year, you find that everybody has their mannerisms and these can be quite

Grounded icebergs on the Fram Bank.

amusing or intriguing to start with, but when they go on and on and on and bloody on, they become intolerable. One of our members who was a meteorologist was required to leave the hut on regular occasions to go up to his met quarters to take certain observations, and this went on throughout the year.

This laddie brought the house down on one occasion. Very early on—in the middle of a blizzard—he held the snow door open so that everybody got a good dose of snow coming sweeping in through the door, closed the door slightly so that things could settle down and then announced, 'Gentlemen, I may be gone some time'—that's a quote from Titus Oates who died on Scott's expedition.

So, roars of laughter, and he left and disappeared into the swirling mists. The next time it happened again, and again, and again . . . and we could have quite cheerfully crucified that man on that simple thing alone.

History does not record how that particular situation was dealt with by the group, but station records do not chronicle a murder. Kevin Donovan also had similar experiences at Mawson Station two decades later.

KD: A group at Mawson were complaining about how hard their particular duties were, and how they only ever had time to work and sleep. So, from then on, one particular person was called 'Work And Sleep'. Another in the group was called 'Moan and Groan' because everyone said that was all he did. And whenever they came into the room, you'd say, 'Oh work and sleep, work and sleep, that's all we get to do', which was unkind in a way, but he then stopped saying that, and stopped getting on other people's nerves. So everyone adjusted to a reasonable relationship.

TB: What about bizarre behaviour engendered by this isolation? I've noticed head shaving in a punk way. What about more personal idiosyncrasies?

KD: When we arrived at Mawson in 1986, Mohawk hair cuts were all the rage and several people had Mohawks. It is the sort of situation where you can do strange things with your hair, knowing that it will grow out by the time you get back to civilisation. People go through fads. It might be ear-piercing. They may pick up comments from videos and old movies and use those as a sort of in-joke, then when the new crowd arrives, who haven't been a part of it, they find it all very strange. You probably noticed on the ship that *The Blues Brothers* has become a cult film with the group. That certainly happens on the base.

TB: I've heard of a tradition involving a 'Bad Taste Night'.

KD: They do have Bad Taste Parties where they come as pregnant nuns, or President of the Colostomy Club or something like that. It varies from year to year, what the group decides to do. On the first Saturday of every month at Mawson we had a different theme for a party. We had an Arabian Nights one where someone actually shaved his beard off, made a sort of copper uplift bra and sort of pushed his pectorals into that, stuck a ruby in his navel and turned up as a dancing harem girl—which I suppose anywhere else would be considered strange behaviour.

People would shave their heads for parties if it suited. We had a Woolshed Dance where a lot of people covered themselves with brown boot polish to come as local Aboriginals. It took them a couple of days to get it off afterwards. They would do that there, but in Australia they wouldn't, because next day they'd have to be dressed and clean.

183

TB: A lot of imagination seems to go into these occasions.

KD: There's the old classic pantomime, *Cinderella*, that is done every mid-winter. The casting is often done in such a way as to take a dig at some people's stereotypes. In 1986 we did *Snow White and the Seven Dwarfs* because we had seven people who were deemed to be shorter than average. One of the carpenters wrote the script. We had a particular bloke who was considered to be terribly ugly when he smiled, so he was made the Wicked Witch. He was also terribly clumsy, so he brought all the scenery tumbling down in the first act. We also had a cult following of *The Blues Brothers*, and we did a skit where we stood up on stage and played the Rawhide theme and lowered a screen mesh down in front of us so people could throw things at us, as they do in the movie. That was good fun and got the night going.

TB: Did you have any women on the base that year?

KD: We had one woman who arrived on Easter Saturday. She came in by helicopter to replace one of the meteorological blokes that left about half-way through the summer. It was going to be an all-male year, but because of that she came in, and was the only girl on the base during the winter.

TB: I should imagine, for her, that would be a difficult situation, coming in after the group had been established. How did it work out?

KD: It worked out well. She certainly knew a couple of people on the base, as she had been south before. She wasn't coming in completely cold. But she could only get limited gear in, so she had to borrow lipstick and make-up and things from the blokes who were there. Somehow they seemed to produce those sort of things from their kits. They were probably saving them for dressing up later in the year. She certainly fitted in well, but did comment she missed having someone female to talk to. She was particularly skilful in forming a sibling relationship rather than a male/female relationship with the men in the wintering party. That certainly took away any sexual stereotypes. They treated her like an older or younger sister. I don't think anyone made any approaches—or certainly none that were spectacular enough to come to general notice.

TB: Did the inclusion of one woman change the behaviour of the men during that year at all?

KD: I think there was a certain apprehension as soon as she arrived. There were some people who made comments that they had never ever wintered with an all male group, and were looking forward to the difference. I suppose there is a slight difference, in that you tend to be a bit rowdier in the celebrations than you would be if there was a girl present. She certainly established a rapport with everyone in that there wasn't anything you wouldn't talk about in her company that you wouldn't discuss in an all-male situation. When she came into the room, you weren't aware there was a girl in the room. She fitted into the group and was just another member of the wintering group—not standing out as a girl. I'm not sure whether she'd appreciate me saying that or not! She certainly fitted in extremely well with that group.

TB: Women on bases are a relatively recent development. What is your view on women in the Antarctic, Kevin?

KD: I could say 'No comment', but I suppose I should be a little honest. I suppose the easy way out is to say that there are enough complications down there without adding another, and I think mixing a group of women and men does add another complication to social relationships. It would be a lot easier if those complications weren't there. It is inevitable that women will go south. There are going to be problems because of that, I can't envisage that there wouldn't be problems.

TB: Have there been sexual jealousies and pairings off, or even promiscuity on some of the stations?

KD: I can't really say, because there weren't any women on mainland Australian Stations in 1975. The first woman wintered on mainland Antarctica in 1981. There was the woman I described at Mawson in 1986. I can't envisage putting males and females together under those circumstances and not having those situations arising. Whether it causes great disruption is hard to say. It would depend on who it was that did it. If they sent a married couple down, and then the husband or wife formed a liaison with some one else, it would certainly be a problem. If a couple came down—not married but who were on friendly terms when they left Australia—and that relationship broke up in Antarctica and another formed, that would cause some sort of jealousy, especially if the people concerned had to work in the same office, eat with them every day of the year, sleep with them— well, in the same building anyway—that is going to add another complication to life down there.

To all intents and purposes the debate on women in Antarctica is over. Equal opportunity and changing attitudes have seen to that. And there are many expeditioners who applaud the changes, saying that, apart from reflecting a more balanced community and any other pluses, women have encouraged more civilised behaviour on the stations.

FEBRUARY 8

We are on the move again, back to have another go at breaking through the fast ice and getting in to Mawson Station. I stood looking over the bow as *Icebird* steamed east through strips of open water and broken pack ice. Our speed exactly matched the following breeze, so I looked down into a perfect mirror image reflection of the ship's bow slicing through the water. It was so quiet that you could actually hear the splashing of the Adelie penguins as they 'porpoised' along beside the ship. They looked as though they were flying underwater.

We are steaming as close as possible to the Amery Ice Shelf, one of the largest glaciers to stream off the Antarctic continent. The idea is to make a radar profile of its ice cliffs. It shows up splendidly on the radar, but it is frustrating not to be able to see it close up.

FEBRUARY 9

I got up at 6 am to see a most spectacular sight—the grounded icebergs that form the Fram Bank, named by the Norwegians after Nansen's *Fram*, in the 1930s. It is formed by icebergs calving from the Amery Ice Shelf, which are moved out to sea by the current, and run aground on the 200 metre line. We are steaming past a great tumbled line of bergs, some tilted over at crazy angles beside other more symmetrical tabular bergs. Even the blase old Antarctic hands are bringing

out their cameras as we pass by the spires, towers and jagged crevassed tops of this amazing display of stranded icebergs.

'Wok' Bromham, the weather man, gave me a print-out of the Russian satellite weather picture for the day. The Fram Bank is clearly visible, a major feature curving out like a comet's

Imagine waking up to this kind of view through your bedroom window.

tail from the relatively featureless line of the coast. The technology for forecasting is remarkable. Wok told me that while he was camping with the Prince Charles Mountains party inland from Mawson, he was able to receive similar satellite pictures on portable gear.

Scored a seat at the Captain's table again tonight. The conversation turned to the future of tourism, and the problem of conservation in Antarctica. Ewald favours

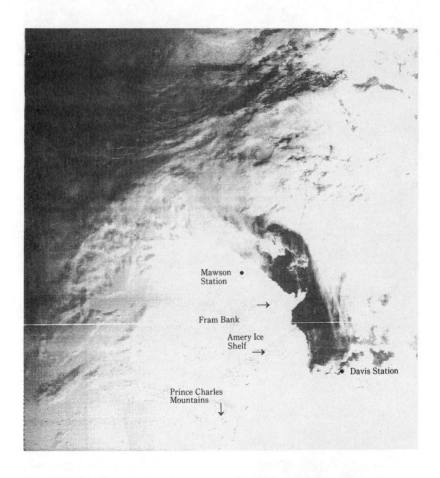

The Fram Bank can be seen clearly from this Russian weather satellite photo I managed to souvenir from obliging weatherman 'Wok' Bromham.

188

ship-based tourism because all the wastes can be secured in tanks on board and removed from the area. Tourists can be taken on short boat or helicopter trips to scenic vantage points, again with minimum impact on the environment.

The Antarctic Division already has a policy of removing all wastes from the field. After all, nothing ever decays in this permanent deep-freeze. Ewald Brune told me of one Antarctic voyage (not *Icebird* on this occasion) when the Voyage Leader issued strict instructions that all waste had to be brought back from the field. The frozen collections from the portable toilets had been put in paper bags, not plastic, which as it happened was unfortunate.

A helicopter was sent out piloted by a Canadian, normally a very quiet person, Ewald said, who had done a lot of flying in the Arctic regions of Canada. The interior of the chopper was heated, and the flight time was one hour.

Those on the ship who watched the chopper land were puzzled why the engines were shut down immediately. The procedure usually takes about five minutes. Observers saw the pilot leap out of the aircraft, red in the face and shouting wildly. His malodorous cargo had defrosted during the flight, melted through the paper bags, and was sloshing all over the floor of his helicopter.

Ewald believes that the concern for the environment, while important, is sometimes taken too far.

EB: During the 1987 summer season I was supposed to land a party at Scullin Monolith, sixty miles further east of Mawson, and they were supposed to stay there for twenty-four hours. Our cook made some lunch packets and tried to do a good job with pork chops, schnitzel and some hard-boiled eggs. But the field party leader became very upset about the eggs, and said there must be absolutely no eggs at all.

I said, 'What is wrong with eggs?' He said, 'They are not good for the penguins'. I said, 'But they are not for the penguins, they are for you'. He said, 'If we have to go to the toilet and we have eaten eggs, that is not good—perhaps some chicken sickness will be brought to the penguins'.

Ewald then asked him what he had eaten for breakfast that morning. 'No eggs', said the field leader triumphantly. Ewald said, 'But you had pancakes served. Did you eat any?' The field leader said he had four.

EB: Well, I said, pancakes are made from eggs. So I'm sorry, if you are serious about eggs we can't let you ashore—unless you take a laxative first that will make you go to the toilet.

That was a joke from my point of view, but they took it seriously. So a group of twelve came to me, and I happened to have a bottle of Ferne Branca in the bar, which is not a medicine, but a liqueur with a bitter taste. It is certainly not a laxative—if anything it has the opposite effect! I made them drink a glass each, and six of them went straight to the toilet and the other six were in trouble because they were due to fly to Scullin Monolith the next morning and they had not been to the toilet.

They did finally get there.

CHAPTER THIRTEEN

Mawson Ice Edge Again! • A Mini Mega Jolly • Some Gloomy Predictions • How Not to Harness a Husky • World's Longest Golf Drive • Naked Journalists On Ice • Dogs Attack Doctor's Nether Regions • Delights of Dog Sledging Experienced • The Lost Tractor Train of Frustration Dome • Boy's Own Antarctic Era Revisited

FRIDAY, FEBRUARY 10

Once again, dare I say, off the ice edge at Mawson! This time Ewald seems fairly gung-ho about getting through, but I can't see how *Icebird* can do it. It's still solid fast ice for seven nautical miles. Maybe only six, because we broke in some way during the day, but had to pack it in and retreat to the ice edge because of engine trouble. It is something to do with the pneumatic control that controls the pitch of the propeller, and it alters our ability to reverse.

While we waited, yet again, with *Icebird*'s bows gently embedded in the fast ice edge, I was listed for a flight to Taylor Rookery, the only known rock rookery for Emperor penguins. I shared a chopper with 'Babs' Graham and Robin Taylor, piloted by Dave Pullinger. Graham Robertson, in the lead chopper, thought there was a sporting chance some Emperors might still be hanging about. I noted in my diary that the flight was a 'mini-mega-jolly'.

Slightly overcast day with high cloud as we flew over several glaciers west of Mawson Station; great wrinkled crevasse-split rivers of ice, tumbling down to spectacular ice-cliffs on the coast. A little red apple hut stood out amongst the brown rocks of Taylor Rookery,

but we did not land as Graham could see there were no Emperors. With some extra time to exploit, we were treated to a wonderful scenic coastal tour while returning to *Icebird*, hovering occasionally to photograph an ice cave, and swooping past the whorled curves of grounded icebergs. Yet another photographic orgy.

Keith Scott came the closest yet to beating me in our daily Scrabble joust. He drew a game!

FEBRUARY 11
This is the day we were due back in Hobart on the original schedule and here we are with our bows thrust in to the ice edge at Mawson, in exactly the same situation we were almost four weeks ago.

I found out later that one reason for the earlier-than-usual departure from Hobart was that Ewald expressed great confidence he could break ice and get *Icebird* in to Mawson Station ahead of schedule. Now our second attempt has been stalled by engine trouble. Ewald has faxed and phoned the *Icebird*'s owners in Hamburg to see if the engineers there think he can continue breaking ice. Apparently there are two pneumatic pumps to control the pitch of the propeller, and if the second one were to fail we would not be in good shape.

A briefing in the mess that evening canvassed some bleak options: wait for the ice to break out; evacuate the bulk of the Station's personnel; go home without doing anything more.

The problem is that Voyage Six is the major resupply effort for Mawson Station. Without the fuel oil we carry, the Station could not maintain full operation through the year. Another option would be to leave a skeleton staff there, using the old wooden huts and abandoning the red and green 'Taj Mahal' sheds to conserve fuel.

As is so often the case in the Antarctic, this kind of speculation evaporated within the hour with the news that we would resume breaking ice in the morning. Apparently the Hamburg experts gave the green light to go for broke on the one remaining pneumatic pump. Or perhaps the failed pump has been fixed by psychokinesis from Germany?

FEBRUARY 12

Des Lugg put a notice up on the board this morning:

'On the 13th of February, 1954, Mawson Station was officially opened with a flag-raising ceremony after *Kista Dan* had broken through some miles of fast ice . . . '

I don't think he is impressed with *Icebird*'s or Ewald's performance.

Visiting rights to Mawson Station seem a lot easier to obtain this time around. I wonder if Diana Patterson has become aware that our first visit was not remembered fondly by most involved? Mind you, there is still a certain brittleness between ship and shore. I heard the following exchange on the radio from the bridge this morning.

Diana: Good morning Des. We've got work programs arranged for all those coming ashore from *Icebird* this morning.
Des: Negative Diana. Some people have their own work projects, and others will volunteer.

It was an absolutely glorious Antarctic summer's day with almost no wind, a deep blue sky, and perfect conditions for a dog-sled run on the sea ice. Keith Scott had asked one of the Mawson expeditioners, Peter Crosthwaite, to go on one, and said I could go along. I was unlikely to say no! How many times in my life would I be able to ride (and run beside) a Nansen sledge drawn by seven huskies?

The party consisted of Keith Scott, me, Robin Taylor (wife of 'Pud' Taylor, our cargo supremo) and Major Tony Gill (to be known from this point as 'The Galloping Major'). Our guide and dog handler, Peter Crosthwaite, sensibly involved us in the mechanics of the operation right from the start. First harness your dog. The sledge was positioned and staked down on a snow slope leading directly down on to the sea ice. The line of seven (or nine) dogs is attached by a single trace, but branching out left to right at intervals behind the lead dog.

The huskies live staked out in the open on long chains on a snow bank at the western side of the Station. They all knew

193

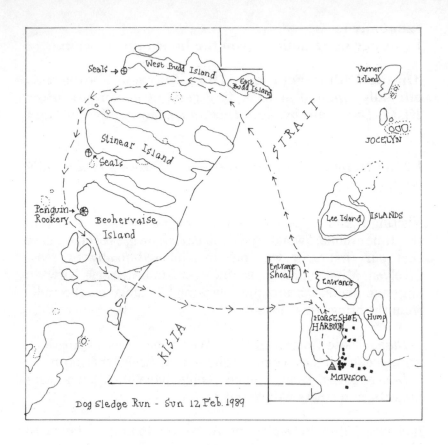

Seals → ⊕ West Budd Island

East Budd Island

STRAIT

Verner Island

JOCELYN

Stinear Island

⊕ Seals

Lee Island ISLANDS

Penguin → ✦ Beohervaise Island
Rookery

Entrance Shoal

Entrance

HORSESHOE HARBOUR

Hump

KISTA

▲ Mawson

Dog Sledge Run – Sun 12 Feb. 1989

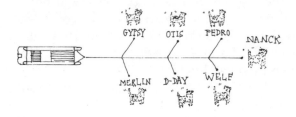

GYPSY   OTIS   PEDRO

NANCK

MERLIN   D-DAY   WELF

The route of our sledge run.

194

that a sledge run was on, and began a terrific barking and howling as we approached. Peter showed us how to fit the harness by straddling the dog, lifting up its front legs and guiding them through loops that encased its chest. You can do absolutely anything with these amazing animals, they will never attack or bite a human. But, given the chance, they will fight and even kill an unpopular dog. It was extremely important that I didn't let my dog off the leash because they love to take off and roam the camp having a high old time— and they are difficult to catch.

As I unclipped my dog from the permanent chain he lunged forward, throwing me off balance. My rubber boots slipped on the icy surface and I fell over, grimly hanging on as the excited husky towed me down the bank, the Bowden chin carving a furrow through the turd-stained snow as we went. I knew I would be in deep disgrace if I let go! When I could get a purchase on the rock with my boots, I stood up and lifted the dog's front feet off the ground with the harness, and half carried him to the waiting sledge. I was breathing heavily and sweating before we actually got going!

The twenty-six huskies at Mawson Station on the dog lines had their origins in Greenland. They are a Labrador/Greenland husky cross, and their ancestors were acquired by ANARE following their use by a French Antarctic expedition in 1948/49. The French dogman of that time, M Pommier, commented on the characteristics of the different breeds:

LABRADOR: 'Very artistic, in general capricious and nervous. More difficult to live with than the Greenlanders. They will obey only the strongest law. Feeble or timid dogs ought to be watched closely because they will be killed sooner or later by the others.'

GREENLAND: 'Good dogs, rough and sober. Family spirit very well developed. Arrange their affairs amongst themselves and require less supervision than the Labradors.'

The then ANARE Director, Dr Phillip Law, managed to override Australia's tough quarantine laws by keeping the French dogs he acquired in the Melbourne Zoo. They were bred and cared for there until January 1950 when twelve dogs were loaded on to HMAS Labuan for transport to Heard Island—a staging post for the eventual move to the Antarctic Continent. In a

1987 article in Aurora (the ANARE Club journal) Patrick Moonie wrote:

At Heard Island the dogs did valuable haulage work around the station and across the 'Nullabor Plain', pulling sleds in winter and dogmobiles (wheeled carts) in the summer. Apart from useful haulage work, the other objective was to enable the expeditioners to gain experience in dog-team management and to maintain a training regime for eventual destinations further south. A cross-breeding program was initiated to retain from the Labrador only their heavier build and greater strength, whilst eliminating their long shaggy hair in favour of the Greenlander's short thick coat.

In January 1954, thirty huskies were loaded on board *Kista Dan* for passage to Mawson and formed part of the station when it was commissioned on 17 February 1954. In February 1963, per favour of J Lauritzen Lines, an additional three Greenland huskies arrived on *Nella Dan* to vary the blood line. Over the years some of the Mawson dogs were sent to Davis and Wilkes/Casey Stations, and in 1956, twenty-six were made available to New Zealand for their station at Scott.

In the first decade the Mawson huskies were the primary means of transportation in exploration work east to the Amery Ice Shelf, west to Enderby Land, south throughout the vast Prince Charles Mountains and over the sea ice for coastal work.

The dog sled run I was about to begin was linked to the 'Heroic' era of polar exploration. Scott had not put much faith in dogs, but the man who beat him to the South Pole, Roald Amundsen, had actually lived with Eskimos in the Arctic to study their sledging techniques. He had put this knowledge to good effect in his dash to the pole in 1911. He used Nansen sledges, similar to the New Zealand-built models at Mawson. Their design has not altered very much: a wooden construction bound together with rawhide strips which can cope with the constant flexing and jarring as the sledge crashes and batters its way over the roughly surfaced ice. No modern materials do the job as well.

We were all asked to sit on the sledge for the start. It is not advisable for anyone to say the word 'ready'

as the dogs can race off with a false start. 'Ready—
MUSH BOYS MUSH!' and we were off, careering down
the snow slope, crashing across ice tide-cracks and off
onto the fast ice still covering the surface of Horseshoe
Harbour, which didn't look too safe to me, but the dogs
certainly didn't seem to have any worries. It took a
while to master the art of jogging beside the sledge
in my cumbersome felt-lined Antarctic rubber boots,
over the razor-sharp edges of the ridged sea ice, and
trying not to slip on the greasy smooth patches
preferred by the dogs.

*Perfect weather for the tourist excursion of a lifetime—by husky power
across the sea ice on a Nansen sledge off Mawson Station.*

197

Six weeks of soft life on board ship had not done a great deal for my fitness, and it was a relief to collapse on to the sledge every now and then. The only two of our party not to do this were our dog man, Peter Crosthwaite, who looked fit enough to run 600 K east to Davis Station without stopping, and Tony Gill, 'The Galloping Major', who also revelled in the exercise and ran like a man possessed. Robin, who is not tall, found her legs a bit short for the occasion and took good advantage of the sled. You could either ride by sitting on the sledging box on the main platform of the Nansen sledge, or stand behind, being careful not to stand on the brake—except when Peter Crosthwaite asked you to. The brake was a lever that simply scraped down on the icy surface when you stepped on it.

Peter ran ahead with the lead dog, Nanok, partly to head the team off if they cottoned on to a seal or penguin. The dogs will head towards anything that isn't ice or rock, and have to be dissuaded from having a penguin snack. I recalled interviewing Nils Lied, a Norwegian dog handler who worked with the original huskies on Heard Island, and then drove them at Mawson and Davis Stations in the 1950s and 1960s. The huskies' penchant for heading towards any unusual object was instrumental in Nils making the Guinness Book of Records for the longest golf drive ever achieved. It took place at Mawson Station in 1956:

NL: When the sea ice first forms in autumn and before the snowfalls make it knurly and knobby, it is as smooth as glass. We had brought down a Number 1 wood with us, to have a bit of a hit around. We took some golf balls into the engine room and carefully dipped them into black enamel engine paint; our tees were huge wood screws which we counter-sunk on the emery wheel to make the tops concave and which could be screwed into the ice.

One morning two or three of us went down in front of the station to Horseshoe Harbour to have a hit around. The sea ice had not long been formed but it was strong enough to support a dog team and sledge. We screwed a tee in to the sea ice, placed a black golf ball carefully on top, and I had first hit. I was dressed up like a real polar explorer in windproofs, mukluks and crampons. The crampons raise you two or three inches higher off the ground, which didn't do much for my golf swing.

It was a blustery day. The wind was gusting from practically nothing up to fifty knots. So I waited for a lull and I let her have it. For once, I made a good hit. It was a beauty! That ball fairly flew out of the harbour. And just as I finished my drive, in came a tremendous gust, and the wind took the ball and propelled it out of the harbour mouth; it bounced over the tide crack, and just kept going. It finished up in the tide crack near Flatoy Island, some four kilometres off shore.

So we saddled up Oscar, my lead dog, with a sledge behind him. We knew if any dog could sniff the ball out, Oscar would. And he did. There it was sitting very nicely in the tide crack near the island, thank you.

When I came back to Australia, I was having a drink with a journalist friend of mine in Lou Richards' pub in Flinders Street, Melbourne, and the talk came around to golf so I told him the story. Everybody roared with laughter, but the Melbourne *Herald*'s golf writer happened to be in the group next to us, and he sidled over and said, 'Is that fair dinkum?' I said 'Yes, would I lie to you?' And he said, 'It's a good story, do you mind if I use it'. I said, 'Feel free'.

So he ran the story the following day in the *Herald* about the longest golf drive known to man and, so help me, some time later I found I was listed in the Guinness Book of Records for 'the longest golf drive in the world'.

I believe there have been long drives along airport runways and so forth, but nothing like mine.

Once you set out over the ice with a dog team, there is no stopping, because the huskies are trained to pull, and if they stop and are not properly pegged down on their traces, they usually fight. Peter kept a watchful eye on them, ready to belt them with his doubled up piece of rope if they got out of hand.

From time to time I threw myself gasping onto the sledge, to dwell on the sight of seven husky posteriors, tails high, pulling me along at a steady four to five knots. The only sounds to be heard were the rasping breaths

of running humans, the clatter of the wooden runners over the ice, and the panting of the dogs. I count the sledge run over the sea ice near Mawson as one of the most exhilarating experiences of my life. As we moved further away from the coast, we could see the stony peaks of Mt Henderson and the Masson Range thrown into relief against the great ice sheet, curving up and away into the interior of the continent. We were heading into the sun, and the razor-edged shards of surface ice glistened like crystal. In the distance, the scramble of buildings that was Mawson looked like a toy settlement built of Lego blocks.

We were bound for one of the rocky off-shore islands between Horseshoe Harbour and the open sea, named after early expeditioners. We broke our two-hour run on the shores of West Budd Island, securing the sledge, and staking out the dogs in their traces on a snow drift on the island's stony beach.

Keith Scott and I indulged ourselves in a piece of photographic nonsense. I had a plan to pose, with beach towel casually draped over one shoulder, on the sea ice dressed only in Y-fronts and boots. In bright sunshine, and with almost no wind, it was possible to strip down and have photos taken in this spectacular location without great discomfort. The dogs seemed unimpressed. I was grateful that we did not have to answer any urgent and serious calls of nature during the trip, recalling a story Nills Lied had told me on tape about his 1961 wintering at Davis Station:

> *NL*: We had a doctor who was a magnificent middle distance athlete, and he loved coming on sledging runs, but he was a bit of a know-all. He thought he knew everything about the Antarctic even though he'd been there for about five minutes.
>
> We were going up to the plateau, inland, with a team of dogs, and I was driving. He was always running in front of the dogs, which was all right, as it gives them something to aim at. He told me that he wanted to relieve himself, and he'd just run on and squat up ahead. I said, 'I'd advise against it'.
>
> He said, 'Oh no, it'll be all right'.

So off he went, and as we progressed I could see his posterior glistening in the setting sun. He was at peace with the world, and doing what he set out to do.

Then the dogs got a sniff of this on the slight down-slope breeze. Now huskies will eat just about anything, even human excrement, because they get trace elements from it. Unfortunately for the doctor, a team of huskies runs silently. They don't yap or bark, so he couldn't hear them while he was crouched there with the wind blowing past his ears.

The next thing he knew was my lead dog Oscar's nose and a vicious snap about a fraction of an inch behind that little part of the body that men treasure more than anything!

I am not sure why Keith Scott (right) and I decided to pose in our jocks on the Antarctic sea ice, but we did!

That's the only time I ever saw a man go into orbit. It was hilarious. He was trying to clean himself up, do up his straps and zippers and his bits and pieces, and run at the same time. There were bits of paper floating around in the breeze and vicious snaps either side as the other dogs in the team tried to get at them. They hoped the doctor was the source of more of this good stuff! And he ran and he ran and he ran, until I finally managed to stop the team. I couldn't do it before, I was laughing too much. It looked so ridiculous. I think the dogs enjoyed it just as much as I did.

Safely dressed, Keith and I took off again as we continued our sledging run around the outlying islands, while the dogs rather worryingly preferred the smooth, obviously thinner ice that had refrozen over melted channels. It must have been considerably easier on their paws and pads than the fractured, sharp, mottled surface of the older ice. Peter, shouting commands, steered the team in a wide arc past an Adelie penguin colony as we veered around for the run home.

I feel privileged to have joined the select band of people who have sledged on sea ice, on a Nansen sledge behind a working husky team. It is an experience I will never forget. On the return journey the light from the low sun caught the flanks of the dogs, tinging their black, white, and brown fur with gold.

There were more adventures ahead. Station Leader Diana Patterson said Keith Scott and I could join a helicopter expedition that evening to try and locate some equipment that had been abandoned about sixty miles inland by a field party in 1967. A sled and other gear had been sighted from the air by one of the diesel mechanics, Dave McCormack, in 1986, but bad weather had prevented any closer inspection.

Phil Barnaart, Mawson Station Leader for 1988, told us that a 1967 traverse party comprising John Manning, Pat Moonie and Tony Jacques had been on a field expedition to chart the exact location of Church Mountain, east of Mawson. Intense cold and a heavily crevassed area forced them to abandon their broken-down vehicles and walk back to Mawson Station in appalling blizzard conditions. The crevassing was caused by the ice sheet riding over a hidden rock dome, since named 'Frustration Dome'. The tractors and snow vehicles had been recovered not long after, but the other gear had been lying out on the ice sheet for twenty-two years until sighted by Dave McCormack.

We flew from Mawson at 8 pm in perfect weather. The plan was for our two helicopters to fly on previously calculated bearings at 2500 ft to 'Frustration Dome' and then search at lower heights. We flew past the brown rocks of Mt Henderson into the nothingness of the ice cap. To our left was the deep blue of the ocean, spotted with dazzling white icebergs. On the right, the slow curve of the ice sheet to a featureless horizon.

Keith Scott and I shared a helicopter with Dave McCormack, piloted by Pip Turner. Leigh Hornsby, the senior pilot, led the way, with Station Leader Diana Patterson and Phil Barnaart on board. The crevassed area containing what Keith and I agreed from now on to call 'The Lost Tractor Train Of Frustration Dome', could be seen clearly. Dave was the first to spot the abandoned gear and Pip radioed to the other chopper. We touched down on 'blue' ice, swept clean of any snow by the wind, which also made it easy to see where the crevasses were. It was −12C, and we were two-and-a half thousand feet above sea level, but because of the still air and bright sunshine we didn't notice the cold.

A sledge, about two metres long and a little more than a metre wide, was sitting on the ice looking as though it had been left there a week before. A rope was hanging over the rail, looking brand new. Some abandoned ration packs had burst open, and their contents were scattered about. In the dry deep freeze of Antarctica, they were perfectly preserved. I picked up some bars of MacRobertson Supreme Milk Chocolate, with coloured pictures of London's Tower Bridge, and the Egyptian pyramids!
It is difficult to comprehend how all this stuff can just sit there on the blue ice, and not be blown away. I suppose it drifts up a bit in the winter, and then becomes

Examining perfectly preserved twenty-two-year-old food supplies after finding 'The Lost Tractor Train of Frustration Dome'.

more exposed in the summer. Dave picked up a small piston head from a two-stroke motor, slightly embedded in the ice. It didn't have a trace of rust on it. The cocoa in plastic packets was still dry and crumbly, as were the rolled oats in similar packets. An open tin of butter still had some kind of buttery substance inside. I have no doubt the unopened tins of butter (marked 'for tropical use'!) would still be as good as new.

There were also plenty of packets of HF6 Bars, and the famous 'sledgies'—Swallow and Ariel sledging biscuits. The HF6 Bar is a 6 oz emergency ration, prepared by Horlicks Ltd, of Slough, England.

'In emergency can be eaten uncooked. For cooked meal, crumble 3 oz of Bar, add half a pint of water, bring to boil and simmer at least five minutes whilst stirring. If desired 1 oz of Instant Potato Powder can be stirred into the hot mixture until completely absorbed. Serve.'

The indestructibility of this ration is illustrated by the fact that somewhere in Antarctica is a surveyor's cairn, with the

I wasn't allowed to bring an actual HF 6 Bar back to Australia in case I returned a deadly disease (!) so here's the label.

central surveying point (usually a brass pin or plaque) officially designated as an HF6 Bar!

We flew back low over the huge crevasses resulting from the hidden bulk of Frustration Dome, some of them big enough to swallow our helicopter. These enormous 'slots' follow the curve of the dome as they run down towards the coast. The low sun threw a crisp and almost perfect shadow of our helicopter on the ice as we returned to Mawson Station.

FEBRUARY 13
It is the thirty-fifth anniversary of the founding of Mawson Station, and a cause for celebration. Appropriately enough, one of the original 'sledge caravans',

designed to float to help get it ashore, was recovered from the ice behind the Fischer Nunatak, about twenty kilometres south of Mawson, and brought back to the Station. It had been completely entombed in ice, following its early use as a weather station. Dave McCormack was involved with this, too. He has a great sense of Antarctic history, as has Phil Barnaart who also worked on this project.

There is much debate about whether this plyboard sledge caravan (still sporting its original coat of red paint) should be left at the Station as an historical artifact, or taken back to Australia. I peeked in one of its tiny windows (it was still three-quarters full of ice) and saw an old red packet of Craven A cigarettes sitting there as though it had been dropped yesterday. Later in the evening we watched a film, narrated by Frank Hurley, of the original landing at Mawson in 1954, and saw that very sledge caravan being towed ashore. A nice coincidence. The film also showed the Danish ship *Kista Dan* breaking fast ice on its way into Horseshoe Harbour, which seemed to accord Des Lugg some grim satisfaction. The unmistakable figure of Phil Law could be seen standing on the sea ice in front of the charging ship, filming it!

At 5.45 pm we all went down to the old aircraft hangar, one of the first major buildings to be erected at Mawson and the first hangar built on the Antarctic continent. It had almost been filled up with drift, but Dave McCormack (again) had fixed the huge swinging door and cleared the interior of snow. The shelves for spare aircraft parts were made from wooden Penfolds wine boxes and, in some of the side rooms, the flight plans of early aerial mapping operations of the 1950s and 60s were still pinned to the walls.

Earlier, Diana Patterson had rung Phil Law, now living in retirement in Melbourne, on the satellite telephone. He was absolutely delighted and said it was the first time he had ever been phoned from Mawson Station.

Station Leader Diana Patterson pays tribute to the 'Boys Own' era of Antarctica by donning ancient ventiles and beard for the thirty-fifth anniversary celebrations of the founding of Mawson Station. Helicopter Resources mechanic Tony Taylor is pictured left.

After drinks and savouries in the hangar we went to the brewing shed for some 1950s stew and station-made bread. Some of the early brown Japara silk ventile jackets had been liberated from the store and the women present also dressed for the occasion by sporting black Ned Kelly-style beards. The Antarctic was solidly *Boys Own* in the early years.

I thought the whole thing was done with considerable style.

CHAPTER FOURTEEN

We Reach Mawson At Last • A Blizzard Strikes • The Dangers of Rock-Filled Clouds for Pilots • What is a Vague-Out? • 'Blood Chits' and the Hazards of Unloading Cargo • More Antarctic Practical Jokes; Junk Mail and Rice Pudding Episodes • Amazing Nude Behaviour at South Pole

FEBRUARY 14

The *Icebird* is getting closer to Mawson. The ice-breaking seems to be going much better this time. On one occasion we made about a kilometre without having to back and charge forward again. There are patches where the fast ice is clearly older and rotten.

The Philosopher has been misbehaving himself. He wanted to spend the night on the Station instead of being helicoptered back to the ship like the rest of the *Icebirders* after the Mawson Station's thirty-fifth birthday celebrations, and stacked on quite a turn. 'Pud' Taylor had to order him to leave the Station saying that he wouldn't get ashore again if he didn't. On reaching the ship he stormed up to the bridge to have a slice of Des, and then repaired to Stoppy's Bar to iron himself out.

We broke ice all day, making significant progress. I played Scrabble with Keith Scott in the afternoon and he was doing quite well until I cleared my board on my last go! I did have two blanks, and the word was TARGETED.

Towards evening it became apparent that we would get into Horseshoe Harbour that night. I think we took the Station by surprise and, to announce our arrival, Ewald blew three

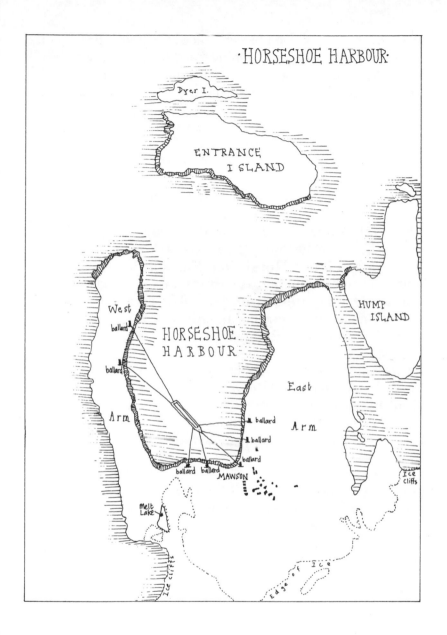

Mawson Station's Horseshoe Harbour is the only sanctuary on the coast of Greater Antarctica where a ship can lie moored to solid rock.

blasts of the ship's siren which echoed eerily off the ice cliffs and hills. It was a superb evening, dead still, with a wonderful low light highlighting the Station buildings and immediate surroundings. We put a line ashore but cast off again while Ewald used the *Icebird* to try and smash up some of the fast ice in the harbour to help with barge operations during the unloading. Then we were moored to the big stanchions anchored into the rocks of the Western Arm of Horseshoe Harbour. It is the best deepwater harbour on the coast of Greater Antarctica where a ship can moor in reasonable shelter.

The Philosopher rose from the dead this afternoon partly because he had bet a six-pack of beer that we *would* make it into Horseshoe Harbour by evening and wanted to claim his bet. He appeared in the bar dressed like a Western dude from the OK Corral. He sported a bootlace necktie, matching shirt and pants in cowboy style. It was a surprising sight.

As we called it a day (there being no real night), I looked out the cabin porthole to see the work boat *Chicken* busily buzzing about pushing slabs of ice out of the way to be ready for the unloading operations. Des confidently predicted we would be discharging cargo by 6 am next day.

FEBRUARY 15
Awoke to a full Antarctic blizzard! Eric Percival, from the Tasmanian Fire Service, had left his cabin porthole slightly ajar and woke to find his cabin full of swirling snow. It is gusting up to 100 knots so it is just as well we made it into harbour yesterday otherwise we would have had to retreat yet again to the ice edge off Mawson. There will be no unloading today.

The Antarctic is at last behaving like the Antarctic after so much amazingly good weather. Kevin Donovan is spreading a rumour that an iceberg has drifted in and blocked the entrance to the harbour and we are blizzarded in for the winter unless a Chinese icebreaker arrives in time to push it away. He got some anxious looks from the gullible.

I couldn't help thinking of the huskies staked out in the

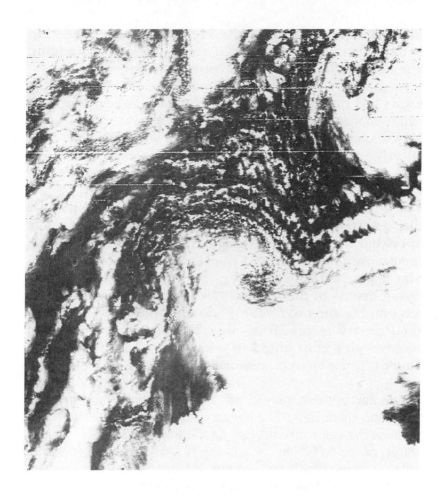

It's official. We endured a hurricane on our first day moored in Horseshoe Harbour, as the satellite photo clearly shows.

open in the middle of it all. They just hunker down, apparently, and let the snow build up around them.

We have been forbidden to venture outside the air-conditioned interior of the ship. I went to the bridge and couldn't even see the bow through the howling wind and driven snow. The Beaufort Scale, which measures wind strength, ends at Force 12. On several occasions while I was on the bridge it swung right off the end of the dial. The Third Mate, Roger Rusling, told me that

it was gusting over 150 kilometres per hour. **The ship is under power, although we are moored, just nudging ahead into the storm to hold our position.**

Ewald told me of one blizzard in Mawson Harbour where he had to manoeuvre the ship right up to the water's edge. The Mawsonites woke up to find the *Icebird*'s big red bow towering directly over their sleeping huts.

FEBRUARY 16

The wind has dropped and the sun is out. Mawson looks like a Christmas card scene with the dark bare rocks speckled with snowdrifts. The historic hangar building has snow in it again, so there's more work for Dave McCormack. There is furious activity, with helicopters flying drums of fuel directly from the ship up on to the ice plateau for next year's traverse parties to ferry to the Prince Charles Mountains. The barges are working, too, ferrying containers to where they can be lifted by shore cranes on to transporters.

Flying has always played an extremely important part in Antarctic operations. The hangar was built close to the water because the early aircraft operated either on floats from open water, or on skis from the sea ice. It is hard to imagine more difficult flying conditions than in Antarctica: isolation, sudden changes of weather, whiteouts and uncertain landing areas with the temperature permanently below freezing. In 1956, several single-engined aircraft were operating from Mawson Station, landing on the sea ice nearby. During an exploratory expedition to Amundsen Bay, some 200 kilometres west of Mawson, a Beaver aircraft from Canada was the leading aircraft, and the back-up plane was the original Auster aircraft that had been constructed out of the wreck of two Austers on the first voyage to Mawson Station in 1954. Flight Lieutenant Doug Leckie was ferrying fuel to a field party at Amundsen Bay, right on the limits of his aircraft's operating range, when an instrument failure placed him in dire straits. So traumatic was this incident that he had not spoken of it to anyone until I recorded an interview with him more than three decades later.

212

Doug Leckie's Beaver aircraft is winched out onto the sea ice in 1956. Antarctic Division photograph by M. Christensen.

DL: I took off with two drums of fuel aboard and climbed up and found a bank of cloud running over the hills—the ranges towards Amundsen Bay. I could see the mountains poking up through the cloud into another bank of cloud that was above so I climbed above them and got right on top, and I decided to proceed. I was a bit stupid really because I didn't have that much faith in the weather but they had told me the weather wasn't too bad at Amundsen Bay so I continued on. I'd been flying for an hour or so and I looked at my radar altimeter and it indicated 'zero' as though I was over the sea-ice. And I thought; 'Oh, I must've struck a tail wind, and if I'm over sea-ice I'd better smartly let down because I'll have to turn over the sea-ice and come back into Amundsen Bay. In that case I'd be heading back into a pretty strong head wind, if it had taken me across that fast.'

So I let down through a bank of cloud, and there was another bank of cloud below me so I let down through that. And as I broke through there was a sheer rock face coming

213

straight at me! Well, my heart nearly stopped, so all I could do was do a violent turn to the left, and I turned left and there was a rock facing me on the left and I finished up doing a complete 360 turn and I had rock running straight up into the cloud all round me.

I thought, 'This is it!' But I could manage to stay within safe limits with the full power by maintaining a rate-one turn on instruments. My instrument flying was—I'm not ashamed to say—a bit rusty and I wasn't a current 'green card pilot' or instrument pilot at the time although I was a fairly experienced instrument pilot. So I had to settle my nerves and just maintain that rate of turn and maintain height while I worked out my next plan. I had rock all round me. There was only one way and that was to climb up, to climb and turn and maintain that situation and hope that I wouldn't strike any wind that would drift me in towards the mountain peaks all around me. I had to climb up and out and face the music or just circle where I was till I ran out of fuel. If I hit a rock wall while I was trying to climb out I'd know nothing because I had two 44 gallon drums of petrol at my back and it would have been just a ball of flame against the rock.

So I started to climb and turn and just checked everything was right. I got into the cloud—completely on instruments— and kept climbing and it just seemed to go on forever. And then gradually I could see slight breaks above me, and the temptation—particularly when you've been off instrument flying for some time—is to try to get back to visual too soon. I'd see the break and I could see the patch of blue and then look back and find that I was close to stalling the aircraft. So I had to say to myself, 'Forget completely visual flying, go back onto instruments and stay with it'. So I'd go back into the grey murk and turn and break again. And I had to force myself to keep my eyes away from looking into safety and to continue climbing.

Well I broke through—I still wake up with nightmares with this one—and when I broke through I forgot all about Amundsen Bay. All I could think of was to head back toward King Edward Gulf as quickly as I could, which I did. When I got there I didn't think I had the strength to land, refuel the aircraft and carry on. I knew I had enough fuel to get back to Mawson as I was at 10 000 feet and all I had to do was to reduce power and just go down on the idle for about two hundred miles. So I flew all the way back to Mawson, landed there and waited until the next day before refuelling and flying those same two damned drums back to Amundsen Bay.

Doug Leckie's radar altimeter had failed at the time he expected to be over the mountains and he was tricked into descending through cloud. Yet flying in Antarctica in modern times can be tricky even in bright sunshine and clear conditions, as I found out in conversations with Helicopter Resources pilot Pip Turner.

PT: It's different, that's the important part. You have to think on an Antarctic wavelength instead of an Australian wavelength, so you have to take different things into account.

TB: So what are some of the differences?

PT: In Australia when you plan to land an aircraft, it's perfectly obvious that you can put it down on a piece of ground. In Antarctica you can say, 'There's a piece of snow, I'll land on that'. But you have to be aware that the piece of snow you are going to land on may actually be a snow bridge over a crevasse. This year, in the Prince Charles Mountains, we were plotting satellite positions on the Amery Ice Shelf and we went out in the early part of the season to place some automatic stations. Then we went back a month later to find out how far the ice had moved. We came back to one of these positions and it was perfectly obvious that we had placed the station on a snow bridge over a crevasse that was more than fifty feet wide—you could still see the skid marks in the snow where the aircraft had been before. I couldn't see the crevasse then and the aircraft had been landed in the middle of it. If the snow bridge had collapsed, we would have disappeared completely out of sight and no one would have ever found us. The only thing that we can be fairly sure of is that the snow bridge was very thick and probably able to support the weight of perhaps ten heli-copters. It is little things like that which make the difference.

The other thing, of course, is the weather, and the speed with which the weather can change while you're not looking.

You turn your back on the weather for a minute and all of a sudden a snow shower has engulfed you and you are in a white-out. So you have to keep your eyes over your shoulder and keep thinking about what you are doing.

TB: And it isn't only the white-out that occurs, is it?

PT: Yes, there's the 'vague-out'. That's a term I've coined, there is no other way of putting it. A white-out happens when you have an overcast sky, a snow-covered terrain underneath you. The sky is white and the ground is white, and you can't define between up and down. It is very difficult to conceive if you have never seen one. You can't tell which way is up, and it is just like flying at night except everything is white instead of black. That's a very well recognised situation in alpine or polar areas.

TB: You then have to go onto instruments.

PT: Yes, that's right, you fly on instruments instead, but we try to avoid those situations. A 'vague-out' can happen where you have a cloudless blue sky over the top, and you are looking down at the ground, but the ground has so few features on it. When you are looking down on the Antarctic ice cap, you can't see any depth of field, whether you are a thousand feet off the ground or ten feet off the ground. The only way to tell your height above the ground is with your radar altimeter which is bouncing a signal off the ground. You have just to believe that implicitly.

TB: You could have a situation, then, where the ice shelf rises gradually from the coast and you are flying inland and lose any impression at all of height over it.

PT: Yes. There is one location on the Amery Ice Shelf where the ice flows down to the sea and rides up over a rock shelf, and the bulge created by the ice flowing over it is one thousand feet high. One thousand feet is a decent height, and that is a big piece of terrain. But because it is white and looks essentially flat, it has absolutely no depth to look at, and you can't see it. So when you are flying towards it, it is shielding part of the view in front of you and you can't quite work out when you are looking ahead why it doesn't look like it should. Then the only things that tell us that the ground is rising underneath us are our instruments. If you flew on, trusting to your eyesight alone, you would have the situation where the ground came up to ten feet below you. We'd been warned about this, but it still looks exactly the same—as though the ice was one thousand feet below you. The ice sheet is featureless.

TB: Did that happen to you?

PT: It did. We knew it was there, we went out on the Amery and when we turned around to come back again we knew we would fly over this feature. We'd been past it two or three times before, but we still got caught out by it. It still shielded our view of the mountains in the background, and we still looked to the area because it was hiding some of our navigational references. Knowing it is there doesn't always help.

This is one of the things I try to point out to people without Antarctic experience: that the big, overlying factor is there is no scale. There are no trees on the ground that you know are forty feet high, no road that you know is twenty feet wide. Therefore a rock could be a boulder of one foot across, it could be the size of a house, it could be a thousand feet high. It's very hard to tell the difference.

TB: This is partly due to the clarity of the air—absolutely no pollution in the atmosphere.

PT: Yes; at times we can quite clearly see ahead 200 miles. We can see mountains in the distance, and know by the map that they are 200 miles away.

TB: Do you ever stop seeing the beauty?

PT: You have to kick yourself that you don't become blase about it, so you can appreciate what's going on around you; it is so unique and absolutely beautiful.

TB: What survival gear do you have to carry in case you have to put down on this featureless ice-sheet?

PT: We carry a survival pack, which is the standard ANARE aircraft survival pack containing two sleeping bags, a fuel stove, a makeshift tent for protection, food, water and odds and ends like that. But because we are operating so far from base, we also carry on top of that a full sleeping arrangement, an air mattress with an insulating blanket over the top, two more sleeping bags for insulation and a more sophisticated tent system. The theory is that if we were to have to put down in bad weather or something, we could survive in the aircraft—probably indefinitely—and gain protection from the blizzard and blown snow.

TB: Have there been situations where choppers have had to put down?

PT: Yes, there have been occasions when helicopters have been caught in a blizzard, have put down, and the two or three in the cabin sat there for two days waiting for the weather to improve.

TB: Have you ever had to do that?

PT: No, I haven't, and I don't relish the thought of it.

TB: After two or three days can you start and fly off easily?

PT: Hopefully. It depends on the cold soak. We do have problems with the batteries in the aircraft getting a cold soaking, because as a battery freezes, it loses its amps. But if you are able to warm it up again, it regains its original charge. The theory behind it is that you put down, take the battery out of its battery compartment, put it in the cabin with you and, if necessary, put it in your sleeping bag with you and keep it warm. Because it is your life-line.

TB: How big is the battery?

PT: Fortunately quite small! It has sharp corners and it is not very comfortable to sleep with, but it is an important part, our life-line and communications link. It powers the radio and it is the key to starting the aircraft when the weather improves.

TB: So you'd sleep with your battery happily would you?

PT: I certainly would—love it to death! But the thing that impresses me most about Antarctica, and flying down here, is the power. We all know about the power of nature—fire and floods and that kind of thing—but here it is the power of the wind, and the power of the wind-driven snow. In the Prince Charles Mountains to the east of our little field camp, when the weather turned really bad and started blowing from the east, the driven snow was blown and picked up and thrown over the tops of the mountains, which are standing up 1500 feet high above the ice plateau. The snow was being thrown up over the tops of these mountains in great rooster tails. We would look, from where we were to the east, to see these massive plumes of snow being thrown into the air and on one hand it filled your heart full of awe— the power of nature—but on the other there was the fear of being caught up in turbulence on the lee side of these mountains. It was very, very impressive.

While Pip Turner and his fellow pilots were airborne, ferrying drums of fuel up to the plateau, all passengers were asked to help with the unloading, and most were willing. I spent a morning stacking cases of frozen food into a cold store, which was less hazardous than the last time I lumped similar cases at Davis Station in alarming proximity to maurauding helicopters. Any one travelling south with the Antarctic Division signs a 'blood chit' absolving the Division of all responsibility in the case of accidents.

One of the problems of having so many well-meaning people helping is that not everyone knows what they are doing, when they are working in highly dangerous circumstances. On one occasion during the day, two barges collided, nearly knocking into the water a passenger who was trying to secure lines. Then a load of passengers on the barge going ashore found themselves underneath a sling load of oil drums coming out of *Icebird*'s hold. There was much shouting and recrimination. There is no doubt a serious accident is lurking around just waiting to happen at these times.

Captain Ewald Brune cons Icebird *into Mawson Harbour from the flying bridge. Mawson Station can be seen in the background as can the peak of Mt Henderson. We had to break ice to get in, and we had to break ice to get out.*

I keep hearing wonderful stories about human relationships on the stations, and the painstaking care with which people will set up practical jokes. Des Lugg told me about one expeditioner who had very little mail arrive with the first resupply ship of the year.

DL: He got about one letter from mum, another from a sister, and nothing else. And everyone else was getting ten, thirty or forty letters. He spent the first summer of his last wintering year in the Prince Charles Mountains, and a particular friend of his was there who was returning to Australia after the summer operation, and he decided to see that this particular person got plenty of mail.

So when he returned to Australia he filled out every conceivable coupon in newspapers and magazines for lonely hearts clubs, joining religious groups, better window-cleaning devices, self-help magazines—the whole range of mail order services. He put this fellow's name and address on all the order forms 'care Mawson Station, Antarctica'.

A year later I was back with the same two expeditioners in the field—in the Prince Charles Mountains again, actually—and five large mail bags arrived for this fellow.

He couldn't believe that from several years in Antarctica and only having a handful of letters, suddenly here were five mail bags. He couldn't get into it fast enough and opened up the first letters, and found religious tracts, dating club introduction forms, various contraptions for contraception, free samples, recipes—it just went on and on.

He was delighted at first, then quite annoyed that he'd been set up. 'You've set me up!' 'No I haven't'. 'Yes, you have'. He saw it as a compliment in the end. He left the mail behind, and the winterers opened it during the year. When anyone had a dull moment, they would open some of it.

The irrepressible Dr Kevin Donovan told me of another joke played on the Officer in Charge at Davis, during his wintering year there in 1975. The OIC was an Englishman who was passionately fond of rice pudding as a dessert.

KD: Everyone else thought of rice pudding as a dish you had if nothing else was available. The chef knew his liking for rice pudding and put it on at reasonable intervals. The only problem was, whenever he made it, he would make it the night before and put it in the fridge to set, but when he got up in the morning there would be a serving gone. And he knew that the OIC was the only one who would eat the stuff at that time of night.

So one night we got some plaster of Paris and made an imitation rice pudding with it and boiled up rice and put nutmeg on top so it looked like the real thing, and just left it in the fridge. The next day there were a couple of bent forks, the rice pudding was still whole, and the OIC didn't mention a word about it. Then we swapped it with a real one, and helped ourselves in front of him. That cured him from pinching the rice pudding in the night.

Some people become Antarctic recidivists. One regular, Doug Twigg, has actually had twenty birthdays in Antarctica, but that is because he travels south in the summer season almost every year, although he has wintered several times as well.

Graeme 'Chompers' Currie who, like Doug Twigg, started as a radio operator, has notched up (on the last count when I interviewed him) eleven winters in Antarctica. In 1981 he was accorded the rare privilege of being allowed to winter at the American base, actually situated at the South Pole. Much of the base is tunnelled under the ice cap and, because of its geographical location, has almost exactly six months' light, and six months' darkness. Temperatures can drop down to −70C and even lower. When I interviewed Graeme, I found he had qualified for membership of a most exclusive club.

GC: One of the things I found out about not long after I arrived at the South Pole was the 300 Degree Club. The Americans measure their temperature in degrees Fahrenheit. There was a sauna in the underground section of the base and, when the temperature outside got to minus 100F, I was told 'The 300 Degree Club's on'.

So I stood near the entrance to the sauna. Everyone was standing in the nude except for socks and sandshoes. You had to do it in two groups, because the others had to take your photograph to prove you had properly joined the club. The temperature in the sauna was plus 200F, and just as you began to perspire you ran out of the sauna, down the ramp through a corridor, and up through the big open doorway at the entrance to the underground polar station.

Now they actually have a symbolic South Pole about a hundred yards from the main entrance. So you run naked around the Pole, have your photo taken, and head back down into the sauna. And then you have joined The 300 Degree Club. Plus 200F to minus 100F with nothing on but your sandshoes. They warn you not to fall over, because the snow is so cold it would burn you like dry ice. I was told that the snap freezing of the sweat on your body actually helps protect you from the intense cold for those few moments.

There was one girl in the party—I'd never seen a naked lady at the South Pole before—but Cindy joined The 300 Degree Club with everyone else. They took a photo and she didn't mind, but she did put her hands over the 'map of Tasmania'. We all got our certificates, suitably stamped as members of The 300 Degree Club.

TB: What was it like when you were out there?

GC: Basically you were running so fast that you really didn't notice the cold, because of the heat from the sauna. But, as you were waiting to get your photograph taken, the air was so dry that the moisture in our breath was making a fog in front of everyone's face, so we all had to hold our breaths while the photo was taken.

TB: I was once told that when it gets that cold and you have a pee, it actually hits the ground as ice crystals.

GC: It's true! But you have to aim high, to give it time to freeze.

TB: Forgive me for asking, but have you ever done the peeing trick yourself and seen your urine turn to ice?

GC: Yes. It got down to minus 108F once, (−78C) and we were out taking some photos of some very good auroras that night. The shutter actually wouldn't work at those temperatures, so you had to open the shutter inside, leave it out on a time exposure, and take it in again to close the shutter. So while we were out there, someone said, 'Let's have a pee, and see if it'll freeze'. So three of us stood there and aimed very high, and frozen droplets did actually rain down.

I'm sure we are all better off for knowing about that.

CHAPTER FIFTEEN

The Difficulty of Farewelling a Continent • 'The Art of Patience Before Immovable Floes' • We Break Out From Mawson • Compliment to Cook Misplaced • The Importance of Finger Nail Growth to Antarctic Research • Medical Emergencies Discussed • Linda Ronstadt Day and George Washington's Birthday Celebrated • Reflections on the Antarctic Experience • The Smell of Home

FEBRUARY 18

It is official: we are to leave Mawson Station today to sail for Hobart. It is as cold as charity with a strong katabatic wind blowing down from the ice plateau and an overcast sky.

The thought actually of going home is hard to grasp. Although the voyage has been an unexpectedly long one, the knowledge that many of us will probably never return to the Antarctic is on all our minds. I have plundered the diaries of my shipmates at this time. Chris Sattlberger:

. . . One last time I walk out to East Arm, a peninsula which reaches out a long way into the sea. On the far side of it I sit down and just look one last time on the ice-cliffs, the plateau, the frozen ocean. A strange thought, to know that in all probability this is the last time in my life that I stand on this continent.

Fellow journalist Keith Scott asked The Philosopher how to say goodbye to a continent but

. . . Having failed to get an answer by 8 am I found the best angle I could. I patted an old dog by the husky lines which is due to be put down and went to a windy

Mawson Station in benign mood after the hurricane-strength blizzard.

place away from the station where the snow was driving horizontally across low, brown rocks. It was the west arm of the bay and from the western side you could see over the sea ice to the plateau. At different times this ice can be pink, or orange, or bright white. It can be split into great slabs like concrete, or it can be a solid sheet like an airport.

The plateau is more spectacular and unforgiving. It can be blue or any of those other colours. It can be still and so quiet it hurts your ears, or it can be hidden in blizzards, whipped harsh by the strongest winds on earth.

On the west arm, I took off a glove and touched a rock which was sharp, hard and cold. I took some photographs—hoping to catch the wind and the cold— and said goodbye. It was the best I could do.

We were all back on board *Icebird* by 10.30 am, after everyone on the Station had come down to the harbour's edge to see us off. Not everyone left will be wintering. There are still some construction staff and summer scientists to be taken out by

Icebird on her last voyage of the season before the ring of fast ice clamps firmly around the edge of Antarctica for another winter.

We had to break ice to get out of Mawson Harbour— which Ewald said was another 'first'. We could see our track in, but the tumbled blocks of ice had been refrozen. A number of seals had taken advantage of the temporarily open water to make blow holes. They took no account of *Icebird* at all as we passed within metres of some of them. One Weddell seal just rolled over on his or her back and gazed up languidly without concern as the steel wall of our starboard side crunched by. At times we had to back and charge during our progress to open water.

Keith Scott wrote a poem to celebrate our return to open water and gave it to me 'in memory of Voyage Six and countless games of Scrabble'. Very generous in view of the fact that he didn't roll me in a one-to-one game the whole voyage.

THE ART OF PATIENCE BEFORE IMMOVABLE FLOES

In some respects it was a sad day today. The ice blew away for the first time since we arrived here two weeks ago.

We had grown used to it in some ways—its solid presence. It was teaching us the art of patience before immovable things.

It was also a new view for on the bridge, the mob with cameras— the 'sunset watchers'. You don't get sunsets over water like you get over ice. You lose a bit when the waves break, take some of the light down with them.

We watched the ice when it changed colour—constantly, like Ayers Rock, or Uluru. One morning soft pink, the next 'night' a sort of see-through blue then orange.

The sun liked it too, I think—basking in its own reflection at midnight in the millpond water between slabs.

We also watched the penguins this month—stupid as sheep but delightful in their human attitudes. Panic-struck when the bow shattered 'night' on the floe.

225

The wind changed all that in two hours. Suddenly, like things happen here.

We'll get to land soon and we're glad of that. But a world we knew for two weeks is gone.

I'm told I'll come back to test someone else's patience.

KEITH SCOTT, FEB. '89.

There was a party that night to say thanks to those passengers who had helped with the cargo handling. As I had a broadcast scheduled for Macca's *Australia All Over* program (at the rather uncivilised hour of 2.30 am Mawson time) I thought it prudent to give it a miss and retire early.

FEBRUARY 19
Woken by alarm and went to the bridge at 2 am where Captain Ewald was at the helm. The Antarctic night has started to re-establish itself. Only a month ago I broadcast to Macca from Mawson at the same time and watched dusk turn into dawn behind mountains sticking up through the ice plateau like broken teeth. This morning was a vastly different eerie scene: *Icebird* was surging forward in total darkness with an occasional shudder every now and then as we hit an isolated platform of floating pack ice. Icebergs showed up on the radar, and were also illuminated by search-lights on the bow which Ewald said could pick them up a nautical mile ahead at least.

On the horizon to the south, the silhouettes of grounded icebergs could be seen against the Antarctic dawn—just a faint lightening of the horizon. It was fascinating to be on the bridge at such a time, with quite large bergs suddenly flashing past on either side in ghostly form. But solid enough if we were unfortunate enough to hit one.

My call from the ABC did not come through, but I did not regret my visit to the bridge in the small hours. Perhaps it was my way of farewelling Antarctica.

At morning tea, I talked with the former Mawson Station

Leader, Phil Barnaart, about the need for an organised history project to record the memories of early expeditioners before it was too late. Australians have been voyaging south since 1948—more than forty years—and many of the early pioneers have since died. Our conversation also touched on the major traverse that Phil Barnaart had led from Mawson Station to the Prince Charles Mountains during last winter, to lay down supplies and take in huts for the 1989 summer program. He reminded me that summer visitors do not see the splendours of the *aurora australis*, the southern lights, flickering like giant searchlight beams across the night sky, or flaming the sky with bursts of colour almost psychedelic in their intensity.

It is one of many civilised and fascinating conversations I have enjoyed with Antarctic professionals on Voyage Six. Men like Voyage Leader Des Lugg, who has been visiting Antarctica since the 1960s, or biologist Don Adamson who has a strong sense of Antarctic history as well as an almost incandescent enthusiasm for his scientific projects. He told me of the push to save the large granitic boulders scattered about Mawson Station, which the construction people wanted to crush into aggregate for the foundations of the great metal boxes that are replacing the wooden huts. One of them, poised seemingly precariously above the sleeping huts, has a chilling piece of graffiti painted across it. PLEASE DO NOT REMOVE THE CHOCKS. There **are** chocks under it too!

Our program of lunch time lectures is continuing, where various professionals share their expertise. I have been asked to do one on my Antarctic oral history project. Glaciologist Ian Allison has lectured us about his work measuring the speed and flow of glacier ice down into the sea from the Lambert Glacier. Some of the glaciers draining into the sea, and squeezed between mountain ranges, surge along at the extraordinary speed of a metre a day, while in other areas of Antarctica the ice sheet moves more sedately. With the spectre of global warming, and the enormous reserves of fresh water held in Antarctica being liberated, Ian Allison is keen to measure how much ice is breaking off the continent and floating away as icebergs, compared with the amount of precipitation being added to the main bulk of Antarctica as ice and snow. Initial results indicate that more ice is going on than is coming off. So if the level of the oceans is rising, it is due to thermal

A large granitic boulder with its chilling piece of graffiti.

expansion, not any extra ice coming off the ice cap. Perhaps that is good news for the environmental alarmists.

FEBRUARY 20
After all the criticism of Roger and his 'thaw it, burn it and serve it' cooking, he seemed to make an effort to lift his game. We haven't had any more boiled-dishcloth flavoured stews or curries. Last night's main course was marinated chicken and fried rice and was quite tasty. I congratulated Roger and his face fell. I found out later it had been prepared by Horst, his deputy, who usually cooks for the German crew.

There is some concern about the health of Ilsa, one of the stewardesses, who may have appendicitis. The ship is rolling quite heavily most of the time now as we punch back through the storms of the Southern Ocean, so if an operation is necessary it will be quite difficult. One reassuring aspect of this possible emergency is that we are well off for medicos—four doctors at the last count. Kevin Donovan (the ship's doctor), Des Lugg, John Gill (a general practitioner on his way back from a year at Mawson) and Konrad Muller, Professor of Pathology at the University of Tasmania.

Because all expeditioners have to be extremely fit to qualify for Antarctic service, the wintering doctors do not have to do a great deal of actual 'doctoring' unless there are emergencies. Kevin Donovan told me that there were certain basic things the Division required, like regular measurements of body weight, blood pressure, pulse rate, oral temperature and skin-fold thicknesses. However, doctors were encouraged, and generally wanted, to undertake special research projects.

In 1975, during his year at Davis Station, Kevin Donovan intended to do some blood-clotting studies, theoretically connected with fat metabolism. But the equipment he needed for this was sent to Mawson Station by mistake. He did have a little comparator with which he planned to measure nail growth, so that became his major project:

KD: It just consisted of scratching a small groove in the nail, measuring the distance from the base of the nail up to the groove, and when that grew out, just marking again and measuring the distance between the two marks. By doing that you got a continuous assessment each month of how much the nail grew.

TB: And what was the point of that?

KD: It's just that McLean had mentioned in his reports that nail growth in the Antarctic for the 1912 group Australians on Sir Douglas Mawson's expedition was one-tenth the rate of that in temperate areas. The French had done some measurements in about 1955, and had mentioned the figure of one-fifth the rate in temperate climates. It was mainly to see whether both had made mistakes, or one was wrong, or it was a steady change.

TB: And what did you find out?

KD: I found that it was the same as temperate climates, so I suppose the conclusions that could be drawn are either the other two were right and I was wrong, or that conditions had changed over the last fifty years, so that cold exposure for expeditioners is much less now than it was for the 1912 wintering party.

TB: That is likely isn't it?

KD: Oh yes. They got down there, the 1912 party, and had to build their own base, and during that period they would have had a lot of cold exposure. The base hut was

British Journal of Dermatology (1977) **96**, 507.

Antarctic environment and nail growth

K.M.DONOVAN*

Antarctic Division, Department of Science, Baker Medical Research Institute, Melbourne, Victoria, 3181,
Australia

Accepted for publication 23 October 1976

SUMMARY

Nail growth of all fingers was measured on 13 men wintering in Antarctica. A mean rate of 109·5 μm/
day was found with the longer digits having faster growth. No significant difference was demonstrated
between the warmer and colder months of the study period. Monthly variations suggested that sub-
jects had an individual rate irrespective of environmental influences.

Comparison with previous studies both in polar and temperate conditions showed growth rates in
Antarctica have increased progressively; present values being comparable with observations in temperate climates.

just Mawson's original hut, so most of their activities took
place outside. The French, when they arrived, also had to
build a base, and they lived in tents for several months before
the base was built and they could move in.

TB: Did you only measure fingernails? What about toe
nails?

KD: Toe nails were done in subsequent years by other
doctors. They found they grew faster. The reason that was
put forward is that the feet are in a sort of semi-tropical
environment wrapped up in mukluks—felt-lined boots. In
the old buildings, opposed to the newer ones, the heating
was waist heat, from the radiator on the wall, so the
temperature inside the building was zero degrees on the floor,
maybe eighteen degrees on the roof. The people tended to
leave their mukluks on inside, because their feet would get
cold if they wore ordinary shoes, and just wear shirt-sleeves
from waist level up because that was the ambient temperature. By the mukluks staying on, the feet were warmer
than toast, so they got excess heat. And the theory states
that nails grow depending on the heat of the environment.

TB: To summarise then, I gather the result was that,
because of hot-house conditions in the boot, toe nails grow
faster but fingernails grow exactly the same as fingernails

grow elsewhere. Were you pleased with the conclusions of your research?

KD: Well the British Journal of Dermatology published my paper in 1977, so my findings must have been reasonable. I suppose it's a simple experiment that showed something of value.

TB: So you are now probably one of the top world authorities on fingernail growth.

KD: Oh yes, but there are better authorities though. W B Bean in the United States since the Second World War has been measuring his thumb nail growth.

TB: Just the thumb?

KD: Just his thumb, and publishes a paper every five years on five years of nail growth, ten years of nail growth, fifteen years of nail growth, twenty-five years—he must be up to about forty-five years of nail growth now.

TB: What about actual doctoring on the bases?

KD: You hope that no one gets injured or sick at all. If that happens it is a successful year. In 1975 when we arrived at Davis one of the people going to Mawson had developed appendicitis—it was an eighty per cent possibility. As we were there with the wintering Mawson doctor, myself as the wintering Davis doctor and the Davis doctor who had just finished wintering, it was a much safer procedure to do the operation there than perhaps take a punt and let the patient go around to Mawson where there would only be one doctor. So we radioed ahead for the doctor at Davis to get the theatre ready, duly arrived and squeezed all three of us and the patient into the small operating theatre. The wintering Davis doctor did the anaesthetic and the Mawson doctor and myself did the surgery successfully in that he recovered fairly quickly after that.

TB: And it was appendicitis?

KD: Well it looked red! There was something going on. That was the usual thing, once you hopped in there it was a bound down retrocaecal appendix. It's Murphy's Law that if there is going to be an operation it will be the most difficult one that happens. So it was probably a good thing it was done then as it would have been a problem to do it by myself. A retrocaecal appendix is when the appendix is bound down underneath the large bowel so that you actually have to dissect it away, get it up and take it out in a kind of reverse order to what it usually is. You take off at the back and work to the front, instead of starting at the front and working to the back.

TB: That's obviously a fairly major event. What are some of the other medical things that happen more commonly?

KD: I suppose the most common injuries are cuts which need suturing, sprains from people tripping over. There are no pavements, just lumps of rock and roughly cleared paths, so certainly as the year goes on they get covered with ice and snow and people are forever falling over, bumping knees and twisting ankles.

TB: Hypothermia?

KD: Well I haven't had any real cases of what I'd classify as hypothermia. That is something that you keep in mind and work out a procedure in case you get it. You certainly get frost nip, that's fairly common; from just superficial freezing of the skin you get some sores that arise. They are just really like localised sunburn. The skin peels and gets hard and cracks. Every year you seem to get a couple of fractures of some description, fingers, wrists, ankles, feet. That's mainly from falling. The biggest thing you do, or so it seems to me—I don't know whether I'm lucky or unlucky—is dentistry. Fillings are forever falling out because of the cold, usually taking half the tooth with them so that it becomes a regular thing to have to put a filling back in. It is not just a matter of filling up the hole, you have this defect that has to be repaired. That is certainly something that tries your skills, because it's usually something you've never ever done before.

TB: They give you a bit more than a pedal drill these days don't they?

KD: Certainly the difference between 1975 and 1986 at Mawson was that the Black and Decker flexible coupling with the dental head on it had been replaced with a high speed air turbine drill, which is certainly much more effective and makes it much easier to use. The old electric one was a hazard, and there was always a smell of burning teeth— you had to cool it with a separate jet of water from another little squeeze bottle and puffs of air, and you needed four hands. The air turbine drill makes life a lot simpler.

As it happened Ilsa's suspected appendicitis subsided, and the *Icebird*'s surgery did not have to be turned into an operating theatre.

FEBRUARY 21

George Washington's Birthday, and 'Linda Ronstadt Day'. This came as a surprise to us all. Bearded weather man 'Wok' Bromham turned up at lunch in a spotted dress, with matching bandana, and declared it was Linda Ronstadt Day. Linda Ronstadt music dominated the ship's music system all day and into the night. Wok did not reveal why he was so obsessed with the lady in question, but cut quite an unexpected figure in his outfit. Ah well—there is a strong tradition of drag in the Antarctic it seems!

The second surprise of the day was when The Philosopher shouted the bar on the occasion of George Washington's birthday—but the drink had to be bourbon. All this after a turkey dinner (in George's honour) preceded by bean soup.

It was a *very* windy night in Cabin C2.

Everyone's thoughts are turning towards home. I am thinking not only of the future, but of how to make sense of the past. Barry Batts has also been keeping a kind of audio diary on his pocket tape recorder for his wife Judith:

BB: It really has been very hard to sum up in my mind. We have seen an awful lot, I have seen things I'd never dreamed I would see and seen beauty that photographs may not really reveal. I think also I've learnt a lot, about people we've had on board, soldiers, tradesmen—we've had a whole host of people whom in normal academic life I don't come upon. I would never call them friends because I'm sure most of us will never see one another again. But I met some people whom I would like to meet again and that, of course, is what makes life interesting.

I think, though, the problems that we anticipated before we left home are certainly very real. There's very little time to talk to you on my recorder, very little time to be by myself. You clearly cannot talk to this box when people are around; I mean, it's too personal. I think the other thing is that one

233

*The surprising sight of bearded weather man 'Wok' Bromham
celebrating Linda Rondstadt Day, squired by helicopter pilot Pip
Turner.*

needs time-to-be-by-one's-self time, to sit and to think and
to put it into perspective. I do a little bit of writing, but
that's only just on my day book and that doesn't really help
very much either, but it will be good to get back.

I miss my music. I'd love to hear some decent music again
because with a ship's complement such as we've got, any
music you have is more bang than tune. But I can think
the beauty that we've had in the last couple of days. There
are a number of albatrosses following the *Icebird*—about four
or five of them. They really are magnificent birds, with large
wing spans that must be some ten feet across, and beautiful
white bodies. They just fly along about one or two inches

above the water and then meet the updraft and soar up close to the ship and then sail off down the side. They really do make quite an impression. I think the whole concept of nature in this part of the world is something that we don't really see and consider enough.

I think then, in those rather strange or plaintive tones which are really somewhat unlike me, I should finish off this tape and say that I hope someday somebody might listen to it. I might one day have a listen to it myself. I'm not certain what I have rambled on about on these last sixty days wandering in the wilderness. But, as I think I said earlier on this morning, it really is and has been and will continue to be quite an experience. And, on the same thing, it's rather strange to think that tomorrow I'll be having lunch with Judith. That's something really that is going to be very hard to think about, because it is such another, different, world and a world that you miss so much you put it aside.

You put it aside really because you cannot bear to think about it. I know that sounds strange but I think the whole ability to live in this very beautiful but violent area of the world depends in a way on *not* talking about home. You cannot think about home because really home is such a special place—a special place that you keep in the back of your mind and that keeps you going from day to day. But you cannot really afford to dwell on it.

It's time I came back to reality, anyway. I really begin to wonder how on earth I'm going to front up to work next week with all its petty considerations.

FEBRUARY 23

It's raining! It is the first rain we have seen for eight weeks. Graham Robertson went out on deck and just stood in it. The Head Prefect has just beaten me in Scrabble. I fear that puts him in the lead, with time running out to play again. I think he reads the dictionary every night. My sleep rhythms have gone crazy. I didn't get to sleep until 5 this morning and slept until lunch time. This has got to stop!

Those who have wintered in Antarctica are looking more and more pensive as we get closer to Hobart. It will be an enormous adjustment for them. Even Hobart's modest traffic will hit them like a hammer blow. Social contacts will be difficult after so much isolation with a small group—even with close family. The Antarctic *is* a marriage hazard. You also hear stories about expeditioners, unused to handling money, forgetting to pay for drinks in a pub or food in a restaurant.

Then again, no one goes to the Antarctic without being profoundly affected by it—even contemptible round trippers like me. Although The Philosopher did not manage to answer Keith Scott's question at the time, how to farewell a continent, he did later publish a paper 'Reflections on Distant Ice' in which he commented, among his other conclusions: 'If a person can look at Antarctica and not be moved, there is *something* wrong with that person.'

Phil Law is on record as saying:

> *PL*: I think there are several aspects to this. There's the sheer adventure of it—the beauty of the environment, and there's a sort of philosophical attraction resulting from one's involvement with nature on a grand scale. I think it's fair to say that no man ever goes to Antarctica without its having an immense impression upon him.
>
> There's the beauty and the grandeur of it all and the feeling that one is so insignificant in this scale of nature. The fact that you have enough time down there to sit and ponder and philosophise and sort yourself out enables you to look back on civilisation from a stand-off view point. You can review your own attitudes and your own life and you can make new resolutions as to how to proceed in the future. And I think most men in Antarctica for any length of time do go through some sort of personal re-assessment.

FEBRUARY 24
Following sea, mist, some wind and a more pronounced roll. Awoke at noon and had breakfast instead of lunch. It is getting distinctly warmer. I have had to take the doona off my bunk.

There is a curiously static quality to life on board on this homeward run, an unspoken realisation that the voyage is really over, but we are still on board. The Antarctic is behind

Biologist Don Adamson reflecting on his many Antarctic expeditions.

us and each throb of the screw takes us closer to Australia.
We are going through our well-worn routines almost like auto-
matons. The sea-sick-prone are indeed prone in their bunks
day and night. Even Stoppy's Bar is a relatively subdued scene,
although the helicopter pilots—their job well and truly done
for the year—tied one on last night and were extremely noisy
in the corridors.

We eat, sleep and lie in our bunks reading or listening to
music tapes. I wonder when I will ever have as much 'down'
time again. Fortunately, the ship has the odd Macintosh
computer available, and I am able to summarise all my interview tapes ready for processing when I get back to Sydney.
The days blur into each other, and even the weather is misty
and overcast in sympathy with the overall mood.

**Following seas are moving *Icebird* around in quite a
lively fashion, but, as on the voyage down, we have
managed to avoid any dramatic storms. One of the great
delights is to watch the albatrosses swooping and
soaring in our wake. The photographers are delighted,
but the ship's film supplies are exhausted. In fact most
things are running out.**

It's just as well we are getting close to home. The ship has been drunk dry of beer. Another first, says Ewald. It has never happened before. He has been preparing some statistics to summarise our voyage.

'The two most joyful events on a polar voyage are the first and last sight of the ice.' (Anon)

The first thing that must be said about Voyage 6, 1989, is that it has created a number of firsts.

• It is *Icebird*'s longest charter for the Australian Antarctic Division, from January 3 to February 28.

• *Icebird* recorded the fastest time from Mawson to Hobart—exactly ten days.

• We carried the largest crew—twenty-five—ever to go south on *Icebird*.

• Five politicians were carried south, but did not return on *Icebird*.

• Among the passengers were the first full-time philosopher to visit Antarctica and the first professional fly-catcher.

• Sandra Fahey, the lottery-winning Antarctic wife, spent a record three weeks with her husband on Mawson Station.

• More food and drink was consumed during Voyage 6 than on any other voyage so far. Some statistics may be of interest:

999 rolls of toilet paper
57 cases of toast bread
200 kilos of bacon
625 cartons of beer
98 bottles of gin
150 bottles of Scotch

As you will be aware, the problems caused by the excess consumption of food and drink caused grave stability problems, and had to be addressed by me on January 31, off the ice edge of Mawson.

Despite searching inquiries I was not able to find out who was responsible for a false news item appearing on the ship's Telex which stated that the Australian Treasurer Paul Keating had resigned from Parliament to take up a position with the World Bank. I am aware that this caused our then resident politicians some concern, and enclose a copy of this false message in case further light can be thrown on this unfortunate happening.

Shortly after arrival at Davis Station on the morning of February 1, 1989 precise navigation enabled me to find the uncharted rock close to the anchorage. I think that ANARE expeditioners have for too long monopolised the naming of Antarctic landmarks and believe the time has come to break the pattern with underwater features. I propose the uncharted rock at Davis be named 'Brune's Barrier', and will press my claims through the correct channels. I must say, however, that I consider the naming of a new ship's cocktail ICEBIRD ON THE ROCKS by unknown persons was in extremely bad taste.

Despite delays caused by fast ice at Mawson and Davis Stations, all our cargo and fuel was discharged, and thanks are due to all passengers who assisted. I also thank everyone for sharing so harmoniously in such an extended and eventful Voyage Six, 1989.

Ewald Brune
Captain

FEBRUARY 28 (Final Antarctic diary entry)

Calm sea, overcast, and WARM. Ewald invited me to his cabin for a gin and tonic—a signal honour as it is not only the last bottle of gin left on board, but certainly the last of the tonic.

3 pm. Walking up the stairs inside the module, and despite the gin fumes, I suddenly smelt the smoky eucalyptus fragrance of the incomparable Tasmanian bush! Rushed on deck to see the misty mountains of the South West just visible on the horizon. Oh, that wonderful aroma of the Australian bush after the splendid but sterile wastes of Antarctica. I cannot describe the exultation of the prospect of returning to contact with living vegetation.

It is a hot summer's day. The *Icebird* is moving smoothly across a low, oily swell, while we drink in the perfume of the bush. Oh my Gawd, it's good to be back!